D1616589

DOMINO'S PIZZA®

Celebrates

Acknowledgements

Cookbook Chairman: *Polly Minick*
Assistant Chairman: *Cheryl McCormick*

A portion of the proceeds from the sale of this cookbook will be donated to charity.

Editor: *Mary Ann Fowlkes, CF Marketing Associates, Inc.*
Associate Editor: *Ann Cox, CF Marketing Associates, Inc.*
Photographer: *Mike Rutherford, Rutherford Studios*
Food Stylist: *Pat Coker, Elise Walker, CF Marketing Associates, Inc.*
Publisher: *Favorite Recipes Press, A Division of
                 Great American Opportunities, Inc.*

Library of Congress Catalog Number is as follows: 86-22795
ISBN: 0-87197-214-X

Manufactured in the United States of America
First Printing 1986

Recipes for cover on pages 11, 22, 23, 25, 36, 174, 186 and 191.

Domino's Pizza, Inc.

30 Frank Lloyd Wright Drive
P.O. Box 997
Ann Arbor, Michigan 48106-0997
313/668-4000

Dear Friends

The Domino's Pizza 25th Anniversary Cookbook is a dream come true. The project became an idea of mine more than ten years ago. Today it is a reality.

Our cookbook is symbolic of the family atmosphere at Domino's Pizza. The tantalizing recipes in this book were selected from thousands of entries submitted by Domino's Pizza staff around the world. The contents of this publication truly represent a family effort.

Recipes are like family heirlooms. Hopefully we can share our family treasures with you through the Domino's Pizza 25th Anniversary cookbook.

This book is a thanks to over 100,000 members of the Domino's Pizza family who contribute daily to the success of our company.

A very special thank you to Polly Minick and Cheryl McCormick who contributed many hours of their personal time towards the completion of this project.

I am confident that the cookbook will provide many of us in the Domino's family with increased pride and unity.

Marge Monaghan

Contents

Domino's Pizza Celebrates 25 Years   *5*
Appetizers   *9*
Beverages   *27*
Soups and Stews   *37*
Salads   *47*
Main Dishes   *65*
    Beef and Veal   *79*
    Chicken   *91*
    Pork   *107*
    Seafood   *119*
Vegetables   *131*
Breads   *149*
Desserts   *167*
    Cakes   *181*
    Cookies   *189*
    Pies   *203*
Miscellaneous   *211*
Nutrition Conversion Chart   *221*
Equivalent and Substitution Charts   *222*
Index   *224*
Index of Contributors   *228*

Domino's Pizza Celebrates 25 Years

The Domino's Pizza story is so closely tied to the personal story of its founder, president and chairman of the board that it is impossible to tell one without also telling the other. It is a story of hardship, persistence, love and success.

Life did not begin easily for Thomas S. Monaghan. His parents were poor and his family's hopes of escaping poverty virtually ended with the death of his father when young Monaghan was four years old. With his family unit destroyed, Monaghan spent his childhood in foster homes and orphanages. As a teenager he worked as a laborer on several northern Michigan farms before enlisting in the U.S. Marine Corps in 1956.

In 1959, Monaghan enrolled at the University of Michigan in Ann Arbor. While attending college, he held three part-time jobs to support himself, but despite his efforts the lack of funds stopped his attempt at a college education.

Tom Monaghan was 23 years old when, along with his brother James, he borrowed $500 and bought a small pizza store in Ypsilanti, Michigan. The year was 1960, and the store was named Domi Nick's. Like the name of the store, things just weren't quite the way they were supposed to be for Tom Monaghan. He sold his car and rented a room for $6 a week. His diet consisted of pizza, the burned ones! In less than a year, Tom traded James a Volkswagen for his share of the business and, with a new partnership, soon opened pizza stores in Ann Arbor, Mount Pleasant, and a second store in Ypsilanti.

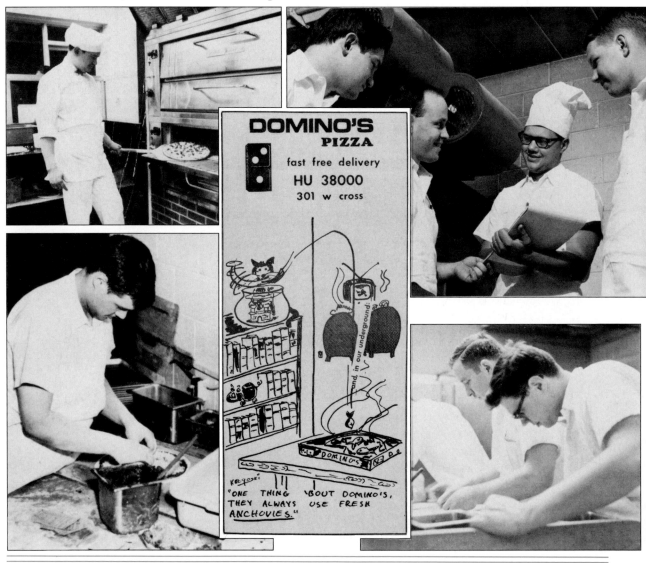

Although the business was struggling and the future still held many pitfalls, Thomas Monaghan's prospects for future success took a definite turn for the better the day he made his first pizza delivery from the new Mount Pleasant store. For it was on that delivery that he met Marge. Tom and Marge were married in 1962.

In 1965, after dissolving the second partnership, Monaghan re-named his business Domino's Pizza, Inc. and became sole owner of the company. Within the year sales had doubled and by 1967, Domino's Pizza sold its first franchise. The future did indeed look promising.

The period from 1968 through 1972 was a major crossroad in the history of Domino's and in the lives of Tom and Marge Monaghan. The hint of Domino's Pizza, Inc.'s future corporate personality came in 1968, when the first out-of-state store opened in Vermont.

But his initial progress was followed by a series of setbacks. A devastating fire in 1968 burned the corporate offices and the commissary. A financial crisis which followed forced Monaghan to lose controlling interest in 1970. Instead of giving up, Monaghan ragained his company the following year and began a slow rebuilding process. He repaid creditors, settled some 150 lawsuits, and aimed the company down the path to prosperity. By 1977, a total of 159 stores were located in 18 states.

Most of America is familiar with the remainder of the story . . . More than 3,000 stores . . . Locations in all 50 states and six foreign countries . . . System-wide sales in 1985 of $1.08 billion . . . Not a bad record for a company that's celebrating its twenty-fifth birthday.

As for Tom and Marge Monaghan are rewarding them for their years of adversity. Things seem to get easier the 1980's struggle and for Tom. In October, 1983 he realized a boyhood dream when he became the sole owner of the Detroit Tigers Baseball Club. Unlike his pizza empire which took years to build, Monaghan's Tigers presented him with a World Series Championship after only one year. In 1985, Domino's Pizza Team Shierson with driver Al Unser, Jr. finished second in the 1985 Indy Car World Series. The team and Unser lost the championship by one point . . . the winner was Unser's dad, Al Unser, Sr. In June, 1985, Domino's Pizza joined with Commissioner Billy Jean King to become the national sponsor of Team Tennis.

Perhaps most important is not so much what has happened to Domino's Pizza and Tom Monaghan, but rather how it happened. For Tom and Domino's Pizza the ingredients were there. A country where freedom allows an individual to overcome hardships and make the best of his or her talents, a strong faith in God that gives an individual the character and strength to deal with life, an enterprise system that ensures that the quality and dedication that goes into a product will be recognized by customers who want to buy the product, and finally the belief that giving back as much or more than you are taking out is the real key to success.

This book is dedicated to the thousands of persons and their families who helped make Domino's Pizza what it is today.

Appetizers

Appetizers

Benedictine Sandwich Spread

1 (3 to 4 inch) cucumber, peeled, seeded and chopped
¼ small onion, grated
2 (8-ounce) packages cream cheese, softened
⅛ teaspoon salt
4 tablespoons mayonnaise
2 drops of green food coloring

Combine all ingredients, mixing well. Ready to spread!! Makes 2½ cups.

Naomi Funkhouser
San Antonio, Texas

Beer Cheese In Rye Boat

1 small onion, quartered
2 cloves garlic
1 teaspoon Worcestershire sauce
½ teaspoon hot sauce
½ ounce Roquefort cheese
2 teaspoons butter or margarine, softened
3 (6-ounce) rolls Kraft nippy cheese
¾ cup heated beer (heat to almost boiling and cool slightly)
Whole loaf of unsliced rye bread

Combine onion, garlic, Worcestershire sauce and hot sauce in the container of electric blender; process for 45 seconds or until finely chopped. Add Roquefort cheese and butter; process until smooth. Add cheese and beer; process until smooth, scraping sides of blender often. Cut about ¼-inch from top of loaf of bread. Scoop out bread leaving ½-inch shell; reserve bread. Spoon cheese mixture into shell. Cut reserved bread into 1-inch cubes; use to dip into cheese mixture. Makes 24 appetizers servings.

Susan Thomason
Elgin, Illinois

Supervisors

1 (12-ounce) can Spam
1 package sharp Cracker Barrel cheese
1 small onion
1 small green pepper
½ cup melted butter
1 package English muffins

Grate Spam and cheese into mixing bowl; set aside. Mince onion and green pepper. Add to cheese and Spam mixture. Add butter; mix well. Spread on muffin halves. Cut with scissors into sixths. Bake at 350°F. for 20 to 30 minutes. Yum Yum. Freezes well. Makes 10 servings.

Patrick (age 5) couldn't remember the word Appetizer but had heard Supervisor so often he created the name for these by accident.

Timothy and Patrick Romano
Boulder, Colorado

◆Recipes for this photograph on pages 13, 15, 18 and 21.

Cheese Ball

2 cups (8 ounces) shredded Velveeta
    cheese, at room temperature
1   (3-ounce) package cream cheese,
    softened
1 clove garlic, finely chopped
1 cup finely chopped nuts
Chili powder

In mixing bowl blend, by hand, cheeses, garlic and nuts until thoroughly blended and uniform in color. Shape mixture into ball. Sprinkle all sides of ball with chili powder. Cover and refrigerate. Serve with crackers.
Makes 1 ball.

Can be made the night before a party. Leftovers (if any) will last up to 2 weeks in plastic wrap if refrigerated.

Robert Daniel
Chelsea, Michigan

Hot Cheese Balls

1 cup (4 ounces) shredded Cheddar
    cheese
3 tablespoons butter or margarine,
    softened
½ cup flour
Dash of cayenne
Dash of salt
1   (4-ounce) jar pimento-stuffed
    olives, drained

In a small bowl, blend cheese, butter, flour, cayenne and salt together to make a dough. Mold 1 teaspoon dough around each green olive, covering completely. Place in ungreased pan. Bake in preheated 400°F. oven for 12 minutes.
Makes about 16 appetizers.

Tala Arnowitz
Trotwood, Ohio

Microwave Cheese Ball

1   (2½-ounce) jar dried beef,
    shredded
1 cup water
1   (8-ounce) package cream cheese,
    softened
½ cup grated Parmesan cheese
1 green onion, finely chopped
2 tablespoons sour cream
¼ cup chopped nuts
    (walnuts are good)
2 tablespoons parsley flakes

Combine beef and water in microwave oven container. Microwave on HIGH (100% power) for 3 to 4 minutes. Drain beef well. Combine cream cheese, Parmesan cheese, onion, sour cream and drained beef; mix thoroughly. Form into a ball; roll in chopped nuts and parsley. Chill.
Makes 1 ball.

May be frozen for later use.

Ann Krueger
Canton, Minnesota

Taco Cheese Ball

2   (8-ounce) packages cream cheese,
    softened
1   (1¼-ounce) package taco
    seasoning mix
1 small onion, finely chopped
1 cup (4 ounces) shredded Cheddar
    cheese
½ small head lettuce, shredded
1 medium tomato, chopped
½ cup sliced black olives
1   (11-ounce) bag tortilla chips

Combine cream cheese, seasoning mix and onion together; mix thoroughly. Form into a ball and chill. Roll in shredded cheese. Place cheese ball on a serving platter. Garnish with lettuce, tomato and olives. Serve with tortilla chips.
Makes 1 ball.

Doug Galusha
Kettering, Ohio

Cheese Pastry Hors D' Oeuvres

1 cup butter or margarine, softened
1 cup sour cream
2½ cups flour
½ teaspoon seasoned salt
¼ teaspoon pepper
½ teaspoon paprika
3 cups shredded sharp Cheddar cheese
1 egg yolk, beaten

Cream butter and sour cream until fluffy. Gradually add flour and seasonings. Mix well until blended. Divide dough into 4 portions. Wrap each portion in plastic wrap and chill overnight. Roll out, one at a time, on floured surface to 12x6-inch rectangle. Sprinkle with ¾ cup cheese. Starting with long side, roll up jelly roll style. Seal edges and ends with beaten egg yolk. Place seam-side down on an ungreased cookie sheet. Score roll halfway through at 1-inch intervals. Repeat procedure with remaining dough. Bake in preheated 325°F. oven for 30 to 35 minutes. Serve hot after slicing.
Makes 48 appetizers.

Roileen Domingues
West Sacto, California

Cheese Sables

¾ cup flour
½ teaspoon salt
¼ teaspoon pepper
¼ teaspoon cayenne
½ cup butter or margarine, melted
2 egg yolks, slightly beaten
¾ cup grated Cheddar cheese
¼ cup grated Parmesan cheese
½ cup ground walnuts
1 egg beaten with ½ teaspoon salt
  (for glaze)

Sift flour, salt, pepper and cayenne together on clean surface; make well in center. Pour butter and egg yolks in well and incorporate into flour gradually with fingertips until mixture resembles crumbs. Add cheeses and work into dough. Knead on lightly floured surface for 2 or 3 minutes; chill dough for 30 minutes. Roll dough out on floured surface into rectangular shape, ⅜-inch thick. Cut into 1-inch squares and cut each square into triangles. Sprinkle with walnuts, pressing nuts lightly into dough. Place on ungreased cookie sheet, nut-side down. Brush with egg glaze. Bake in preheated 375°F. oven for 15 to 18 minutes or until browned. Transfer to rack to cool.
Makes 2 dozen.

Katherine Hilboldt Curtis
Ann Arbor, Michigan

Cheese Spread

½ (8-ounce) package cream cheese,
  softened
1 cup (4 ounces) sharp Cheddar
  cheese, shredded
3 tablespoons mayonnaise
2 tablespoons chopped green onion
2 teaspoons prepared mustard
1 teaspoon Worcestershire sauce
⅓ cup sliced black olives
Crackers or French bread, sliced
  lengthwise
Chopped tomatoes
Bacon, cooked, drained and crumbled

Combine cream cheese, Cheddar cheese, mayonnaise, green onion, mustard, Worcestershire sauce and black olives. Spread on crackers or French bread. Top with tomatoes and bacon; broil for 10 minutes.
Makes 32 appetizers.

Very good!!

Sharon Richwine
Bayville, New York

Fried Cheese

1 (8-ounce) package Mozzarella
   cheese
2 eggs, beaten
1 cup fine bread crumbs
Oil for frying
Salsa or Marinara Sauce
Sour cream

Cut cheese into ½ inch sticks or cubes. Dip cheese into beaten eggs and then into bread crumbs. Heat oil to 375°F. and fry cheese for about 25 seconds. Cool slightly. Serve warm with Salsa or Marinara Sauce. Sour cream may be used.
Makes 4 servings.

Connie Lynn Frisbee-Goden
Jacksonville, Florida

Puffy Cheese Slices

2 cups (8 ounces) shredded Cheddar
   cheese
1 egg, slightly beaten
½ teaspoon dry mustard
½ teaspoon salt
6 slices bread, toasted on one side

Combine all ingredients, except bread, mixing well. Spread mixture on untoasted side of bread. Broil 3 inches from heat until cheese is bubbly.
Makes 6 servings.

Serve with slice of tomato, if desired.

Craig Stevens
Fair Oaks, California

Artichoke Dip

1 (14-ounce) can artichoke hearts
   in water, drained
½ cup grated Parmesan cheese
½ cup mayonnaise

Chop artichoke hearts into ½ and ¼-inch pieces. Place in baking dish. Add cheese and mayonnaise, mixing well. Bake in a preheated 350°F. oven for 1 hour or until golden brown. Cool for 5 minutes and serve with crackers. We prefer the buttery Keebler Club or Town House crackers.
Makes 8 servings.

The taste is uniquely delicious. This recipe is very easy to prepare and can be mixed, baked and served in the same dish. It's always a conversation starter.

Anna Schmitt-Heatlie
Ann Arbor, Michigan

Chili Con Queso Dip

1 large onion, chopped
1 (16-ounce) can stewed tomatoes,
   chopped
1 (4-ounce) jar hot chili peppers
½ cup whipping cream
8 ounces Monterey Jack cheese,
   finely diced
Tortilla or corn chips

In large saucepan, combine onion and tomatoes. Cook over medium heat for 25 to 30 minutes or until moisture evaporates, stirring occasionally. Stir chilies into tomato mixture (adding more or less, depending on individual taste). Remove from heat and let stand for 15 to 20 minutes. Return to heat and stir in cream and cheese. Cook over medium heat just until cheese is melted and mixture is hot. Serve with chips.
Makes 2½ cups.

Jill Curby
Saline, Michigan

Company Clam Dip

1 (10¾-ounce) can cream of
    celery soup
1 (8-ounce) package cream cheese,
    softened
1 (6½-ounce) can minced clams,
    drained
¼ cup chopped green onions
1 tablespoon Worcestershire sauce
Crackers or chips

Combine soup and cream cheese; beat until smooth. Add remaining
ingredients, mixing well. Chill for at least 1 hour. Serve with crackers
or chips.
Makes 3 cups dip.

Tammy R. Lynn
Cape Girardeau, Missouri

Crab Dip

1 cup chopped onion
1 stalk celery, chopped
¼ cup butter or margarine
½ cup flour
1 cup evaporated milk
2 egg yolks, beaten
1 teaspoon salt
½ teaspoon red pepper
¼ teaspoon black pepper
2 cups crab meat, picked to
    remove shell
4 cups (1 pound) shredded
    Cheddar cheese

Sauté onion and celery in butter in a medium saucepan. Add flour,
stirring until smooth. Gradually add milk, stirring constantly. Add
egg yolks, salt, red pepper and black pepper. Cook, stirring
constantly, for 5 minutes or until mixture thickens. Stir in crab; cook
an additional 1 to 2 minutes. Spoon mixture into a greased 1½-quart
shallow baking dish. Sprinkle with cheese. Bake at 375°F. for 20
minutes. Serve with crackers.
Makes 48 appetizer servings.

Joyce A. Archenbronn
Ypsilanti, Michigan

Crab Dip

1 (8-ounce) package cream cheese,
    softened
½ cup mayonnaise
½ cup chopped chives
2 tablespoons prepared horseradish
½ cup seafood cocktail sauce
Crab or shrimp

Combine cream cheese, mayonnaise, chives and horseradish, mixing
thoroughly. Chill for 1 hour. Spread cocktail sauce on top and cover
with crab or shrimp. (I use mock crab legs.) Serve with crackers.
Makes 24 appetizers.

Debra Bores
Mankato, Minnesota

Dill Mustard Dip

¾ cup sour cream
¾ cup mayonnaise
2 teaspoons prepared mustard
1 teaspoon dillweed
½ teaspoon lemon pepper
¼ teaspoon salt
Potato chips or fresh vegetables

Combine all ingredients, except potato chips or vegetables, in a small
bowl; mix well. Serve with potato chips, or fresh vegetables.
Makes about 1½ cups.

Gail Newsome
Rainbow City, Alabama

Festive Egg Dip

1 (8-ounce) package cream cheese, softened
3 tablespoons milk
3 hard-cooked eggs, finely chopped
2 tablespoons mayonnaise
2 teaspoons chopped chives
1 teaspoon prepared mustard
¼ teaspoon salt
⅛ teaspoon pepper

Combine cream cheese and milk in small mixing bowl; beat until creamy. Add remaining ingredients, mixing until light and fluffy. Serve with fresh vegetables (crudites).
Makes about 1½ cups.

Cindi L. Wright
Largo, Florida

Horseradish And Cream Cheese Dip

2 (3-ounce) packages cream cheese, softened
¼ cup sour cream
4 tablespoons freshly grated horseradish
Salt and freshly ground black pepper to taste
Paprika to taste
Tabasco sauce to taste
2 tablespoons chopped parsley

Beat cheese until fluffy; gradually blend in sour cream. Add horseradish, salt, pepper, paprika and Tabasco sauce; beat well. Chill and sprinkle with parsley. Serve with raw vegetables cut into bite-sized pieces.
Makes about 1 cup.

Barbara Eckel
South Lyon, Michigan

Jalapeño Dip

2 pounds ground beef
1 large onion, chopped
1 (8-ounce) can tomato sauce
2 pounds Velveeta cheese, cut into chunks
¼ teaspoon garlic powder
¼ teaspoon Worcestershire sauce
4 whole jalapeño peppers, chopped
⅛ teaspoon jalapeño juice

In large deep pan, brown ground beef; drain. Add onion and cook until the onion is transparent. Add tomato sauce, Velveeta, garlic powder, Worcestershire sauce, jalapeños and juice. Heat through but do not let boil. Serve hot.
Makes 20 servings.

Freezes well.

Sally Tanner
Colorado Springs, Colorado

Mushroom Dip

1 (8-ounce) package cream cheese, softened
2 egg yolks
1 clove garlic, crushed
½ cup grated Parmesan cheese
Juice of ½ lemon
½ pound fresh mushrooms, finely chopped
¼ cup butter or margarine
Triscuits

Combine cream cheese, egg, garlic, cheese and lemon juice, mixing thoroughly. Sauté chopped mushrooms in butter. Combine mushrooms with cheese mixture and bake in preheated 350°F. oven for 20 minutes. Serve hot with Triscuits.
Makes about 2 cups.

A 9-inch quiche pan makes an ideal cooking and serving dish.

Sally A. Watson
Adrian, Michigan

Pumpernickel Dip

1½ cups sour cream
1½ cups mayonnaise
2 teaspoons Beau Monde Spice
2 tablespoons minced onions
2 tablespoons parsley flakes
½ teaspoon dillweed
2 (2½-ounce) packages chopped
 beef
1 loaf pumpernickel bread

Combine all ingredients, except bread. Mix until well blended. Refrigerate overnight. Cut center out of round loaf of pumpernickel bread and fill with dip. Place cut out bread cubes around loaf and serve.
Makes 8 to 12 servings.

If loaves are small, this recipe will fill 2 loaves.

Colleen Mull
Chelsea, Michigan

Shrimp Dip

1 (4½-ounce) can shrimp, chopped
1 (3-ounce) package cream cheese,
 softened
2 tablespoons mayonnaise
2 tablespoons minced onion
3 tablespoons finely chopped celery
Dash of chives
Dash of pepper
½ teaspoon Worcestershire sauce

Mix all ingredients together in a small bowl. Chill overnight. Serve with assorted crackers.
Makes about 1 cup.

Goes well with Town House crackers. Recipe can be doubled or tripled without adjusting ingredients.

Pam Waleri
Norwalk, Ohio

Slow-Ball Dip

1 large round loaf bread
3 (6½-ounce) cans clams
2 (8-ounce) packages cream cheese,
 softened
2 tablespoons grated onion
2 tablespoons beer
2 teaspoons Worcestershire sauce
2 teaspoons lemon juice
1 teaspoon hot sauce
½ teaspoon salt
Celery, carrots and jicama sticks

Cut off top of loaf to serve as lid and hollow out loaf. Reserve bread from inside of loaf and cut into chunks; set aside. Drain clams, reserving ¼ cup of the liquid. Combine all remaining ingredients, except raw vegetables and mix well. Pour into center of loaf. Place lid on loaf and wrap the entire loaf in aluminum foil. Bake in preheated 250°F. oven for 3 hours. To serve, remove bread from foil and use as a dip for raw vegetables and bread cubes.
Makes 6 to 8 servings.

After the dip is gone, you can eat the bowl!

Randall and Linda Nelson
Mesa, Arizona

Spinach Dip

1 (10-ounce) package frozen
 chopped spinach, thawed
1½ cups sour cream
1 cup mayonnaise
1 (8-ounce) can water chestnuts,
 drained and chopped
1 (¾-ounce) package dried
 vegetable soup

Squeeze excess moisture from spinach. Combine spinach and remaining ingredients in a small bowl; mix well. May be served with raw vegetables or crackers.
Makes 4½ cups.

Also great served in a hollowed out round loaf of bread such as Hawaiian bread. Reserve the removed bread for "dipping."

Carol Carr
Ann Arbor, Michigan

Tantalizing Tuna Dip

2   (8-ounce) packages cream cheese,
      softened
1   (6½-ounce) can tuna, drained
2 tablespoons mayonnaise
1 medium onion, finely chopped
3 tablespoons parsley flakes
1 teaspoon garlic
1 teaspoon cayenne pepper
Dash of pepper
Crackers or fresh vegetables

Combine all ingredients, except crackers or vegetables, in a medium mixing bowl; mix thoroughly. Chill at least 1 hour. Serve as dip with crackers or fresh vegetables.
Makes about 3 cups.

Marianne Bussey
State College, Pennsylvania

Vegetable Dip

1   (10-ounce) package frozen
      spinach, thawed
1 cup sour cream
1 cup mayonnaise
1 teaspoon lemon juice
¼ cup finely chopped onion
Fresh vegetable pieces

Squeeze excess moisture from spinach. Combine spinach and remaining ingredients, except vegetables; mix thoroughly. Serve with fresh vegetables.
Makes 3½ cups dip.

Vicki Dean
Chattanooga, Tennessee

Easy And Good

1 slice bread
1 teaspoon grated Parmesan cheese
¼ teaspoon instant onion (to taste)
1 tablespoon mayonnaise

Remove crust from bread. Cut bread into 4 pieces. Brown in broiler. Add cheese and onion to mayonnaise, mixing thoroughly. Spread mixture on uncooked side of bread. Place under broiler until golden brown.
Makes 1 serving.

Mary B. Holmes
Ann Arbor, Michigan

Mary's Fondue

1 clove garlic
1½ cups dry white wine
1 tablespoon Kirsch, Brandy, lemon
   juice or Sherry
1 pound natural Swiss cheese,
   shredded
3 tablespoons flour
Dash of pepper and nutmeg
French or Italian bread, cubed

Twenty-five minutes before serving time, rub inside of medium saucepan with garlic clove. Add wine and Kirsch and heat until wine is hot but not boiling. In a medium bowl, toss the cheese with the flour to coat cheese. Add the cheese by handfuls to hot wine. Stir constantly until all the cheese has been added and mixture is creamy and smooth. Add pepper and nutmeg. Serve immediately in a fondue pan. Use fondue forks for dipping cubed bread.
Makes 4 servings.

Good served with apple slices.

Sara Ann Briggs
Okemos, Michigan

Spiced Nuts

¼ cup sugar
1 tablespoon cinnamon
⅛ teaspoon each ground cloves,
   nutmeg
1 cup pecan halves
1 egg white, slightly beaten

In small bowl, combine sugar and spices. Add nuts, a few at a time, to egg white, stirring to coat thoroughly. Toss with sugar and spice mixture, coating completely. Place on well-buttered cookie sheet. Bake at 300°F. for 30 minutes.
Makes 1 cup nuts.

Rhea Y. Fetzer
Ann Arbor, Michigan

Clam Bites

2 (2-pound) loaves Pepperidge
   Farm bread
1 cup butter or margarine, melted
1 teaspoon Worcestershire sauce
8 drops of Tabasco sauce
½ teaspoon garlic salt
½ teaspoon onion salt
Juice of 2 large lemons
1 (10¾-ounce) can cream of
   mushroom soup
6 tablespoons minced onion
3 (8-ounce) packages cream cheese,
   softened
2 (7-ounce) cans minced clams,
   drained

Cut 12 dozen 1½-inch rounds of bread. (Easily done with cookie cutter.) Toast one side; brush toasted side with melted butter. Mix remaining ingredients in mixer or food processor. Generously spread mixture on untoasted side of bread, covering entire top. (May be frozen or chilled at this point.) To serve, broil for approximately 6 minutes, or until tops begin to brown. If frozen, lengthen cooking time.
Makes 12 dozen appetizers.

Sherri Seiber
Arlington Heights, Illinois

Elegant Crab Meatballs

2 (6½-ounce) cans crab meat,
   drained and flaked
1 cup soft bread crumbs
3 tablespoons cooking Sherry
1 tablespoon lemon juice
1 tablespoon grated onion
1 teaspoon dry mustard
½ teaspoon salt
Pepper to taste
12 bacon slices, halved

Combine crab meat with remaining ingredients except bacon in a small mixing bowl; mix well. Shape into walnut-sized balls. Wrap each ball with bacon; secure with toothpicks. Broil under medium heat until bacon is crisp, about 10 minutes, turning to brown evenly. Makes 2 dozen.

Can garnish with parsley and lemon.

Nancy DeWeese
Pasadena, Maryland

Company Crab Mold

1½ envelopes unflavored gelatin
¼ cup cold water
1 (10¾-ounce) can cream of
   mushroom soup, undiluted
8 ounces crab meat, canned or fresh
1 (8-ounce) package cream cheese,
   softened
1 cup mayonnaise
¾ cup chopped celery
½ cup chopped onion

Soften gelatin in cold water. Combine gelatin mixture and soup in a small saucepan. Cook over low heat, stirring constantly until gelatin dissolves. Remove from heat and stir in remaining ingredients. Spoon mixture into a greased 4-cup mold. Chill until set. Unmold and serve with assorted crackers.
Makes 3 dozen appetizers.

Susan Peterson
Diamond Bar, California

Finger Steaks

1 round steak, cut in 3-inch by
   1-inch strips
1 (3-ounce) package oven fry for
   pork (regular or crispy)
2 eggs
2 tablespoons water
2 tablespoons oil

Prepare round steak according to directions on package of oven fry. Bake in a preheated 350°F. oven for 20 minutes.
Makes 3 to 4 servings or 20 to 25 appetizer servings.

Peg Henerdine
Champaign, Illinois

The One Pounder

1 pound bulk pork sausage
1 pound hamburger
1 pound Velveeta cheese, cut in
   chunks
2 loaves party rye bread

Brown sausage and hamburger; drain well. Reduce to low heat. Add cheese to meat, stirring until melted. Spread on party rye slices. Place on cookie sheet and bake in preheated 400°F. oven until cheese bubbles. These can be made ahead of time and frozen.
Makes about 70 appetizers.

Variation: Use 1 pound hot pork sausage and ½ teaspoon oregano and ½ teaspoon garlic salt, and rest of above ingredients. This will taste like pizza.

Deanna Brusinski
Lathrup Village, Michigan

Mom's Spicy Meatball Recipe

1 pound ground beef
½ cup milk
1 egg, slightly beaten
½ cup fine-dry bread crumbs
2 tablespoons finely minced onion
⅛ teaspoon ground cloves
⅛ teaspoon ground allspice
1 teaspoon garlic salt
1 teaspoon minced parsley
2 cups catsup
½ cup brown sugar
2 tablespoons Worcestershire sauce
1 clove garlic, finely minced
  (optional)

In a large bowl, combine beef, milk, egg, bread crumbs, onion, cloves, allspice, garlic salt and parsley; mix thoroughly. Shape into 1-inch balls and place on lightly greased shallow baking pans. Bake in preheated 350°F. oven for 20 to 25 minutes (or broil for 10 to 12 minutes). While meatballs are baking, combine catsup, sugar, Worcestershire sauce and garlic in a medium saucepan; heat until sauce is bubbling and sugar has dissolved. Place baked meatballs in a chafing dish or Crock•Pot; pour sauce over them. Heat together for at least ½ hour before serving. Serve hot.
Makes 40 meatballs.

The longer the meatballs have to absorb the sauce, the better they are, which makes this a nice appetizer for an all afternoon or all evening buffet.

Joan Curran
Ann Arbor, Michigan

Quick Party Meatballs

2 pounds ground chuck
1 pound sausage, mild or hot
½ teaspoon salt
½ teaspoon ground black pepper
½ teaspoon garlic powder
1 (8-ounce) can water chestnuts,
  drained and diced
20 saltine crackers, ground
2 eggs
Sweet and sour sauce

In a large bowl, combine all ingredients, except sweet and sour sauce, mixing thoroughly. Roll in 1-inch balls and place in ungreased baking pan. Cover with aluminum foil and bake in preheated 350°F. oven for 15 minutes. Remove aluminum foil and bake an additional 10 minutes. Drain excess grease and place in a warmed casserole or chafing dish. Serve with toothpicks for spearing and sweet and sour sauce for dipping.
Makes approximately 50 meatballs.

Recipe may be doubled if needed for large crowd.

Mary Ott
Smyrna, Tennessee

Mock Oysters Rockefeller

1 onion, diced
2 tablespoons butter or margarine
1 (8-ounce) can mushrooms
1 (10-¾ ounce) can cream of
  mushroom soup
1 (10-ounce) package chopped
  broccoli, cooked according to
  package directions, drained
1 (6-ounce) roll Kraft garlic cheese
Hot sauce to taste
Chunks of toasted French bread

Sauté onion in butter. Add mushrooms and mushroom soup, combining thoroughly. Add broccoli and cheese; heat just until cheese is melted and mixture is hot. Stir in hot sauce. Serve with toast for dipping.
Makes about 3 cups.

Sara Hickey
Ann Arbor, Michigan

Shrimp Mold

1 (10¾-ounce) can cream of
  tomato soup
1 (8-ounce) package cream cheese,
  softened, broken into pieces
2 (¼-ounce) envelopes unflavored
  gelatin, dissolved in ½ cup cold
  water
1 cup mayonnaise
3 (5-ounce) cans shrimp, drained
  and rinsed
½ cup celery, finely chopped
½ cup onion, finely chopped

In a medium saucepan, heat soup; add cream cheese, stirring until smooth and heated through. Remove from heat. Add gelatin mixture, mayonnaise, shrimp, celery and onion, combining thoroughly. Pour into greased mold. Refrigerate for several hours or overnight. Makes 12 to 14 servings.

Make one day ahead, will keep for at least 4 days. Can be put into small molds and frozen. Serve with favorite crackers.

Janet Przybylski
Canton, Michigan

Shrimp Spread

1 (8-ounce) package cream cheese,
  softened
2 tablespoons milk
½ small diced onion
1 clove garlic, crushed
½ teaspoon garlic salt
2 teaspoons lemon juice
½ teaspoon Worcestershire sauce
1 (4½-ounce) can chopped baby
  shrimp, drained and finely
  chopped

Combine cream cheese, milk, onion, garlic, garlic salt, lemon juice and Worcestershire sauce, mixing thoroughly. Add finely chopped shrimp. Blend together and chill.
Makes about 1½ cups.

This is really delicious.

Jennifer Menges
Dunkirk, New York

Mini Quichettes

½ cup butter or margarine
1 (3-ounce) package cream cheese,
  softened
1 cup flour
4 ounces small shrimp
1 medium onion, chopped and lightly
  sautéed
½ cup grated Swiss cheese
2 eggs, slightly beaten
½ cup milk
⅛ teaspoon nutmeg
Fresh ground pepper to taste

Beat together butter and cream cheese until smooth. Add flour and form into a ball. Wrap in waxed paper and chill for at least 30 minutes. Make miniature pie shells by shaping dough into 1-inch balls and pressing into bottom and sides of small muffin cups (about 1½-inch diameter). In each miniature pie shell, place a few small shrimp, some of the sautéed onion and grated cheese. Combine eggs with milk, nutmeg and ground pepper and divide among cups. Bake at 450°F. for 10 minutes. Reduce heat to 350°F. and bake an additional 15 minutes. Serve immediately.
Makes 8 to 12 appetizers.

The filling can also be made with crabmeat, chopped ham and spinach, or sautéed bacon bits.

Lily Ernst
Dallas, Texas

Exotic Filipino Raw-Style Shrimp

¼ pound small shrimp, shelled and
   deveined
2 tablespoons minced gingerroot
2 tablespoons chopped green onion
Juice of ½ lemon
3 tablespoons soy sauce
Salt and monosodium glutamate
   to taste

Combine all ingredients, mixing thoroughly. Refrigerate for 10 minutes and serve.
Makes 2 servings.

Mario Talledo
Honolulu, Hawaii

Sweet And Sour Wing Dings

3 pounds chicken drumettes
Garlic salt to taste
2 eggs, beaten
1 cup cornstarch
1 cup firmly packed brown sugar
¼ cup water
1 tablespoon soy sauce
½ cup vinegar
3-4 tablespoons catsup
½ teaspoon Accent
Dash of salt

Sprinkle chicken drumettes with garlic salt; let stand for 1 hour. Dip chicken in eggs and roll in cornstarch. Deep fat fry until browned; drain well. Place chicken in a large pyrex dish. In a small saucepan, combine brown sugar, water, soy sauce, vinegar, catsup, Accent and salt; heat thoroughly. Pour sauce over chicken and bake in a preheated 350°F. oven for 40 minutes. Drain slightly before transferring to chafing or serving dish.
Makes 6 to 8 servings.

Susan J. Gates
Norcross, Georgia

Won Ton

1 (12-ounce) can spam, finely
   chopped
2 teaspoons sugar
3 teaspoons cornstarch
½ cup finely chopped green onions
1 (16-ounce) package won ton skins

In a bowl, combine spam, sugar, cornstarch and onions. Place 1 teaspoon meat mixture in center of each won ton skin. Fold won ton skin into a triangle; seal edges with water. Fry won tons in deep fat-fryer until golden brown (about 2 minutes). Serve hot.
Makes about 40 appetizer servings.

Mrs. Scott Kubota
Pearl City, Hawaii

Seasoned Oyster Crackers

1 (14 to 16-ounce) package
   unsalted oyster crackers
¾ cup vegetable oil
1 (1-ounce) package dry buttermilk
   ranch dressing mix

Place crackers in large plastic container. Pour oil over crackers and mix thoroughly. Add dressing mix and shake vigorously. For extra flavor, add ½ to 1 teaspoon dillweed. Keep tightly covered for 24 hours, shaking occasionally. Keep in closed container for up to three weeks.
Makes 1 quart nibblers.

Becky Belknap
Ann Arbor, Michigan

Antipasto

½ cup olive oil
1 small cauliflower, broken into
  bite-sized pieces
1 (13-ounce) can ripe olives
1 (8-ounce) jar pickled onions,
  drained
1 (12-ounce) jar green olives with
  pimento, drained
1 (4-ounce) can whole mushrooms,
  drained
1 green pepper, cut into 1-inch
  squares
1 (4-ounce) jar whole pimentos,
  drained and cut into bite-sized
  pieces
1 (12-ounce) jar sweet mixed
  pickles, drained
5 cups catsup
1 (14-ounce) can green beans
1 (2-ounce) can anchovies
½ cup vinegar
2 (6½-ounce) cans tuna, broken
  into chunks

In a large saucepan, combine olive oil, cauliflower, ripe olives, pickled onions and green olives. Simmer for 10 minutes over medium to low heat. Add mushrooms, green pepper, pimentos, pickles, catsup and green beans. Simmer for 10 minutes longer. Add anchovies, vinegar and tuna. Simmer for 1 or 2 minutes; remove from heat and place in containers. Freeze or chill. Serve cold with crackers. Makes about 15 cups.

This does not taste at all the way it sounds! The combination of all these ingredients is great!

Sharon Golzan
Kingston, Ontario, Canada

Hot Artichoke Spread

1 (14-ounce) can artichoke hearts
1 cup grated Parmesan cheese
1 (8-ounce) package cream cheese,
  softened
Paprika
¼ to ½ cup slivered almonds

Drain artichoke hearts and chop very fine. Add Parmesan cheese and cream cheese, mixing well. Pour into greased 1-quart casserole. Sprinkle paprika and almonds on top. Bake in preheated 350°F. oven for 20 minutes. Serve with crackers or party rye bread.

Shirley Tranquill
Pittsburgh, Pennsylvania

"There's-Never-Any-Left" Celery Sticks

2 (8-ounce) packages cream cheese,
  softened
2 tablespoons milk
1½ teaspoons Worcestershire sauce
½ teaspoon pepper
2 green onions, minced
½ teaspoon minced parsley
1 cup green olives, chopped
1 bunch of celery, washed and cut
  in 4-inch pieces
Whole olives
Radishes

In a medium bowl, combine cream cheese, milk, Worcestershire sauce and pepper; blend until smooth. Add onions, parsley and chopped olives; mix thoroughly. Fill celery with cream cheese mixture. Refrigerate for 20 minutes. Arrange on serving dish. Garnish with whole green olives and radishes.
Makes 36 appetizers.

Valerie Mueller
Gulfport, Michigan

Cheese-Stuffed Mushrooms

2 cups water
1 tablespoon lemon juice
1 pound medium mushrooms
1 (8-ounce) package cream cheese, softened
½ cup chopped walnuts
1 teaspoon Worcestershire sauce
½ teaspoon curry powder
Fresh parsley sprigs
Paprika

Place water and lemon juice in large saucepan. Bring to a boil and add whole mushrooms. Return to a boil and simmer gently for 2 minutes. Drain and cool. Remove stems from mushrooms; finely chop, reserving ½ cup for filling. Blend cream cheese with walnuts, Worcestershire sauce and curry powder; stir in chopped mushroom stems. Place a sprig of parsley in each mushroom cavity and fill with cheese mixture; sprinkle with paprika. Chill for 2 to 3 hours before serving.
Makes 6 to 8 servings.

Paul K. Derouin
Culver City, California

Spinach-Crab Stuffed Mushrooms

1 (10-ounce) package frozen chopped spinach, thawed
6 to 8 ounces Alaska Snow Crab, frozen or canned
1 pound fresh large mushrooms
2 teaspoons finely chopped onion
2 tablespoons butter or margarine
½ teaspoon garlic salt
¼ teaspoon pepper
2 tablespoons butter or margarine, melted

Cook spinach according to package directions; drain well. Set aside. Drain crab, reserving 2 tablespoons liquid. Remove stems from mushrooms; mince. Sauté mushroom stems and onion in 2 tablespoons butter until tender. Remove from heat and stir in reserved spinach, garlic salt and pepper. Brush inside of mushroom caps with melted butter. Spoon spinach mixture into mushrooms. Place filled mushrooms in 13x9x2-inch baking pan. Bake at 350°F. for 15 minutes.
Makes 24 appetizer servings.

Karen Shipman
Norcross, Georgia

Stuffed Mushrooms

1½ pounds medium to large mushrooms
1 (8-ounce) package brown-and-serve sausage links, chopped
½ cup shredded Mozzarella cheese
¼ cup seasoned dry bread crumbs

Remove stems from mushrooms; chop and set aside. Reserve mushroom caps. Brown sausage; drain, reserving 2 tablespoons grease in skillet. Sauté chopped mushroom stems in reserved grease until tender. Remove from heat and stir in sausage, cheese and bread crumbs. Spoon mixture into mushroom caps; place mushrooms in 15x10x1-inch jelly roll pan. Bake at 450°F. for 15 minutes or until mushrooms are tender.
Makes 2 dozen appetizer servings.

Kay Shook
Ypsilanti, Michigan

Spinach Balls

2 (10-ounce) packages frozen
   spinach, thawed
2 cups croutons
2 small onions, finely chopped
6 eggs, lightly beaten
¾ cup butter or margarine, melted
½ cup grated sharp Cheddar cheese
½ cup grated Parmesan cheese
1 tablespoon Accent
1½ teaspoons garlic salt
½ teaspoon thyme
¼ teaspoon pepper

Squeeze excess moisture from spinach. Combine all ingredients, mixing well. Allow mixture to stand ½ hour. Form into walnut-sized balls. Bake in a preheated 350°F. oven for 10 minutes or until lightly browned. Serve hot.
Makes about 50 balls.

Tammy Jo Galdikas
Anderson, Indiana

Spinach Squares

2 eggs, lightly beaten
1 cup milk
1 cup all-purpose flour
1 teaspoon baking powder
1 teaspoon salt
1 (10-ounce) package frozen
   spinach, thawed and drained well
½ pound Monterey Jack cheese,
   cubed

Combine eggs, milk, flour, baking powder and salt, mixing well. Stir in spinach and cheese. Place in greased 13x9x2-inch pan. Bake in a preheated 350°F. oven for 35 to 40 minutes. Cool for 10 minutes and cut into squares. Serve immediately.
Makes 48 appetizers.

May be made ahead and frozen. Heat in oven or microwave.

Ruth Hendricksen
South Lyon, Michigan

Water Chestnut Appetizer

½ pound bacon
1 (8-ounce) can water chestnuts,
   drained
1 cup catsup
½ cup firmly packed brown sugar

Cut bacon into thirds and wrap around water chestnuts; secure with toothpicks. Place on a cookie sheet with sides and bake in a preheated 350°F. oven until bacon is crisp. Place water chestnuts wrapped in bacon in serving dish and keep warm. In a small saucepan, combine catsup and sugar; cook for 5 minutes on medium heat, stirring occasionally. Pour over chestnuts. Serve warm.
Makes about 16 appetizers.

Ildiko Marcus
Xenia, Ohio

Beverages

Beverages

Aunt Julie's Bloody Mary Mix

2 (46-ounce) cans tomato juice
2 teaspoons celery salt or 2 teaspoons
   celery seed plus 2 teaspoons salt
2 teaspoons coarsely ground pepper
3 ounces horseradish
1 ounce Worcestershire sauce
1 ounce Roses lime juice
Vodka

In gallon container, combine all ingredients except vodka; mix well. Keep refrigerated. Serve over ice in tall 16-ounce glasses with one-shot (1-ounce) vodka.
Makes 12 to 16 servings.

Janet Przybylski
Canton, Michigan

Irish Cream

3 eggs, beaten
1 tablespoon Hershey chocolate
   syrup
1 teaspoon instant coffee
1 teaspoon coconut extract
2 pints whipping cream
1 (14-ounce) can sweetened
   condensed milk
1¼ cups Scotch

Combine eggs, chocolate syrup, instant coffee and coconut extract; mix well. Stir in whipping cream, sweetened condensed milk and Scotch. Refrigerate. Keeps for 1 month.
Makes about 1½ quarts.

Stephen M. Ley
Zionville, Indiana

Kahlua

2 cups water
4 cups white sugar
2 ounces instant coffee
1 fifth vodka
1 vanilla bean, cut into ½-inch
   pieces

In large pan, bring water to a boil; dissolve sugar in boiling water. Stir in instant coffee. Allow to cool. Pour vodka into jug. (An old large wine bottle works well.) Add coffee mixture and vanilla bean pieces; seal and shake. Let stand for 30 days in dark place.
Makes ½ gallon.

Timothy J. Ryan
Ann Arbor, Michigan

Boiled Custard

2 quarts milk
1½ cups sugar
6 eggs, beaten
4 tablespoons flour

Heat milk in top of double boiler just to simmering. Mix sugar and flour. Add eggs; mix well. Stir egg mixture into hot milk. Cook at low boil until slightly thickened, stirring constantly. Serve cold and garnish with ground nutmeg.

Valeria Russell
Ann Arbor, Michigan

◀*Recipes for this photograph on pages 31 and 33.*

Root Beer

4½ gallons water
5 pounds sugar
2 (2-ounce) bottles Hires Root
    Beer Extract
10 pounds dry ice

In 5-gallon nonmetalic container, combine water, sugar and Root Beer extract. Add dry ice slowly using wooden spoon. Let stand for 20 minutes before serving.
Makes 5 gallons.

Rachel Elbert
Marietta, Georgia

Tom & Jerry Mix

4 eggs, separated
1 pound confectioners' sugar
Milk
Rum or whiskey, if desired
Nutmeg

Beat egg yolks until thick. Beat egg whites until stiff. Gradually add confectioners' sugar to egg whites. Fold in egg yolks gently. Store mixture, covered, in refrigerator.
To Serve: Heat 1 cup milk per serving to desired temperature. Place 2 tablespoons egg mixture in each mug with desired amount of rum. Add hot milk to the egg and rum mixture. Sprinkle with nutmeg. Serve warm.
Makes 12 to 15 servings.

Susan L. Parker
Bedford, Ohio

Chocolate Milk Shake

¾ cup milk
3 tablespoons chocolate syrup
1 pint chocolate ice cream

In covered blender container, at high speed, blend all ingredients until smooth. Pour mixture into chilled glasses.
Makes 2 servings.

For Banana Milk Shake—Prepare as above but substitute 1 large ripe banana for chocolate syrup and 1 pint vanilla ice cream for chocolate ice cream.

Robyn Villarreal
Belleville, Illinois

Merry Berry Mint

4 scoops vanilla ice cream
2 ounces half and half
1 (heaping) tablespoon cranberries
5 small mint patties
Whipped Cream
Candy Cane
Sprig of fresh mint (if available)

In blender container, combine ice cream, half and half, cranberries and mint patties; blend until creamy. Pour into wine glasses. Top with whipped cream; garnish with candy cane and sprig of mint.
Makes 2 servings.

Janet Tilley
Troy, Michigan

Orange Cow

8 ounces orange juice
3-4 large scoops vanilla ice cream

Place ingredients in blender container; blend until smooth. Serve immediately in chilled glasses.
Makes 1 or 2 servings.

Coleen Butterick
Edgerton, Wisconsin

Peanut Butter Cup

5-6 scoops vanilla ice cream
½ ounce dark Creme de Cacao
¾ ounce chocolate syrup
1 teaspoon chunky peanut butter
1 Reese's chunky peanut butter cup

In mixer or blender, combine vanilla ice cream, Creme de Cacao, chocolate syrup, peanut butter and only ½ of the peanut butter cup; mix until smooth, thick consistency forms. Pour into large champagne, sherbet or dessert dishes. Place remaining ½ of the peanut butter cup on top. Serve with spoon or straw.
Makes 2 servings.

Kathleen Krpan
Mt. Prospect, Illinois

Uncle Bob's Moose Milk (Eggnog)

1 dozen eggs, separated
1 cup sugar
1 quart whipping cream, whipped
1 quart milk
1 cup light rum
2 cups whiskey
Nutmeg to taste

Beat egg yolks until light and lemon colored. Beat egg whites, gradually adding sugar until stiff. Whip cream until stiff. Fold egg yolks, egg whites and whipped cream gently together. Add milk, rum and whiskey. Place in large punch bowl; chill. Sprinkle with nutmeg before serving.
Makes 16 servings.

Sylvia Miller
Colorado Springs, Colorado

Ultimate Eggnog

1 dozen eggs, separated
1 pint whiskey or rum
3 cups sugar
1 tablespoon nutmeg
1 quart half and half
1 pint whipping cream

Mix egg yolks, whiskey, 2 cups sugar and nutmeg together. Let ripen for 24 hours. Add half and half. Beat egg whites with 1 cup sugar until soft peaks form. Add to egg yolk mixture. Beat whipping cream until stiff; gently fold into egg mixture.
Makes 25 servings.

Kim Kuz
Canton, Michigan

Hot Buttered Rum

1 quart vanilla ice cream, softened
1 pound butter or margarine,
  softened
1 pound brown sugar
1 pound confectioners' sugar
2 teaspoons cinnamon
1-2 teaspoons nutmeg
Rum
Cinnamon sticks, optional

Combine ice cream, butter, brown sugar, confectioners' sugar, cinnamon, nutmeg and rum; stir until well blended. Place mixture in a freezer container and freeze.
To Serve: Spoon 3 tablespoons of above mixture into each mug; add 1 jigger rum and enough boiling water to fill mug; stir. Place 1 cinnamon stick into each mug for an added touch and flavor.
Makes 30 servings.

Kathleen Krpan
Mt. Prospect, Illinois

Hot Cider

3 cups water
6 cups apple cider
1 (.25-ounce) package presweetened
   orange drink mix
1 (6-ounce) can frozen orange juice
1 (6-ounce) can frozen pink
   lemonade
1 teaspoon whole cloves
3 cinnamon sticks

In a 15-cup percolator, combine water, apple cider, drink mix, orange juice and pink lemonade. Place cloves and cinnamon sticks in percolator basket. Perk and serve hot.
Makes 12 servings.

Rebecca Waltz
Peyton, Colorado

Hot Chocolate Mix

1 (25.6-ounce) package instant
   nonfat dry milk
1 (6-ounce) jar powdered nondairy
   creamer
2 cups confectioners' sugar
1 (16-ounce) can instant chocolate
   drink mix

In large bowl, combine dry milk, creamer, confectioners' sugar and chocolate drink mix. Mix well. Place in large airtight container. Label and store in cool, dry place. Use within 6 months.
To Serve: Add 3 tablespoons Hot Chocolate Mix to 1 cup hot water. Stir to dissolve.
Makes 17 cups chocolate mix.

Gayle W. Ruby
Ponca City, Oklahoma

Spiced Mocha

1/2 cup whipping cream
1 tablespoon instant coffee granules
3 tablespoons sugar
1/2 teaspoon ground cinnamon
1/4 teaspoon nutmeg
Dash of ground cloves
6 tablespoons chocolate syrup
Hot coffee

Combine whipping cream, instant coffee, sugar, cinnamon, nutmeg and cloves. Chill for several hours. Beat until soft peaks form. Refrigerate until ready to use. Spoon 1 tablespoon chocolate syrup into each coffee mug. Fill with hot coffee, stirring well. Top each with generous spoonful of spiced whipped cream. Serve with cinnamon sticks.
Makes 6 servings.

Tammy Jewell-Greer
Pasadena, California

Mama's Good Tea

2 1/2 cups sugar
2 cups orange breakfast drink mix
1/2 cup instant tea with lemon
1 teaspoon cinnamon, ground
1/2 teaspoon cloves, ground

Combine sugar, orange drink mix, instant tea, cinnamon and cloves. Store in canister.
To Serve: Mix 2 teaspoons of mix with 1 cup hot water.
Makes 5 cups tea mix.

Rachel Elbert
Marietta, Georgia

Brandy Slush

7 cups water
2 cups sugar
2 cups water
4 tea bags
1 (12-ounce) can frozen lemonade
1 (12-ounce) can frozen orange juice
2 1/2 cups Brandy
1 (25-ounce) bottle Sweet and Sour Mix

In a saucepan, combine 7 cups water and 2 cups sugar; boil for 10 minutes. Cool to room temperature. Bring 2 cups water to a boil using 4 tea bags; steep tea for 5 minutes. Remove tea bags. Allow to cool to room temperature. Combine tea, sugar-water mixture, lemonade, orange juice and Brandy. Freeze in several small freezer containers.
To Serve: Partially thaw; fill glasses 2/3 full slush mixture. Fill glasses with Sweet and Sour Mix.
Makes about 20 servings.

Diana Thorp
Victoria, Texas

Candy Apple Punch

⅓ cup red cinnamon candies
½ cup lemon juice concentrate
4 cups apple juice or cider
2 tablespoons brown sugar
6 whole cloves
2 red apples, cored and sliced into rings, (optional)

In heavy saucepan over low heat, melt candies in lemon juice, stirring frequently. Add apple juice, brown sugar and cloves. Simmer for 15 minutes to blend flavors. Remove cloves; pour into heatproof punch bowl or individual mugs. Garnish with the apple rings, if desired. Best served warm, but can be cooled and iced.
Makes 4 servings.

Kathy McCracken
Bradford, Pennsylvania

Fruit Punch

6 cups sugar
3 tablespoons citric acid (Fruit Fresh)
5 pints warm water
5 pints cold water
1 (46-ounce) can orange juice
1 (46-ounce) can pineapple juice
1 (28-ounce) bottle ginger ale
1 quart lime sherbet

Mix sugar, citric acid and warm water until sugar is dissolved. Add cold water, orange juice and pineapple juice. Refrigerate until cold. (This may be made days ahead of time.) When ready to serve, pour mixture into punch bowl. Add chilled ginger ale and spoon in sherbet.
Makes 50 (6-ounce) servings.

Valeria Russell
Ann Arbor, Michigan

Health Shake

Juice of 1 large orange
Juice of 1 lemon
Juice of 1 lime
1 banana
¼ cup honey
¾ cup cracked ice
Wheat germ
Orange slices

Place juice from orange, lemon and lime in blender with banana, honey and cracked ice. Blend at high speed until smooth and frothy. Pour into 2 tall glasses. Sprinkle with wheat germ. Garnish with orange slice.
Makes 2 servings.

Tom Fast
Palatine, Illinois

Multi-Flavored Juice

12 ounces grape juice
12 ounces apple juice
12 ounces orange juice
12 ounces lemonade
12 ounces Hawaiian punch
1 (6-ounce) can frozen limeade
1 (6-ounce) can frozen tangerine
  juice

Prepare frozen juices by directions on can. In a large container, combine all juices; mix well. Chill or serve over ice. This juice is an ideal party punch.
Makes about 1½ gallons.

Substitute pineapple-orange juice for tangerine juice, if desired. For smaller quantities use only 5 juices of your choice.

Yvonne Grove
Las Vegas, Nevada

Orange Julius

⅓ cup orange juice concentrate
¼ cup sugar
½ cup milk
½ cup water
½ teaspoon vanilla extract
6 ice cubes, crushed

In a blender container, combine orange juice concentrate, sugar, milk, water, vanilla and crushed ice cubes. Blend for 30 seconds. Serve immediately or place in freezer for 1 to 2 hours.
Makes 3 servings.

Sara Ann Briggs
Okemos, Michigan

Peppermint Twist Punch

1½ cups sugar
1½ cups lime juice from concentrate
1 cup vodka or water
2 tablespoons white Creme de Menthe
  or ⅛ teaspoon peppermint extract
2 (28-ounce) bottles of Club soda
Ice Ring
Peppermint candy canes

In punch bowl, dissolve sugar in lime juice. Stir in vodka and Creme de Menthe.
To Serve: Add ice; stir in Club soda. Hang candy canes on edge of bowl or in each punch cup for stirrers. Substitute ⅛ teaspoon peppermint extract for Creme de Menthe if desired.
To Prepare Ice Ring: Fill an ice ring mold with water. Add a few candy canes to bottom of mold. Freeze for several hours. A fluted cake pan or an angel food cake tube pan may used for added designs.
Makes 2½ quarts.

Kathy McCracken
Bradford, Pennsylvania

Punch

4 cups sugar
2 (¼-ounce) packages lime drink
  mix
1 gallon water
1 (46-ounce) can pineapple juice
1 (12-ounce) can frozen orange
  juice concentrate, thawed

Combine sugar and lime drink mix. Add water and stir well. Add pineapple juice and frozen orange juice concentrate. (Do not add water to orange juice.) Mix well. Chill.
Makes approximately 2 gallons.

Yvonne Silvey
Marietta, Georgia

Strawberry Citrus Punch

4 cups unsweetened orange juice,
  chilled
1 cup lemon juice concentrate
1 (32-ounce) bottle lemon-lime
  carbonated beverage, chilled
1 (10-ounce) package frozen
  strawberries in syrup, partially
  thawed

In small punch bowl, combine orange juice and lemon juice. Just before serving, pour in carbonated beverage, then stir in strawberries. Makes 2 quarts.

Great party punch: A round ice ring made with whole fresh strawberries and orange slices may be added for color and flavor.

Kathy McCracken
Bradford, Pennsylvania

Strawberry Slush

4 ounces Strawberry de Bordeaux
2 ounces rum
2 teaspoons lemon juice
1 cup frozen strawberries, partially
  thawed

In a blender, combine Strawberry de Bordeaux, rum, lemon juice and frozen strawberries. Blend for 15 seconds. Serve in chilled goblets. Makes 2 servings.

Suzanne Gibson
Hamden, Connecticut

Sunshine

1 (46-ounce) can pineapple juice
1 (15½-ounce) can cream of coconut
1 (12-ounce) can frozen orange
  juice concentrate
7½ cups water

Combine all ingredients in large container; stir well. Chill. Serve over ice in tall glass; garnish with orange slice. Makes 1 gallon.

Maggie Monaghan
Ann Arbor, Michigan

Soups and Stews

Soups and Stews

Jewish-Style Chicken Soup With Matzo Balls

1 whole chicken, cut into eighths
6 stalks celery, sliced ½-inch thick
6 medium carrots, peeled and sliced
  ½-inch thick
3 medium potatoes, peeled and cut
  into cubes ½-inch thick
¼ cup chopped onions
¼ teaspoon paprika
¼ teaspoon salt
Dash of pepper
Pinch of rosemary
½ tablespoon chopped parsley
2 eggs
1 tablespoon corn oil
1 cup matzo meal

Fill large saucepan or Dutch oven with 14 cups water, approximately ⅔ full. Add chicken. Bring to a boil. Reduce heat and simmer for 10 minutes. Skim fat from top of boiling water. Return to a boil; reduce heat and add next 9 ingredients. Simmer for 60 to 90 minutes. In a mixing bowl, beat eggs with oil; stir in 1 cup matzo meal. Refrigerate mixture for 10 minutes. In a saucepan, bring 6 cups water to a boil. Form matzo mixture into 1-inch diameter balls. Drop balls into boiling water for 5 to 8 minutes. Remove and add to simmering chicken soup. Skim any additional fat from soup.
Makes 8 to 10 servings.

David Arky
Garland, Texas

Mom's Chicken Soup
(Even A Manager Can Make)

2 quarts water
5 chicken bouillon cubes
1 medium onion, diced
1 whole chicken, rinsed
2 cups water
1 (16-ounce) package medium egg
   noodles

I wake up at 11:00 A.M. on Saturday after getting clobbered at the store by a rainy Friday night, which included among other things, 2 sick trainees, 3 no-show drivers and a cooler breakdown. I need vitamins, something special, TLC? Tired of hot dogs and pot pies? I need a simple but darn good recipe for a healthy home-cooked meal? In a large saucepan, combine 2 quarts water, bouillon cubes and onion, bring to a boil. Reduce heat and add chicken. Simmer for 40 minutes. Remove chicken, reserving broth; cool for 15 minutes. Remove all meat from chicken, discarding bones and skin. In a separate 3-quart saucepan, place 2 cups reserved chicken broth and 2 cups water; bring to a boil. Add noodles and cook until tender about 8 to 12 minutes. Add chicken and noodle mixture to remaining chicken broth; add salt. Heat to desired temperature.
Makes 8 to 10 servings.

Soup is finished. Turn on ball game. Feel the strength returning to legs and back; know in your heart that you'll be ready to handle whatever tonight brings.

Daniel R. Shefte
Atlanta, Georgia

◀Recipe for this photograph on page 43.

Italian Soup

1 pound Italian sausage, crumbled
1½ cups chopped onion
2 cloves garlic, minced
¼ pound fresh mushrooms, quartered
2 tablespoons chopped fresh parsley
1 (28-ounce) can Italian plum
    tomatoes
1¼ cups beef bouillon
⅔ cup dry red wine
¼ teaspoon basil
1½ cups uncooked noodles
Fresh Parmesan cheese

Brown sausage in large saucepan or Dutch oven; drain thoroughly. Add remaining ingredients except noodles and cheese. Simmer for 3 hours. Add noodles and cook an additional 30 minutes. Serve hot. Sprinkle with cheese if desired.
Makes 6 servings.

Good with fresh crusty bread and wine.

Polly Minick
Ann Arbor, Michigan

Wedding Soup

1 pound Italian pork sausage
1 pound ground beef
3 eggs
1 cup uncooked regular oats
2 teaspoons oregano
1 teaspoon rosemary
1 clove garlic, minced
6 tablespoons olive oil
2 (14½ ounce) cans chicken broth
2 cans water
1 (5-ounce) package wide noodles
1 cup fresh spinach leaves, broken
    into pieces
1 large white onion, cut into thin
    rings
6 mushrooms, thinly sliced
2 eggs, lightly beaten
Croutons
Parmesan cheese

In a large bowl, combine pork sausage, ground beef, 3 eggs, oats, oregano, rosemary and garlic. Shape into walnut-sized meatballs. In a large skillet, brown meatballs in olive oil; drain and set aside. In a large saucepan, combine chicken broth and water; bring to a boil. Add noodles, meatballs and spinach. Cook gently, uncovered, until noodles are tender, about 11 to 13 minutes. Add onion, mushrooms and 2 eggs, stirring only until eggs are cooked. Remove from heat. Serve with croutons and Parmesan cheese, if desired.
Makes 8 to 10 servings.

Sue Pagniano
Missoula, Michigan

Crab Gumbo

¼ cup diced ham
½ clove garlic, minced
2 cups sliced fresh okra
2 tablespoons oil
½ bay leaf
½ teaspoon salt
⅛ teaspoon thyme
6 peppercorns
6 tomatoes, diced
1 cup hot water
½ pound crab meat, flaked

Sauté ham, garlic and okra in oil. When well coated with oil, but not brown, add remaining ingredients, except crab. Cook for 20 minutes. Add crab and simmer for 15 minutes longer. Serve on mounds of steamed rice.
Makes 6 servings.

Jennifer Seals
Carleton, Michigan

Seafood Gumbo

4 tablespoons flour
1/4 cup bacon drippings
1 onion, finely chopped
1 green pepper, finely chopped
1 teaspoon parsley flakes
1 teaspoon salt
1/4 teaspoon celery seed
1/4 teaspoon oregano
1/4 teaspoon garlic salt
1 (28-ounce) can tomatoes
1 (32-ounce) can tomato juice
5 cups water
1 1/2 tablespoons Worcestershire
  sauce
Dash of hot sauce
4 chicken bouillon cubes
1 teaspoon liquid crab boil
1 (16-ounce) package frozen sliced
  okra
1 pound shrimp, cooked, peeled and
  deveined
1 pound crab meat, picked to
  remove shell
1 tablespoon gumbo filé powder
Hot rice

Brown flour in bacon drippings until deep brown, stirring often, being careful not to burn. Add onion, green pepper, parsley flakes, salt, celery seed, oregano and garlic salt. Cook slowly over low heat for about 15 minutes, stirring frequently. Add remaining ingredients except shrimp, crab and filé powder. Continue to simmer on low heat for 2 hours. Add shrimp and crab and cook an additional 10 minutes. Stir in filé powder. Serve over hot rice.
Makes 10 to 12 servings.

Ann M. Holliday
Gulfport, Mississippi

Navy Bean Soup

4 cups dried navy beans
1/2 pound smoked bacon, diced
3 quarts water
1 large Spanish onion, chopped
2 cloves garlic, peeled and cut in half
1 cup diced celery
1 cup grated carrots
Salt and freshly ground black pepper
  to taste

Rinse and sort beans. Cover with water and let stand one night. Drain. In a large saucepan or Dutch oven, brown bacon; add water, onion and garlic. Bring to a boil; reduce heat; simmer for 30 minutes. Remove garlic. Add celery, carrots and beans. Simmer, covered, until beans are tender, stirring occasionally. Add salt and pepper to taste; simmer for 30 minutes longer.
Makes 12 servings.

Spear garlic cloves with toothpick for easy removal from soup.

Jim Tilley
Troy, Michigan

Broccoli Chowder

2 pounds fresh broccoli, washed and
  coarse stalk removed
3 cups chicken stock
3 cups milk
1 cup chopped cooked ham
2 teaspoons salt
1/4 teaspoon freshly ground pepper
1 cup half and half
2 cups grated Swiss cheese
1/4 cup butter

Place broccoli in large pan with 1 1/2 cups chicken stock. Bring to a boil. Reduce heat; cover. Simmer for 7 minutes, or until broccoli is tender. Remove broccoli from stock with slotted spoon; chop coarsely and set aside. Add remaining chicken stock, milk, ham, salt and pepper. Bring to a boil over medium heat, stirring occasionally. Reduce heat; stir in cream, cheese, butter and broccoli. Heat until cheese is melted. Do Not Boil.
Makes 8 servings.

Pam Carmichael
Jefferson City, Missouri

Cream Of Broccoli Soup

2   (10-ounce) packages frozen
   chopped broccoli, thawed
¼ cup chopped onion
2 cups chicken broth
2 tablespoons butter or margarine
1 tablespoon flour
2 teaspoons salt
⅛ teaspoon mace
Dash of white pepper
2 cups half and half

In a medium saucepan, combine broccoli, onion and chicken broth. Bring to a boil; reduce heat and simmer for 10 minutes or until broccoli is tender. Place broccoli mixture in a blender; blend until very smooth or press through a food mill. Melt butter in medium saucepan. Add flour, salt, mace and pepper, stirring until smooth. Slowly stir in half and half. Add broccoli purée. Cook over medium heat, stirring often, until soup bubbles. Serve hot.
Makes 10 to 12 servings.

Can be prepared a day ahead.

Joan Ebert
Barrington, Illinois

Cauliflower Soup

½ cup chopped onion
1 tablespoon oil
1 cup chopped celery
½ cup shredded carrot
1 small head cauliflower, washed
   and chopped
1 tablespoon minced parsley
6 cups chicken broth
1 bay leaf
½ teaspoon pepper
1 teaspoon tarragon
¼ cup butter or margarine, melted
¾ cup flour
2 cups milk
1 cup half and half
2 teaspoons salt
1 cup sour cream

Cook onion in oil until tender. Add celery and carrot; cook for 2 minutes. Stir in cauliflower and parsley. Reduce heat and cook, covered, for 15 minutes. Add broth, bay leaf, pepper and tarragon; simmer. In a small saucepan, combine butter and flour to make a thick paste. Slowly add milk and half and half. Cook and stir until thick and smooth. Add slowly to simmering vegetables, stirring constantly until thickened. Season with salt. Simmer for 15 minutes. Add sour cream.
Makes 10 to 12 servings.

May substitute broccoli for cauliflower.

Marsha Ikle
Franchise Concern

Cheese Soup

1 chicken bouillon cube
1 cup water
¼ cup diced onions
½ cup diced celery
½ cup diced carrots
3 cups cubed potatoes
3 cups milk
2 tablespoons flour
½ pound Velveeta cheese, cubed

In a medium saucepan, dissolve bouillon in water. Add remaining ingredients, except cheese. Simmer until vegetables are soft, about 15 minutes. Add cheese and heat over low heat until melted.
Makes 4 to 6 servings.

Amy Hamill
Brighton, Michigan

Gazpacho (Cold Spanish Soup)

1 (32-ounce) bottle clamato juice
3 tablespoons Italian dressing
2 tablespoons red wine vinegar
¾ teaspoon salt
Garlic powder to taste
⅛ teaspoon basil
1 green pepper, chopped
1 onion, diced
4 stalks celery, chopped
1 cucumber, peeled, seeded and
    quartered
Croutons (optional)

Combine juice and seasonings in large bowl; add vegetables and mix. Cover tightly; let stand at room temperature for 1 hour. Refrigerate for at least 2 hours. Serve chilled with croutons on top, if desired. Makes 6 to 8 servings.

Variations: Above method yields cool, crunchy soup. For a smoother texture, put all vegetables in a food processor before adding to juice.

Cheryl L. McCormick
Hendersonville, Tennessee

French Onion Soup

2 cups thinly sliced onions
¼ cup butter
1 tablespoon flour
¼ cup Burgundy wine
4 cups beef stock
1 tablespoon Worcestershire sauce
1 teaspoon salt
⅛ teaspoon pepper
⅛ teaspoon garlic powder
Garlic bread slices, frozen loaf is
    easiest
Mozzarella cheese

In a large saucepan or Dutch oven, sauté onions in butter until golden brown. Sprinkle flour over onions; stir. Add wine and allow to evaporate. Add beef stock and seasonings. Simmer, covered, for 45 minutes. In soup bowls or large mugs, place enough garlic bread to cover bottom of bowl. Pour soup into bowls over garlic bread. The bread will float. Place enough cheese on top of bread to cover entire surface. Place bowls in a preheated 350°F. oven to melt cheese, about 4 minutes. Serve immediately.
Makes 4 servings.

Mary Kogelschatz
Belleville, Michigan

Italian Lentil Soup

1 (1-pound) package dried lentils
4 cups water
1 medium onion, chopped
3 carrots, thinly sliced
3 stalks celery, thinly sliced
2 medium potatoes, peeled and diced
1 (16-ounce) can crushed Italian
    tomatoes
Salt and pepper to taste
1 teaspoon oregano
1 teaspoon garlic salt

Rinse and sort lentils. Combine lentils and water in large Dutch oven. Cover and let stand overnight. Drain lentils; add remaining ingredients. Bring to a boil; reduce heat. Cover and simmer for 3 hours, stirring occasionally.
Makes 8 servings.

Lynn LaRosa
Orange, California

Sweet And Sour Lentils

2½ cups lentils
4 cups water
⅓ cup tamari sauce
½ teaspoon crushed bay leaves
2 cups chopped onions
½ cup honey
½ cup vinegar
1 teaspoon ginger
1 teaspoon ground cloves
1 teaspoon allspice

Rinse and sort lentils. Combine lentils and water to cover in small Dutch oven. Cover and let stand overnight. Drain. Combine lentils with 4 cups water, tamari sauce, bay leaves and onions; simmer for ½ hour. Combine honey, vinegar, ginger, cloves and allspice. Add to lentils. Pour mixture into casserole. Bake, uncovered, in preheated 325°F. oven for 1 hour.
Makes 8 servings.

Beth Black
Minneapolis, Minnesota

Egg Drop Potato Soup

3 large potatoes, peeled and diced
1 onion, coarsely chopped
½ cup celery, diced
1 teaspoon salt
1½ cups water
2 cups milk
¼ teaspoon pepper
3 tablespoons butter or margarine
1 egg, beaten
3 tablespoons flour
Chopped parsley

Combine potatoes, onion, celery, salt and water in saucepan. Bring to a boil. Cover and simmer for 15 minutes or until potato is tender. Add milk and bring almost to a boil. Add pepper and butter. Blend egg and flour. Drop by ½ teaspoonfuls into soup. Simmer for 5 minutes; sprinkle with parsley.
Makes 4 servings.

Daphne Gabriel
Ann Arbor, Michigan

Polish Potato Soup

3 pounds beef ribs
1 teaspoon salt
¼ teaspoon pepper
3 stalks celery, thinly sliced
2 medium onions, chopped
2 bay leaves
20 peppercorns
12 medium potatoes, diced
2 (10¾-ounce) cans Campbell's tomato soup
1 (1¼-ounce) package onion soup mix

Cover ribs with water; bring to a boil. Drain; add fresh water to cover ribs. Add salt, pepper, celery, onions, bay leaves and peppercorns. Bring to a boil. Reduce heat and simmer for 2 hours. Remove meat, celery, onions and bay leaves from broth, reserving meat; discard celery, onions and bay leaves. Add potatoes and tomato soup to broth. Cook for 1 hour. Remove meat from ribs and add to soup. Simmer for 10 minutes; stir in onion soup mix. Cook for 10 minutes longer.
Makes 6 servings.

Steve Lipinski
Huntsville, Ohio

"Jim's Vegetable Soup"

2-inch cube beef suet
1½ pounds stewing beef, fat removed
   and cut into 1-inch cubes
Garlic powder to taste
5 to 6 cups water
2 beef bouillon cubes
3 to 4 teaspoons beef extract
2 teaspoons salt
5 medium potatoes
3 carrots
½ pound green beans
3 stalks celery
2 large onions, chopped
3 tablespoons salt
3 tablespoons chili powder
2 tablespoons oregano
2 teaspoons black pepper
1 teaspoon garlic powder
1 teaspoon crushed red pepper
½ teaspoon paprika
½ teaspoon curry powder
½ teaspoon thyme
½ head of cabbage, shredded
½ (10-ounce) package frozen lima
  beans
½ (10-ounce) package frozen corn
1 (14½-ounce) can whole tomatoes
1 (24-ounce) can tomato juice
¾ cup barley

Slowly brown suet in medium metal pan. Remove suet from pan and save. Brown beef in drippings; add garlic powder while browning. When beef is browned, return suet to pan with water. Add bouillon cubes, beef extract and salt. Allow to simmer for 3 to 4 hours. Skim fat from soup. In very large pan, place potatoes, carrots, green beans, celery and onions. Cover vegetables with water and bring to a boil. Reduce heat. Add salt, chili powder, oregano, pepper, garlic powder, red pepper, paprika, curry powder and thyme. Cook for about 20 minutes; add cabbage, lima beans, corn, tomatoes and tomato juice. Continue to cook for 1 hour. Remove from heat and let stand until cooled. Add beef mixture to vegetables. Add barley. Bring to a boil; reduce heat. Simmer for 15 to 20 minutes. Season to taste.
Makes 14 to 16 servings.

Note: This is my father's recipe exactly as he gave it to me. I have made it once, and it was very good. However, I would make a few changes next time I make it:
1. I would increase the stewing beef to about 2½ to 3 pounds. The beef and the stock is what really makes this soup.
2. Be careful not to put too much water in pot when boiling vegetables. Only put in enough to cover vegetables.
3. If possible, use all fresh vegetables.
4. You'll need at least a 12-quart pot to cook this in.

Jay Newby
Huntsville, Alabama

Curried Cream Of Zucchini Soup

1 medium yellow onion, chopped
1 clove garlic, minced
½ cup butter
1 pound zucchini, thinly sliced
1 tablespoon curry powder
1 teaspoon salt
½ teaspoon pepper
1 (12-ounce) can evaporated milk
1 (10¾-ounce) can chicken broth
½ cup water (optional)

In a large saucepan, sauté onion and garlic in butter until transparent. Add zucchini and cook until tender. Add curry powder, salt and pepper to zucchini mixture. Place entire mixture in a blender and blend until smooth. Return to saucepan. Add evaporated milk and chicken stock and cook for at least ½ hour. Add water if soup becomes too thick.
Makes 6 to 8 servings.

Carla Caldwell
Ann Arbor, Michigan

Irish Stew

1 pound boneless lamb, cut into
  1-inch cubes
1 medium onion, cut into thin
  wedges
1 bay leaf
1½ teaspoons salt
¼ teaspoon pepper
4 cups water
2 medium potatoes, peeled and
  thinly sliced
1 medium turnip, peeled and chopped
1 (10-ounce) package frozen green
  beans
1 tablespoon snipped parsley
¼ teaspoon dried basil
¼ teaspoon dried oregano

In large saucepan or Dutch oven, combine lamb, onion, bay leaf, salt and pepper. Add water; bring to a boil and reduce heat. Cover and simmer for 1 hour. Stir in potatoes, turnip, green beans, parsley, basil and oregano. Cover and simmer for 25 to 30 minutes longer or until vegetables are tender. Remove bay leaf. Season to taste.
Makes 6 servings.

Jack Gardner
Ann Arbor, Michigan

Tater Stew

1½ pounds ground beef
1 large onion, chopped
4 medium potatoes, peeled and cubed
1 (10¾-ounce) can mushroom soup
Water or milk
Salt and pepper to taste

In an electric frypan, sauté ground beef, onion and potatoes until meat is cooked and potatoes are tender. Add mushroom soup and enough water or milk to cover potato mixture. Add salt and pepper to taste.
Makes about 6 servings.

Thomas Monaghan
Ann Arbor, Michigan

World's Easiest Stew

1½ pounds stew beef, fat removed,
  and cubed
1 (10¾-ounce) can mushroom soup
1 (1¼-ounce) package dry onion
  soup mix
½ cup sliced mushrooms
½ cup sliced carrots
4 cups cooked rice
4 slices bread, toasted

Combine stew beef, mushroom soup, onion soup mix, mushroooms and carrots in baking dish. Cover. Bake in a preheated 350°F. oven for 2 hours. Serve over rice or toast.
Makes 4 servings.

Karen Shipman
Atlanta, Georgia

Salads

Salads

Cranberry Holiday Salad

1 (3¾-ounce) package strawberry-
flavored gelatin
1 cup hot water
1 (9-ounce) can crushed pineapple
½ teaspoon grated lemon peel
2 tablespoons lemon juice
Dash of salt
1 cup diced celery
1 cup whole cranberry sauce
½ cup broken walnuts

Pour gelatin into bowl. Add hot water and stir to dissolve. Drain pineapple, reserving juice. Add pineapple juice, lemon peel, lemon juice and salt to gelatin mixture. Chill until partially set. Combine pineapple, celery, cranberry sauce and walnuts in bowl; stir to mix. Fold into gelatin mixture. Pour into 5½-cup mold or a 9x9-inch dish. Chill until firm.
Makes 8 servings.

Janet Cromer
Ypsilanti, Michigan

Garden Salad With Fruit

½-1 head lettuce, torn into bite-sized
  pieces
4 green onion tops, thinly sliced
1 teaspoon minced fresh parsley
1-1½ cups chopped celery
2 (11-ounce) cans mandarin
  oranges, drained
1 cup seedless green grapes
½ cup slivered almonds, toasted

Combine all ingredients in bowl, except almonds; chill. Prepare dressing and add to salad. Garnish with toasted almonds and serve. Makes 4 to 8 servings.

Dressing

½ cup salad oil
1 teaspoon salt
¼ teaspoon white pepper
4 tablespoons sugar
4 tablespoons white vinegar
Dash of Tabasco sauce

Combine all ingredients in bowl and mix thoroughly. Pour over salad and toss lightly.

Almonds may be toasted by placing a cookie sheet with small amount of butter. Toast in 300°F. oven until golden brown; be careful not to let burn.

Sarah E. Cochran
Zelienople, Pennsylvania

Mandarin Orange Salad

1 (6-ounce) package lemon-flavored
  gelatin
1 (12-ounce) carton frozen whipped
  topping, thawed
1 (12-ounce) carton cottage cheese
2 (6-ounce) cans mandarin oranges,
  drained
Maraschino cherries (optional)

Combine dry gelatin, whipped topping and cottage cheese in bowl; mix thoroughly. Reserve a few orange slices for garnish. Stir remaining oranges into whipped topping mixture. Chill. Garnish with orange slices and cherries.
Makes 6 to 8 servings.

It is quick to prepare and very good!

Wanda Swanton
Augusta, Georgia

◀Recipe for this photograph on page 52.

Mandarin Congealed Salad

1 (3-ounce) package orange-
  flavored gelatin
1 cup hot water
⅓ cup sugar
¾ cup pineapple juice
1 cup sour cream
1 teaspoon vanilla extract
1 cup crushed pineapple
1 (6-ounce) can mandarin oranges,
  drained
½ cup coconut
1 cup miniature marshmallows

Combine gelatin, hot water and sugar in bowl; stir to dissolve. Stir in pineapple juice. Chill until partially set. Add sour cream and vanilla; whip until fluffy. Fold in crushed pineapple, mandarin oranges, coconut and miniature marshmallows. Chill and serve.
Makes 9 servings.

Shirley Tranquill
Pittsburgh, Pennsylvania

Papaya-Avocado Salad

2 ripe papayas
2 ripe avocados
8 leaves of butter lettuce
½ cup pine nuts
1 tablespoon balsamic vinegar
1 tablespoon lime juice
½ cup walnut oil

Peel and seed papayas and avocados. Slice each into fan shapes. Arrange lettuce on plate; top with 2 slices of each fruit. Sprinkle with pine nuts. Combine vinegar and lime juice in bowl; beat in oil. Pour mixture over fruits.
Makes 8 servings.

Dan Rouse
Santa Monica, California

Pretzel Salad

¾ cup butter or margarine
2⅔ cups crushed pretzels
¼ cup sugar
1 (8-ounce) package cream cheese,
  softened
1 (8-ounce) container frozen
  whipped topping, thawed
1 tablespoon milk
2 cups boiling water
1 (6-ounce) package strawberry-
  flavored gelatin
2 (10-ounce) packages frozen
  strawberries

Preheat oven to 400°F. Melt butter in 13x9-inch baking dish. Add crushed pretzels and mix well. Press evenly into pan. Bake in oven for 10 minutes. Cool. Combine sugar, cream cheese, whipped topping and milk in bowl; beat until smooth. Add more milk if necessary. Spread over pretzel crust. Refrigerate. Add boiling water to gelatin and stir until dissolved. Stir in frozen strawberries. When mixture begins to thicken, spoon over cream cheese mixture. Refrigerate until salad is firm.
Makes 12 servings.

Gail LaButte
Lakeland, Michigan

San Francisco Salad Bowl

1¼ cups milk
1 (3¾-ounce) package instant
    vanilla or banana pudding mix
¾ cup mayonnaise or salad dressing
½ teaspoon rum flavoring
2 cups peach slices
2 cups nectarine slices
2 cups grapes
2 cups pear slices
1 cup blueberries

Combine milk and pudding mix in bowl; beat for 1 minute with electric mixer at low speed. Add mayonnaise and flavoring; mix well. Place fruit in serving bowl, reserving ¼ cup; toss lightly. Top with pudding mixture. Chill. Garnish with reserved fruit.
Makes 12 servings.

When in a hurry, use 6 cans chunky-style fruit cocktail instead of fresh fruit.

Joyce A. Archenbrunn
Ypsilanti, Michigan

Sawdust Salad

1 (3¾-ounce) package lemon-
    flavored gelatin
1 (3¾-ounce) package orange-
    flavored gelatin
2 cups boiling water
1½ cups cold water
1 (13½-ounce) can crushed
    pineapple, drained, reserving juice
2 bananas, chopped (optional)
5 ounces miniature marshmallows
⅓ cup sugar
1 egg, beaten
2 tablespoons cornstarch
1 (8-ounce) package frozen whipped
    topping, thawed
1 (8-ounce) package cream cheese,
    softened
Grated cheese or nuts for garnish

Combine lemon and orange-flavored gelatins and boiling water in large bowl; stir to dissolve. Add cold water, drained pineapple and bananas. Chill mixture until it mounds slightly when dropped from spoon. Fold in marshmallows; pour into 13x9x2-inch dish. Chill until set. Measure reserved pineapple juice and add enough water to make 1 cup. In medium saucepan, combine pineapple juice mixture, sugar, egg and cornstarch. Cook over medium heat until mixture thickens; cool completely. Spread over marshmallow mixture. Chill until set. Combine whipped topping and cream cheese in bowl; beat until smooth. Spread over custard layer. Chill until firm. Sprinkle top with grated cheese or finely chopped nuts to suggest sawdust. Cut into squares to serve.
Makes 16 to 20 servings.

Kathy Bott
Westerville, Ohio

Mom's Special Fruit Salad

1 cup whipping cream
2 (3-ounce) packages cream cheese
2 tablespoons mayonnaise
2 tablespoons pineapple syrup
24 marshmallows, quartered
2½ cups pineapple chunks, drained
2 cups Tokay grapes, halved and
    seeded

Whip cream until stiff; set aside. Combine cream cheese, mayonnaise and pineapple syrup in mixer bowl; blend with mixer until smooth. Stir in marshmallows and pineapple chunks. Fold in whipped cream and grapes.
Makes 8 to 10 servings.

Ann Borchert
Ann Arbor, Michigan

Strawberry-Nut Salad

2 (3¾-ounce) packages strawberry-
  flavored gelatin
1 cup boiling water
2 (10-ounce) packages frozen sliced
  strawberries, thawed
1 (16-ounce) can crushed pineapple,
  drained
3 medium bananas, mashed
½ cup chopped nuts (optional)
1 pint sour cream

Place gelatin in bowl; add boiling water and stir to dissolve. Fold in strawberries, pineapple, bananas and nuts. Pour ½ of the mixture into 18x12-inch dish. Chill until firm. Spread with sour cream. Gently pour remaining mixture over sour cream. Refrigerate until firm. Makes 12 to 15 servings.

Tess Bommarito
Ann Arbor, Michigan

Summer Fruit Salad

1 cantaloupe
1 honeydew melon
¼ watermelon
1 fresh pineapple
½ cup shredded coconut

Cut cantaloupe, melons and pineapple into bite-sized pieces. Place in bowl and toss lightly to mix. Just before serving, sprinkle with shredded coconut. Spoon into individual serving dishes and top with dollop of Honey Cream Dressing.
Makes 10 to 12 servings.

Makes a very colorful salad; good for a light dessert.

Honey Cream Dressing

1 pint whipping cream
¼ cup honey to taste

Pour cream and honey into small bowl; whip until stiff. Refrigerate until ready to serve.
Makes 4¼ cups.

Pam Waleri
Norwalk, Ohio

Waldorf Salad

3 cups chopped apples
2 stalks celery, chopped
1½ cups walnut pieces
Juice from 1 lemon
½ cup mayonnaise
Pinch of sugar
Dash of salt and pepper
4 tablespoons whipping cream

Combine apples, celery, walnuts and lemon juice in mixing bowl. In a separate bowl, mix mayonnaise, sugar, salt and pepper. Whip cream until stiff in small bowl. Fold into mayonnaise mixture. Mix dressing with fruit mixture.
Makes 6 servings.

Petra Oudehengel
West Germany

Artichoke-Rice Salad

1 (4.6-ounce) package chicken-
   flavored rice
2 green onions, minced
1 large green pepper, chopped
8 pimento-stuffed olives, sliced
2 (6-ounce) jars marinated
   artichoke hearts
¼ teaspoon curry powder
½ cup mayonnaise
3-4 chicken breasts, cooked and
   chopped
Lettuce leaves

Cook rice according to package directions, omitting butter. Drain and set aside in a bowl. Let stand until rice reaches room temperature. Add onions, green pepper and olives. Drain artichoke hearts, reserving half the liquid. Combine curry powder, mayonnaise and liquid from artichoke hearts; mix until well blended. Add to rice. Add artichoke hearts and chicken; stir. Chill in covered container. Serve on a bed of lettuce.
Makes 6 servings.

Susan Litman
Lakewood, Colorado

Broccoli Salad

1 bunch broccoli
3 green onions, chopped
1 (8-ounce) package mushrooms,
   sliced
½ cup chopped celery (optional)

Combine broccoli, onions, mushrooms and celery in bowl; set aside. Pour dressing over vegetables and toss.
Makes 6 servings.

Dressing

¼ cup vinegar
½ cup sugar
1 cup oil
1 teaspoon paprika
1 teaspoon celery salt

In separate bowl, combine vinegar, sugar, oil, paprika and celery salt and beat until blended.

Mary C. Brueggeman
Grass Lake, Michigan

Marinated Finger Tip Carrots

1 cup sugar
1 cup apple cider vinegar
⅓ cup vegetable oil
4 (16-ounce) cans finger tip
   carrots, drained
1 green pepper, chopped
1 (4-ounce) jar pimento
2 bunches of green onions, chopped
   (about 1 cup)

Combine sugar, vinegar and oil in saucepan; boil until sugar dissolves, stirring constantly. Cool. When liquid is cool, add remaining ingredients and stir thoroughly. Refrigerate in airtight container for 24 hours.

A delicious dish for serving with chicken, fish or beef; good for picnics. Will keep in refrigerator for 10 days to 2 weeks.

Helen R. Bloodworth
Atlanta, Georgia

Velma's Marinated Carrots

1   (10¾-ounce) can tomato soup
½ cup oil
1 cup sugar (or less)
¾ cup vinegar
1 teaspoon mustard
1 teaspoon Worcestershire sauce
1 teaspoon salt
1 teaspoon pepper
1 purple onion, chopped
1 green pepper, chopped
2 pounds sliced fresh carrots,
    blanched

Combine all ingredients except carrots in bowl; stir well. Add carrots; mix thoroughly. Marinate for at least 12 hours before serving. As carrots are eaten, marinate additional carrots as long as liquid remains. Makes 8 to 10 servings.

Rhonda Brown
Yukon, Oklahoma

Cauliflower-Broccoli Salad

1 head cauliflower, broken into
    flowerets
1 bunch broccoli, cut into flowerets
1 bunch green onions, chopped fine
1   (10-ounce) package frozen peas,
    thawed
1 cup mayonnaise
1 cup sour cream
1½ teaspoons garlic salt

Combine all ingredients in bowl and mix. Marinate vegetables overnight before serving.

Patty Recker
Rock Springs, Wyoming

Cucumber Salad

½ cup sour cream
2 tablespoons snipped parsley
2 tablespoons vinegar
1 tablespoon sugar
1 tablespoon snipped chives
3 small cucumbers, unpeeled and
    thinly sliced (about 3 cups)

Combine sour cream, parsley, vinegar, sugar and chives; mix well. Gently fold in cucumbers. Cover and chill. Makes 6 servings.

Sandra F. Fulcher
Ann Arbor, Michigan

Fumi-Fumi Salad

8 tablespoons slivered almonds
8 ounces sunflower seed
2 tablespoons butter
1 medium to large head cabbage,
  shredded
8 tablespoons green onions,
  (shredded with cabbage)
2 tablespoons butter
2 (3-ounce) packages Ramen
  oriental noodles, crushed

Brown almonds and sunflower seed in butter in skillet. Combine cabbage and green onions in bowl; add sunflower seed, almonds and crushed dry noodles. Pour dressing over salad ingredients and toss. Makes 8 to 10 servings.

Dressing

4 tablespoons sugar
1 cup oil
2 teaspoons salt
6 tablespoons rice vinegar

In separate bowl, combine sugar, oil, salt and vinegar; beat until blended.

Pat Carpenter
Lawrenceville, Georgia

Lentil Salad With French Dressing

1 cup dried lentils, rinsed
2 tablespoons chopped watercress or
  parsley
3 scallions, finely chopped
½ cup French dressing

Place lentils in saucepan with 2 quarts cold water. Bring to a boil; reduce heat. Simmer for 10 to 15 minutes or until lentils are cooked but still firm. Drain immediately; transfer lentils to a bowl. Add remaining ingredients to lentils while still hot; toss gently. (Do not mash the lentils). Serve cooled or at room temperature.
Makes 6 servings.

French Dressing

1 clove garlic
Salt to taste
1 tablespoon red wine vinegar
1 teaspoon Dijon mustard
¼ teaspoon sugar
6 tablespoons olive oil

In bowl, mash garlic with salt to make a paste. Blend in remaining ingredients with a wire whisk.
Makes ½ cup.

Connie DeVantier
Ann Arbor, Michigan

Pebble Salad

1 (6-ounce) package long-grain
  wild rice mix
1 (12-ounce) can whole kernel
  corn, drained
1 small cucumber, seeded and
  chopped
2 medium carrots, chopped
2 green onions, sliced
1/3 cup chopped parsley
1/3 cup salad oil
1/4 cup lemon juice
2 cloves garlic, minced
1/2 teaspoon dillweed
1/4 teaspoon dry mustard
1/4 teaspoon pepper
1/2 cup sunflower seed
1/3 cup slivered almonds

Cook rice according to package directions; cool then rinse. Add corn, cucumber, carrots, green onions and parsley to rice and stir to combine. Combine oil, lemon juice, garlic, dillweed, mustard and pepper in small bowl; mix well. Pour into rice mixture and stir. Chill several hours or overnight. Stir in sunflower seed. Sprinkle with almonds and serve.
Makes 6 to 8 servings.

Nancy McCord
Ann Arbor, Michigan

Hot German Potato Salad

1/4 pound bacon
1/2 cup onion, chopped
1/3 cup vinegar
1/3 cup water
1 teaspoon salt
1/8 teaspoon pepper
1 teaspoon dry mustard
1 tablespoon flour
1 tablespoon sugar
4 cups peeled, cubed, cooked
  potatoes
Paprika

Cook bacon in skillet; reserve drippings. Add onion and cook slightly. Add vinegar, water, salt, pepper, mustard, flour and sugar to skillet. Heat mixture to a boil, stirring constantly. Add potatoes and toss. Sprinkle with paprika. Serve warm.

Nancy Williams
Canton, Michigan

Nancy's Potato Salad

8 potatoes
6 hard-cooked eggs, diced
1 onion, chopped

Cook potatoes in boiling water until done. Peel and dice potatoes. eggs and onions. Place potatoes, eggs and onions in bowl and mix. Add dressing to potatoes and toss. Serve hot.
Makes 8 to 10 servings.

Dressing

2 teaspoons celery seed
2 eggs, beaten
1/2 cup sugar
1 tablespoon salt
1 teaspoon pepper
1 tablespoon prepared mustard
1/2 cup vinegar
2 cups Kraft salad dressing

Combine celery seed, eggs, sugar, salt, pepper, mustard and vinegar in saucepan; cook over medium heat until thick. Remove saucepan from heat and stir in salad dressing.

Gwendolyn G. Bradley
Columbus, Ohio

Spinach Salad With Sweet And Sour Dressing

1 (10-ounce) package fresh spinach,
   torn into bite-sized pieces
½ cup fresh bean sprouts
1 (8-ounce) can drained water
   chestnuts
4 hard-cooked eggs, sliced
¼ pound bacon, cooked crisp and
   crumbled
½ red onion, sliced thin

Combine salad ingredients in large salad bowl. Add dressing to salad and toss just before serving.
Makes 8 to 12 servings.

Remaining dressing may be used for other salads as well!

Sweet And Sour Dressing

1 cup salad oil
½ cup wine vinegar
½ cup sugar
⅓ cup catsup
Dash of salt

Combine dressing ingredients and shake vigorously to mix.

Jan Gentner
Ann Arbor, Michigan

Korean Spinach Salad

8 slices bacon, cooked and crumbled
1 (10-ounce) package fresh spinach,
   torn into bite-sized pieces
3 hard-cooked eggs, diced
½ pound Monterey Jack cheese,
   shredded
1 bunch broccoli, chopped
1 (14-ounce) can bean sprouts,
   drained
1 (6-ounce) can sliced water
   chestnuts, drained
1 (4-ounce) can mushrooms,
   drained
3-4 carrots, sliced
2-3 medium tomatoes, sliced

Combine salad ingredients in large bowl. Pour dressing over salad. Toss thoroughly and enjoy!
Makes 8 servings.

This recipe is always a hit whenever I take it somewhere! After trying the salad, most people ask for the recipe.

Dressing

1 cup salad oil
¾ cup sugar
⅓ cup catsup
¼ cup vinegar (with tarragon
   optional)
1 tablespoon Worcestershire sauce
1 medium onion, grated
1 teaspoon basil
1 clove garlic, crushed

Combine dressing ingredients in covered container; shake vigorously until well blended.

Sally Stansik
Wheeling, Illinois

Red Leaf Lettuce And Mushroom Salad

1 bunch red leaf lettuce, torn into
  pieces
½ pound fresh mushrooms, diced
¼ cup oil
1 clove garlic, minced
3 tablespoons fresh lemon juice
1 teaspoon sugar
½ teaspoon salt
¼ teaspoon fresh ground pepper
Herbs of your choice (optional)

Refrigerate lettuce and mushrooms in airtight container. Pour oil into salad bowl. Add garlic and let stand for 1 hour. Combine lemon juice with seasonings in jar with tight-fitting lid. Shake vigorously to dissolve sugar. Let stand for 1 hour. Just before serving, add lemon juice mixture to oil and blend. Add lettuce and mushrooms; toss lightly to serve.
Makes 6 servings.

Delicious!

Sally Stansik
Wheeling, Illinois

Tomato Fans

¾ cup cottage cheese
⅓ cup shredded Provolone cheese
2 tablespoons grated Parmesan
  cheese
2 tablespoons olive oil
1 small clove garlic, minced
¼ teaspoon salt
⅛ teaspoon pepper
6 small ripe tomatoes
6 spinach leaves

Combine cottage cheese, Provolone and Parmesan cheeses, oil, garlic, salt and pepper in bowl; mix thoroughly. Cut each tomato vertically into 6 slices without cutting through bottom. Spoon heaping teaspoon cheese mixture between each slice. Cover and chill for at least 1 hour. Cut spinach into thin strips. Serve tomatoes on spinach.
Makes 6 servings.

Linda J. Paris
Wixom, Minnesota

Twenty-Four Hour Vegetable Salad

1 medium head iceberg lettuce, torn
  into bite-sized pieces
1 teaspoon sugar
½ teaspoon salt
¼ teaspoon pepper
6 hard-cooked eggs, sliced
1 (10-ounce) package frozen green
  peas, thawed
1 pound bacon, crisp-cooked,
  drained and crumbled
2 cups shredded Swiss cheese
1 cup mayonnaise or salad dressing
¼ cup sliced green onions
Paprika (optional)

Place 3 cups lettuce in bottom of large bowl; sprinkle with sugar, salt and pepper. Layer eggs over lettuce, standing some eggs on edge, if desired. Continue layering peas, remaining lettuce, bacon and cheese. Spread mayonnaise over the top, sealing to edge of bowl. Cover; refrigerate for 24 hours or overnight. Garnish with green onions and sprinkle with paprika. Toss before serving.
Makes 12 to 15 servings.

Terri Rummer
Nashville, Tennessee

Molded Vegetable Salad

1   (10¾-ounce) can tomato soup
1½ cans water
2   (3¾-ounce) packages lemon
      gelatin
1   (8-ounce) package cream cheese,
      softened
½ cup chopped green pepper
½ cup chopped celery
½ cup chopped nuts
½ cup chopped olives
½ cup chopped onions
½ cup salad dressing
Lettuce leaves

Combine soup and water in saucepan; bring to a boil. Remove from heat. Add remaining ingredients, except lettuce, and mix thoroughly. Pour into 2-quart mold or a 13x9-inch baking dish. Refrigerate until firm. Serve on lettuce leaves.
Makes 12 servings.

Sara Ann Briggs
Okemos, Minnesota

Macaroni-Shrimp Salad

¾ cup small macaroni shells, cooked
8 ounces cooked shrimp, peeled,
      deveined and cut in half lengthwise
⅓ cup chopped celery
2 tablespoons sliced pimento-stuffed
      olives
1 tablespoon snipped parsley
½ cup mayonnaise or salad dressing
2 tablespoons red wine vinegar
2 teaspoons lemon juice
¼ teaspoon garlic salt
¼ teaspoon dry mustard
¼ teaspoon paprika
Parsley (optional)

Combine macaroni, shrimp, celery, olives and parsley in bowl; set aside. In separate bowl, blend together mayonnaise, vinegar, lemon juice, garlic salt, mustard and paprika. Pour over shrimp mixture and toss. Chill. Garnish with parsley.
Makes 4 servings.

Terri Rummer
Nashville, Tennessee

Pizza Salad

8 ounces macaroni shells, cooked
4 cloves garlic, chopped
1 onion, chopped
5 tomatoes, chopped
1 cup oil
¼ cup grated Parmesan cheese
½ pound extra-sharp Cheddar cheese,
      cubed
¼ cup cider vinegar
Salt and pepper to taste
Garlic salt to taste
Pinch of oregano

Combine all ingredients in large bowl and mix thoroughly. Chill at least 4 hours before serving.
Makes 6 to 8 servings.

Janet George
South Glen Falls, New York

Pasta Primavera Salad
With Fresh Basil Vinaigrette

1 pound uncooked pasta (shell,
  rotini or mostaccioli)
1 bunch fresh broccoli, cut into
  flowerets
2 yellow summer squash, sliced
2 red peppers, cut in julienne strips
1 small European cucumber,
  quartered and sliced
3 cups artichoke hearts, drained
¼ pound carrots, grated
Salt and pepper to taste
Leaf lettuce

Cook pasta in lightly salted water for 15 to 20 minutes; drain. Rinse with cold water; drain again. Chill. Blanch broccoli and summer squash by immersing in boiling, salted water for 2 to 3 minutes. Rinse in cold water and drain. Combine all ingredients except salt, pepper and lettuce in mixing bowl. Just before serving, season with salt and pepper; drizzle with Vinaigrette Dressing. Arrange on a serving platter lined with leaf lettuce.
Makes 12 servings.

Fresh Basil Vinaigrette

1 clove garlic, pressed or chopped
2 tablespoons fresh basil
Salt and pepper to taste
2 tablespoons Dijon mustard
2 tablespoons fresh lemon juice
¾ cup wine vinegar
3 cups olive oil

Add garlic and basil to blender container; process on Chop. Add salt, pepper and mustard; process a few seconds. Add lemon juice and vinegar and blend. Add olive oil and process until smooth.

Katherine Hilboldt Curtis
Ann Arbor, Michigan

Layered Garden Pasta Salad

1   (8-ounce) package macaroni shells
½ cup sliced green onions
¼ cup bacon bits or crumbled bacon
¼ cup lemon juice
1 cup mayonnaise or salad dressing
1 teaspoon sugar
½ teaspoon garlic powder
3 tablespoons grated Parmesan cheese
4 cups salad greens, torn into
  bite-sized pieces
1 medium zucchini, sliced
1 cup cauliflower flowerets, sliced
1 cup broccoli flowerets, sliced
2 medium tomatoes, cut in wedges

Cook macaroni as directed on package; drain. Rinse with cold water; drain. Combine macaroni, onions and 2 tablespoons bacon in a medium bowl. In separate bowl, mix lemon juice, mayonnaise, sugar, garlic powder and Parmesan cheese; set aside. In 3½-quart salad bowl, layer salad greens, macaroni mixture, zucchini, cauliflower, broccoli and tomatoes. Pour mayonnaise dressing over top; cover and refrigerate for several hours. Sprinkle with the remaining bacon and serve.
Makes 10 to 12 servings.

Denise Ashford
Ann Arbor, Michigan

Linguine Salad

1 pound linguine
1 cucumber, seeded, peeled
  and diced
1 tomato, diced
1   (8-ounce) bottle of Wishbone
  Italian salad dressing
1 bottle of salad seasoning

Cook linguine until tender; drain. Combine in large bowl the pasta, cucumber, tomato, Italian dressing and salad seasoning (This may vary according to individual taste and preference. I use only ¾ of a bottle.) Toss ingredients, mixing well. Chill and serve.
Makes 8 to 10 servings.

Quick and easy. Great for hot summer days and picnics.

Marlena LaScola
Whitehall, Ohio

Shrimp And Rice Salad

3 cups cooked rice
1 cup cooked tiny shrimp
¼ cup chopped green pepper
2 tablespoons minced onion
2 tablespoons chopped celery
Freshly ground pepper
¼ cup mayonnaise
¼ cup sour cream
½ (1.7-ounce) package French
   dressing mix
Lettuce leaves

Combine rice, shrimp, green pepper, onion and celery in a large bowl; mix. Season with pepper. In separate bowl, mix mayonnaise, sour cream and French dressing mix. Pour dressing over shrimp and toss lightly. Arrange lettuce leaves on plate to serve; spoon on salad. Makes 4 servings.

Franfisca Fernandez
Linthicum Heights, Maryland

Wild Rice Salad

1 (6-ounce) package long-grain
   wild rice
2 cups cubed cooked turkey
¼ pound fresh mushrooms
1 cup firmly-packed spinach leaves,
   torn into bite-sized pieces
2 green onions, chopped
⅓ cup dry white wine
¼ cup vegetable oil
2 teaspoons sugar
¾ teaspoon salt
¼ teaspoon pepper
10 cherry tomatoes, halved

Cook rice according to package directions; drain. Refrigerate for 1 hour or until chilled. Combine rice, turkey, mushrooms, spinach and onions; mix well. In separate bowl, combine wine, vegetable oil, sugar, salt and pepper; stir until blended. Pour over salad and toss to mix. Top with cherry tomatoes.
Makes 6 servings.

This is an excellent summer meal, served with fruit salad.

Debra Bores
Mankato, Minnesota

Rotini Salad

1½ cups (6 ounces) rotini noodles
1 green pepper
2 cups shredded Cheddar cheese
1 small onion, diced
1 cup sliced mushrooms
1 celery stalk, sliced
1 tomato, diced
1 carrot, sliced
1 (8-ounce) bottle Italian
   salad dressing
½ cup Parmesan cheese

Cook noodles using package directions. Slice 4 rings from green pepper. Chop remaining green pepper. Place in serving bowl. Add Cheddar cheese, onion, mushrooms, chopped green pepper, celery, tomato and carrot. Mix gently. Pour salad dressing into bowl; toss to coat well. Sprinkle Parmesan cheese on top. Decorate with green pepper rings. Cover and refrigerate for at least 1 hour.
Makes 6 to 8 servings.

Anne M. Wright
North Aurora, Illinois

Hot Chicken Salad

4 cups cubed cooked chicken
2 tablespoons lemon juice
¾ cup mayonnaise
1 tablespoon salt
2 cups chopped celery
4 hard-cooked eggs, sliced
¾ cup cream of chicken soup
1 tablespoon chopped onion
2 pimentos, chopped
1 cup grated cheese
1½ cups crushed potato chips
⅔ cup chopped toasted almonds

Combine all ingredients in mixing bowl, except cheese, potato chips and almonds; mix thoroughly. Place in casserole. Sprinkle cheese, potato chips and almonds on top. Refrigerate overnight. Bake at 400°F. for 20 to 25 minutes.
Makes 8 servings.

Easy to make today for tomorrow's lunch.

Christi Orcutt
Norcross, Georgia

Mexican Chicken Salad

1 large ripe avocado, peeled and sliced
2 tablespoons Wishbone Italian dressing
1 teaspoon instant minced onion
2 tablespoons lemon juice
1 teaspoon sugar
1 tablespoon chili powder
1 clove garlic, crushed
½ to 1 cup sour cream or plain yogurt
Salt and pepper to taste
2 cups shredded iceberg lettuce, chilled
2 medium tomatoes, chopped, chilled
½ cup chopped scallions
2 cups cubed cooked chicken breast, chilled
½ cup sliced ripe olives, chilled
1 cup kidney beans (optional)
1 tablespoon chopped jalapeños (optional)
½ cup shredded sharp Cheddar cheese
1 cup crushed Doritos (plain)

Combine first 9 ingredients for dressing in food processor container or blender; process until smooth. Chill to blend flavors. Just before serving, combine lettuce, tomatoes, scallions and chicken with dressing, then add remaining ingredients, topping with cheese and crushed Doritos.
Makes 4 to 6 servings.

In an emergency, frozen avocado dip can be substituted for the avocado, but the flavor of the dressing depends heavily on the avocado's ripeness.

This can be a very creative dish—just add whatever sounds good to you! Remember, it is not good leftover, because salad becomes soggy. But it is very easy, can be prepared ahead of time, and mixed just before serving.

Ellen R. Cole
Old Lyme, Connecticut

Nutty Chicken Salad

2/3 cup uncooked wild rice
2 chicken breasts
1 (8-ounce) can water chestnuts, drained
2/3 cup mayonnaise
1/3 cup milk
1/3 cup lemon juice
2 tablespoons grated onion
2 cups seedless grapes, halved
1 cup cashews or almonds

Prepare rice according to package directions. Boil or bake chicken breasts; cool and chop. Place rice, chicken and water chestnuts in bowl. In separate bowl, combine mayonnaise, milk, lemon juice and onion; mix thoroughly. Pour over rice mixture and toss. Refrigerate. Before serving, fold in grapes and nuts.
Makes 6 servings.

Debby DeMoss
Ann Arbor, Michigan

Chicken And Pineapple Salad With Poppy Seed Dressing

1 small head iceberg lettuce, torn into bite-sized pieces
5 ounces spinach, torn into bite-sized pieces
8 ounces Cheddar or Colby cheese, cubed
1 (8-ounce) can chunk pineapple, drained
1 whole chicken, cooked, deboned, chopped
1 cup frozen peas, thawed

Place lettuce and spinach leaves on individual serving plates. Top with cheese, pineapple, chicken and peas. Add any other salad ingredient desired. May be prepared ahead and refrigerated. Serve with Poppy Seed Dressing.
Makes 4 to 6 servings.

Poppy Seed Dressing

1/2 cup sugar
1 teaspoon dry mustard
1 teaspoon salt
5 1/2 tablespoons vinegar
1 cup corn or vegetable oil
2 1/2 teaspoons poppy seed

Combine sugar, dry mustard, salt and vinegar in blender container. Add oil slowly while blender is processing to thicken dressing. Process for a few seconds. Add poppy seed. Refrigerate.

Becky Benjamin
Ann Arbor, Michigan

Taco Salad

2 large heads lettuce, torn into
  bite-sized pieces
1 (10-ounce) package mushrooms,
  sliced
1 cup chopped green onion
2 cups shredded Cheddar cheese
4 medium tomatoes, chopped
1 (4-ounce) can black olives
4 green peppers, chopped
½ cup green olives
2 (16-ounce) cans red hot chili
  beans in sauce
2 pounds ground chuck, cooked and
  drained
1 (8-ounce) package Doritos tortilla
  chips, crumbled

To assemble salad, arrange lettuce in bowl. Layer remaining ingredients except tortilla chips in order listed. Spread Dressing on top of salad. Sprinkle with crumbled tortilla chips.
Makes 12 to 15 servings.

Dressing

2 (8-ounce) cartons sour cream
4 cups Thousand Island yogurt
  dressing
2 (8-ounce) jars Lawry's Chunky
  taco sauce (mild or hot)

Combine all ingredients and mix well.
Makes 2 quarts.

Beverly Griffith
Ann Arbor, Michigan

Tortellini Salad

1 pound cheese-filled tortellini
¼ cup olive oil
½ pound prosciutto (or other ham),
  cut into ⅜-inch cubes
½ pound smoked turkey, cut into
  ⅜-inch cubes
1 cup cooked fresh peas or defrosted
  frozen peas
2 medium carrots, cut into 1½ x ⅛-
  inch julienne strips
1 large red pepper, cut into 1½ x ⅛-
  inch julienne strips
½ cup finely chopped fresh parsley
2 garlic cloves, minced
½ cup olive oil
1 bunch red leaf lettuce

Cook tortellini according to package directions. Drain; rinse under cold running water. Drain again. Place in large bowl. Toss with ¼ cup olive oil. Add prosciutto, turkey, peas, carrots and red pepper; stir. Cover and refrigerate until 30 minutes before serving time. Before serving, whisk parsley, garlic and remaining ½ cup olive oil. Pour over salad and toss well to coat. Arrange lettuce leaves around edge of serving bowl or on individual plates and fill with tortellini salad.
Makes 6 to 8 servings.

Karen Metro
Springboro, Ohio

Main Dishes

Main Dishes

Alice's Breakfast Casserole

1 pound sausage, cooked and
    drained
9 eggs, beaten
3 slices bread, torn into pieces
3 cups milk
1½ cups (6 ounces) shredded
    Cheddar cheese
1½ teaspoons dry mustard
1 teaspoon salt
Pepper to taste
Fresh parsley sprigs

Combine all ingredients except parsley in large mixing bowl; stir well. Pour mixture into buttered 13x9x2-inch baking dish. Bake at 325°F. for 1 hour. Garnish with parsley. Serve warm.
Makes 12 servings.

Joan Curran
Ann Arbor, Michigan

Breakfast Casserole

2 cups garlic croutons
1 cup shredded Cheddar cheese
4 eggs, slightly beaten
2 cups milk
½ teaspoon salt
½ teaspoon prepared mustard
⅛ teaspoon onion powder
⅛ teaspoon pepper
4 slices bacon, cooked crisp

Grease 8-inch square or 10x6-inch casserole. Combine croutons and cheese; pour into pan. Mix eggs, milk and seasonings; pour over croutons. Crumble bacon and sprinkle over top. Bake in 325°F. oven for 55 to 60 minutes. Makes 6 to 8 servings.

Cheryl L. McCormick
Hendersonville, Tennessee

Chili-Cheese Pie

1½ cups (6 ounces) shredded
    Monterey Jack cheese
1 cup (4 ounces) shredded longhorn
    cheese
1 baked (9-inch) pie crust
1 (4-ounce) can chopped green
    chilies
1 cup cream or half and half
4 eggs, beaten
¼ teaspoon salt
⅛ teaspoon ground cumin

Sprinkle ¾ cup Monterey Jack cheese and 1 cup longhorn cheese in baked pie crust. Sprinkle 3 ounces chilies over cheese. Blend cream with eggs and seasonings. Pour into crust. Sprinkle remaining ¾ cup cheese over filling. Top with remaining chilies. Bake in 325°F. oven for 40 minutes.
Makes 6 servings.

Randall and Linda Nelson
Mesa, Arizona

◄*Recipes for this photograph on pages 73, 95 and 127.*

John Wayne Cheese Casserole

4 cups (16 ounces) shredded
  Monterey Jack cheese
4 cups (16 ounces) shredded
  Cheddar cheese
1 (4-ounce) can diced green chilies
4 eggs, separated
⅔ cup evaporated milk
1 tablespoon all-purpose flour
½ teaspoon salt
⅛ teaspoon pepper

Combine cheese and chilies, stirring well. Spoon mixture into buttered 2-quart casserole. Combine egg yolks, evaporated milk, flour, salt and pepper in medium mixing bowl; mix well. Beat egg whites until stiff peaks form; fold into yolk mixture. Spoon over cheese mixture and stir slightly. Bake at 325°F. for 45 minutes or until a knife inserted in center comes out clean.
Makes 8 servings.

Michael L. Orcutt
Norcross, Georgia

Fancy Dogs

¾ cup all-purpose flour
2 teaspoons sugar
1½ teaspoons baking powder
½ teaspoon salt
¼ cup milk
1 egg
2 tablespoons vegetable oil
6 hot dogs
1 tablespoon prepared mustard
¾ cup creamed cottage cheese
1 tablespoon catsup
½ cup (2 ounces) shredded Cheddar
  cheese
4 slices bacon, cooked and crumbled

Combine flour, sugar, baking powder and salt; add milk, egg and oil. Beat at medium speed of electric mixer for 2 minutes. Spread mixture in greased 9x5x3-inch loaf pan. Split hot dogs in half lengthwise, taking care not to cut all the way through. Spread cut surfaces with mustard and 2 tablespoons cottage cheese. Arrange hot dogs in prepared pan. Drizzle catsup over hot dogs; sprinkle with cheese and bacon. Bake at 350°F. for 30 minutes.
Makes 4 to 6 servings.

Christina Marie Bitner
Carol Stream, Alabama

Chili Topping for Chili Dogs

10 pounds ground beef
2 cups chopped onions
1½ cups catsup
4 ounces chili powder
2 ounces paprika
2 tablespoons black pepper
3 tablespoons salt

In a large saucepan brown ground beef; drain. Stir in remaining ingredients and simmer for 10 hours. Freeze for later use.

Marge Monaghan
Ann Arbor, Michigan

Glop

¼ cup butter or margarine
3 tablespoons all-purpose flour
2 cups milk
¼ teaspoon salt
Dash of pepper
5 hard-boiled eggs, coarsely chopped
4 slices toast or English muffins
Cooked bacon (optional)

Melt butter in small heavy saucepan over medium heat; add flour, stirring until smooth. Cook for 1 minute, stirring constantly. Gradually add milk; cook over medium heat, stirring constantly, until thickened and bubbly. Stir in salt, pepper and eggs. Spoon over toast or English muffins. Serve with bacon, if desired. Makes 4 servings.

Denise Knapp
Asheville, North Carolina

Lanterna Blu Spaghetti

¼ cup butter
1½ tablespoons olive oil
½ cup thinly sliced onion
1 slice ham, chopped
½ pound asparagus, slivered
½ cup water
1 chicken bouillon cube
½ pound vermicelli
½ cup half and half
½ cup fresh grated Parmesan cheese
Pepper to taste

Heat butter and oil in 1-quart saucepan over medium heat. Add onion and sauté until golden. Do not brown. Add ham and sauté briefly. Add asparagus, water and bouillon cube. Reduce heat and simmer for 15 minutes. Cook vermicelli for 5 to 6 minutes in boiling salted water. Drain and return to pot. Add asparagus mixture and half and half. Cook until heated through. Top with Parmesan cheese and pepper to taste.

Catherine Rector
Ann Arbor, Michigan

Sweet 'N' Sour Smoked Sausage

2 green peppers, cut into 1-inch pieces
2 onions, cut into 1-inch pieces
2 pounds smoked sausage,
    cut into ½-inch slices
6 tomatoes, cut into medium chunks
2 tablespoons cornstarch
1 teaspoon ground ginger
2 tablespoons vinegar
2 tablespoons soy sauce
1 cup apricot or peach preserves
4 cups drained pineapple chunks
Cooked rice (enough to serve 6 people)

Sauté green peppers, onions and sausage for 5 minutes. Add tomatoes. Combine cornstarch, ginger, vinegar, soy sauce and apricot preserves and add to sausage mixture. Cook until thickened. Add drained pineapple chunks and let warm for about 2 to 3 minutes. Serve. Makes 4 to 6 servings.

Caution: depending on the consistency of the fresh tomatoes, more cornstarch may be needed to thicken the mixture.

Mary Vallance
Northville, Michigan

My Mom's Easter Pie

3 pounds ricotta cheese
3 eggs, beaten
8 ounces hard salami, diced
8 ounces ham, diced
4 hard-boiled eggs, diced
Salt and pepper to taste
Pinch of sugar
2 tablespoons chopped fresh parsley
2   (10-ounce) frozen deep-dish
    pastry shells, thawed

Combine cheese and eggs in large mixing bowl. Stir in salami, ham, hard-boiled eggs, salt and pepper, sugar and parsley. Pour mixture into pastry shells. Bake at 350°F. for 1 hour or until knife inserted in center comes out clean.
Makes 12 servings.

Christopher Parray
Uniondale, New York

Chalupas

Tortilla chips
Ground beef
Canned chili
Canned refried beans
Cheddar cheese, grated
Chopped onions
Chopped tomatoes
Shredded lettuce
Sour cream

Toast tortillas in oven until warm. Keep warm on heated platter. Brown ground beef with salt and pepper to taste. Spoon into serving bowl. Heat chili and refried beans in separate saucepans. Spoon into interesting bowls. Arrange on table with individual bowls of remaining ingredients.

Wonderful for a buffet for large crowd. Just need beer or cold drinks to complete dinner.

Lou Anderson
Gainesville, Florida

Ham-Broccoli Bake

1 small onion, chopped
2 tablespoons butter or margarine
1   (10-ounce) package frozen
    chopped broccoli
3 cups cubed ham
1 cup shredded American cheese
2 cups uncooked minute rice
1   (10¾-ounce) can cream of
    mushroom soup
1   (10¾-ounce) can cream of
    celery soup
1⅓ cups milk

Sauté onion in butter. Cook broccoli according to package directions. Combine all ingredients in large bowl; mix well. Pour into 13x9x2-inch baking pan. Bake at 350°F. for 45 to 50 minutes.
Makes 10 servings.

Onda Cymes
Belleville, Michigan

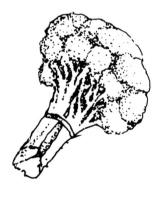

Chicken-Shrimp Spaghetti

2 (3½ to 4-pound) hens
2 cups chopped onions
2 cups chopped green pepper
2 cups chopped celery
4 (4-ounce) cans sliced
   mushrooms, drained
2 cloves garlic, minced
2 cups water
1 (14½-ounce) can whole
   tomatoes, undrained
2 (6-ounce) cans tomato purée
2 (6-ounce) cans tomato paste
1 teaspoon salt
1 teaspoon pepper
2 (16-ounce) packages spaghetti
5 pounds shrimp, peeled, deveined
   and cooked
4 cups (16 ounces) shredded
   Cheddar cheese

Cook hens in boiling water to cover until very tender. Remove meat from bones, discarding bones and skin; chop meat and set aside. Reserve broth. Combine 2 cups broth, onions, green pepper, celery, mushrooms and garlic in large Dutch oven. Cook over medium heat until tender. Add water, tomatoes, tomato purée, tomato paste, salt and pepper; stir well. Cover and simmer for 4 hours, stirring occasionally. Stir in reserved chicken. Cook spaghetti according to package directions in reserved broth; drain. Place half the spaghetti in 13x9x2-inch baking dish. Layer half the shrimp, sauce mixture and cheese over spaghetti. Repeat layers. Bake at 350°F. for 1 hour. Serve immediately.
Makes 10 to 12 servings.

Casserole may be made ahead and frozen. Thaw completely before baking.

Jackie Webb
Smyrna, Georgia

Randy's Baked Italian Sauce

2 pounds ground chuck
1 large yellow onion, chopped
2 large green peppers, chopped
1 pound fresh mushrooms, chopped
1 can tomato paste
1 can tomato sauce
2 cans stewed tomatoes
1 clove fresh garlic, chopped
¼ cup sugar
½ cup Parmesan cheese
2 teaspoons salt
2 teaspoons pepper
2 tablespoons oregano
4 tablespoons parsley flakes

Panfry ground chuck, ½ of the onion, ½ of the green peppers and ½ of the mushrooms; drain. In large oven crock, mix tomato paste, tomato sauce, stewed tomatoes, garlic, sugar, Parmesan cheese, salt, pepper, oregano and parsley flakes. (Adjust these spices to taste). Add ground chuck; mix well. Cover and bake at 300°F. for at least 3 hours. (The longer the better.) If cooking longer, reduce heat to 250°F. Add water as this cooks if needed. One hour before serving, add remaining green peppers, mushrooms and onions. (This allows these vegetables to be firmer when eaten.) Serve over buttered noodles with parlsey flakes and at least one cup of sauce mixed in.

Randy Ostulund
Ann Arbor, Michgan

Cheese Meatballs with Spaghetti Sauce

½ cup chopped onion
¼ cup chopped green pepper
1 clove garlic, minced
2 tablespoons olive oil
3 cups water
2 (6-ounce) cans tomato paste
2 teaspoons chili powder
2 teaspoons salt
¼ teaspoon pepper
¼ teaspoon dried whole oregano
Cheese Meatballs
Hot cooked spaghetti

Sauté onion, green pepper and garlic in olive oil in large Dutch oven. Add remaining sauce ingredients; stir well. Cover and simmer over low heat for 30 minutes. Add meatballs. Cover and simmer an additional 30 minutes. Serve over hot cooked spaghetti.
Makes 8 servings.

Cheese Meatballs

1 pound ground beef
½ pound ground pork
1 cup grated Parmesan cheese
1 cup soft bread crumbs
1 cup milk
1 egg, beaten
½ cup chopped fresh parsley
1 clove garlic, minced
2 teaspoons salt
½ teaspoon dried whole oregano
¼ teaspoon pepper
¼ cup butter or margarine

Combine all ingredients except butter; mix well. Shape mixture into 24 meatballs about 1½ inches in diameter. Melt butter in large skillet. Brown meatballs in butter over low heat.
Makes 2 dozen meatballs.

Tammy Jewell-Greer
Pasadena, California

Tortilla Pie

1 pound ground beef
½ cup finely chopped onion
¼ teaspoon garlic salt
1 tablespoon butter
1 (8-ounce) can tomato sauce
1 (2½-ounce) can sliced ripe olives
1 tablespoon chili powder
1 teaspoon salt
¼ teaspoon pepper
6 corn tortillas
2 cups shredded Cheddar cheese
½ cup water

Brown ground beef, onion and garlic salt in butter; drain. Add tomato sauce, olives, chili powder, salt and pepper. In round casserole dish, alternate layers of tortillas, ground beef, sauce and 1½ cups cheese. Sprinkle remaining ½ cup cheese over top. Pour water down side of casserole. Cover and bake at 400°F. for 25 minutes. Uncover and let stand for 5 minutes before cutting into wedges.
Makes 4 servings.

Karen Lynn Ferns
Rancho Cucamonga, California

Enchilada Casserole

1½ pounds ground beef or ground
  turkey
½ cup chopped onion
1 (15½-ounce) can refried beans
½ teaspoon salt
¼ teaspoon pepper
1 cup vegetable oil
12 frozen or canned corn tortillas
2 tomatoes, chopped
¼ cup butter or margarine
¼ cup all-purpose flour
½ teaspoon salt
¼ teaspoon paprika
2 cups milk
1 (10-ounce) can enchilada sauce
1½ cups (6 ounces) shredded
  Cheddar cheese
¾ cup sliced black olives
4 drops of hot sauce

Brown ground beef and onion in large skillet, stirring to crumble meat; drain. Stir in beans, salt and pepper. Heat oil in small skillet. Dip tortillas in oil for 30 seconds or just until softened. Spoon ⅓ cup meat mixture on tortilla; top with chopped tomato. Roll tightly and place in 13x9x2-inch baking dish. Repeat procedure with remaining tortillas, meat mixture and tomato. Melt butter in medium saucepan; add flour, salt and paprika, stirring until smooth. Gradually add milk and enchilada sauce. Bring to a boil, stirring constantly; boil for 1 minute. Remove from heat and stir in remaining ingredients, stirring until cheese melts. Pour over tortillas. Bake at 350°F. for 30 minutes. Serve with rice or corn.
Makes 6 to 8 servings.

Rebecca Whitelock
Hayward, California

Italian Casserole

1 pound ground beef
1 small onion, chopped
1 (16-ounce) can whole tomatoes,
  undrained and chopped
1 (15-ounce) can tomato sauce
1 teaspoon dried whole oregano
½ teaspoon pepper
¼ teaspooon salt
1 (16-ounce) package egg noodles
2 (8-ounce) cartons sour cream
2 tablespoons lemon pepper
4 cups (1 pound) shredded Monterey
  Jack cheese
1 cup grated Parmesan cheese

Brown ground beef and onion in large skillet, stirring to crumble meat. Drain. Add tomatoes, tomato sauce, oregano, pepper and salt; stir well. Simmer for 30 minutes, stirring occasionally. Cook noodles according to package directions; drain. Combine sour cream and lemon pepper; stir well. Toss noodles with sour cream mixture. Layer half the noodle mixture in buttered 13x9x2-inch baking dish. Spoon half the beef mixture over noodles; sprinkle with half the Monterey Jack cheese. Repeat layers. Sprinkle with Parmesan cheese. Bake at 350°F. for 30 minutes.
Makes 8 to 12 servings.

Doris Ann Baker
Fort Worth, Texas

Lasagne

2 pounds ground chuck
1 medium onion, chopped
1 (28-ounce) can whole tomatoes,
  drained
1 (8-ounce) can tomato sauce
1 (6-ounce) can tomato paste
1 teaspoon dried whole oregano
1 teaspoon grated Parmesan cheese
1 teaspoon salt
½ teaspoon pepper
¼ teaspoon garlic powder
1 bay leaf
Pinch of sugar
Pinch of soda
2 cups large-curd cottage cheese
1 (8-ounce) package cream cheese,
  softened
2 eggs, beaten
Dash of salt
12 lasagne noodles
1 (10-ounce) package frozen
  spinach, thawed
¼ cup grated Parmesan cheese

Brown ground chuck in small Dutch oven; drain. Add onion, tomatoes, tomato sauce, tomato paste, oregano, 1 teaspoon Parmesan cheese, 1 teaspoon salt, pepper, garlic powder, bay leaf, sugar and soda; stir well. Simmer for 2 hours, stirring occasionally. Remove bay leaf. Combine cottage cheese, cream cheese, eggs and dash of salt; stir well. Set aside. Cook lasagne noodles according to package directions; drain. Cook spinach according to package directions. Place ⅓ of the noodles in buttered 13x9x2-inch baking dish. Layer ⅓ of the cheese mixture, meat sauce, Parmesan cheese and spinach over noodles. Repeat procedure twice, using remaining ingredients. Bake at 350°F. for 30 minutes. Let stand for 10 minutes before serving. Makes 8 servings.

Linda Perkowski
Bloomington, Illinois

Lasagne

1 pound ground beef
1 tablespoon sage
1 tablespoon marjoram
1 tablespoon garlic
1 tablespoon basil
1½ teaspoons salt
1 (16-ounce) can tomatoes
2 (6-ounce) cans tomato paste
1 cup water
6 ounces lasagne noodles
2 eggs, beaten
3 cups cottage cheese
1 teaspoon salt
½ teaspoon pepper
1½ pounds Mozzarella cheese,
  sliced very thin

Brown ground beef slowly with sage and marjoram; spoon off excess fat. Add seasonings, tomatoes, tomato paste and water. Simmer, covered, 15 minutes; stir often. Cook noodles in boiling salted water until tender; drain and rinse. Add remaining ingredients, except Mozzarella cheese and stir well. Layer half the noodles in 13x9x2-inch baking dish; layer half the cottage cheese filling, ½ pound Mozzarella cheese and half the meat sauce. Repeat layers. Top with remaining Mozzarella cheese. Bake in 375°F. oven for about 30 minutes (or assemble early and refrigerate; bake for 45 minutes). Let stand for 10 minutes before serving. Makes 8 to 10 servings.

Mary Jo Evans
Warren, Ohio

Plummerville Casserole

1 pound lean ground beef
1 tablespoon butter or margarine
2 (8-ounce) cans tomato sauce
1 (8-ounce) package egg noodles
1 cup cottage cheese
1 (8-ounce) package cream cheese, softened
1 green pepper, chopped
⅓ cup chopped green onion

Brown ground beef in butter in large skillet, stirring to crumble; drain. Add tomato sauce, stirring well; cook over medium heat for 3 minutes. Cook noodles according to package directions; drain. Place half the noodles in buttered 2-quart casserole. Combine cottage cheese, cream cheese, green pepper and green onion; stir well. Spoon over noodles. Top with remaining noodles; spoon meat mixture over noodles. Bake at 350°F. for 30 minutes.
Makes 8 servings.

Jeanne Tabor
Hermitage, Tennessee

Lamb With Spaghetti

2 pounds lamb, cut into pieces
2 medium onions, chopped
½ cup butter or margarine
1 (16-ounce) package spaghetti
1 (6-ounce) can tomato paste
1 cup water
Salt and pepper to taste
Parmesan cheese

Brown lamb and onions in butter in large skillet. Cook spaghetti in boiling water for 5 minutes; drain. Place spaghetti in 13x9x2-inch baking dish; arrange lamb and onion mixture over spaghetti. Combine tomato paste, water and salt and pepper to taste, stirring well; pour over lamb. Add water to cover. Bake at 350°F. for 1 hour. Sprinkle with Parmesan cheese.
Makes 6 servings.

Jill Curby
Saline, Michigan

Moussaka

1 large eggplant, peeled and cut into ½ inch slices
Salt to taste
1 pound ground lamb
2 medium onions, chopped
2 cloves garlic, minced
1 cup chopped canned tomatoes
½ cup dry white wine
2 tablespoons chopped fresh parsley
1 teaspoon salt
½ teaspoon dried whole thyme
½ teaspoon dried whole oregano
¼ teaspoon ground nutmeg
2 eggs, separated
¼ cup fine dry bread crumbs
Olive oil
¼ cup fine dry bread crumbs
3 tablespoons butter or margarine
3 tablespoons all-purpose flour
1½ cups milk
½ teaspoon salt
Dash of pepper
1 tablespoon (or more) grated Parmesan cheese

Sprinkle eggplant with salt; let stand for 30 minutes. Rinse and pat dry. Brown lamb, onions and garlic, stirring to crumble meat; drain. Add tomatoes, wine, parsley, 1 teaspoon salt, thyme, oregano and nutmeg; stir well. Cover and simmer for 30 minutes, stirring occasionally. Let cool. Stir in egg whites and ¼ cup bread crumbs. Brush eggplant slices with olive oil. Broil for 3 minutes on each side or until lightly browned. Sprinkle ¼ cup bread crumbs evenly in 13x9x2-inch baking dish. Arrange eggplant over crumbs; spoon meat sauce mixture over eggplant. Melt butter in small saucepan; add flour, stirring until smooth. Cook for 1 minute, stirring constantly. Gradually add milk; cook stirring constantly until mixture thickens. Remove from heat, and stir in beaten egg yolks, ½ teaspoon salt and pepper. Pour mixture over meat sauce, spreading evenly; sprinkle with Parmesan cheese. Bake at 350°F. for 45 minutes.
Makes 8 servings.

Anna M. Chapekis
Ann Arbor, Michigan

Roast Leg of Lamb

1   (6-pound) leg of lamb, boned
1 teaspoon salt
2 teaspoons seasoned salt
1 tablespoon paprika
½ teaspoon ground ginger
½ teaspoon dry mustard
1 teaspoon dried oregano
1 teaspoon black pepper
Marinade
Medium-sized stuffed olives

Trim excess fat from lamb. Mix next 7 ingredients except olives and rub thoroughly into meat on all sides. Gouge holes ¾ inch deep all over top of lamb with paring knife, pour in a little marinade, and insert a stuffed olive as stopper. Cover meat and refrigerate overnight. Roast, uncovered, for 3 hours at 350°F. or until tender, basting with remaining marinade and small amounts of water, if needed. Remove meat; skim off fat in pan; add enough hot water to make a rich gravy. Makes 8 to 10 servings.

Marinade

4 tablespoons freshly squeezed
    lime juice
2 cloves of garlic, crushed
½ teaspoon salt
½ teaspoon dried marjoram
3 or 4 dashes of Tabasco sauce

Combine all ingredients and mix well.

Alice Sloane
Detroit, Michigan

Stir-Fry Venison

1 pound venison steak, trimmed and
    cut into ⅛ inch slices
¼ cup vegetable oil
2 tablespoons soy sauce
2 tablespoons red wine vinegar
½ teaspoon grated fresh ginger
¼ teaspoon crushed red pepper
2 tablespoons vegetable oil
1 large onion, coarsely chopped
6 large mushrooms, quartered
2 cups sliced Chinese cabbage
1 green pepper, cut into strips
½ cup chicken broth
¼ teaspoon dry mustard
1 tablespoon cornstarch
2 tablespoons cold water
2 cups hot cooked brown rice

Combine venison, ¼ cup vegetable oil, soy sauce, red wine vinegar, ½ teaspoon ginger and red pepper in 1-quart glass container; stir well. Cover tightly and refrigerate at least 2 hours, stirring occasionally. Heat remaining oil in wok. Drain venison, reserving marinade. Stir-fry venison for 3 minutes; remove from wok. Stir-fry onion for 2 minutes; remove from wok. Repeat procedure with mushrooms and cabbage; stir-fry green pepper for 1 minute. Return venison, onion, mushrooms, cabbage and green pepper to wok; add reserved marinade, chicken broth and dry mustard, stirring well. Push venison and vegetables to sides of wok and bring liquid to a boil. Combine cornstarch and water, stirring well. Slowly add to boiling liquid, stirring constantly until thickened. Stir venison and vegetables with liquid. Serve immediately over hot cooked brown rice.
Makes 4 servings.

Any type of meat may be substituted for venison.

William H. Presnar
Franklin, Pennsylvania

Venison Pepper Steak

4 onions
15 mushrooms
3 green peppers
Clarified butter
2 bay leaves
Salt and pepper
2 cloves garlic, crushed
4 venison loin chops, 1-inch thick,
  boned

Quarter onions; dice mushrooms; cut peppers into large pieces. Sauté with clarified butter and bay leaves until tender. Rub salt, pepper and crushed garlic cloves into chops. Fry with onions, peppers and mushrooms. Do not overcook or the meat will be tough. A few shakes of hot sauce or Burgundy wine while cooking is good.
Makes 4 servings.

Jolene Kemppainen
Drummond Island, Michigan

Broccoli-Cheese Burritos

10 large flour tortillas
1 (1½-pound) bunch broccoli,
  cut into flowerets
2 medium tomatoes, chopped
1 medium onion, chopped
1 cup (4 ounces) shredded Cheddar
  cheese
1 (8-ounce) can tomato sauce

Wrap tortillas in aluminum foil; bake at 350°F. for 5 minutes. Combine broccoli, tomatoes, onion and cheese; stir well. Spoon mixture on tortillas; roll tightly. Place in 13x9x2-inch baking dish. Spoon tomato sauce over tortillas. Bake at 350°F. for 30 minutes.
Makes 5 to 6 servings.

Julie Armbruster
Ann Arbor, Michigan

Aubergines Baigan Tamatar
(Eggplant And Tomatoes)

2 medium onions, thinly sliced
½ cup butter or margarine
2 cloves garlic, minced
2 teaspoons ground coriander
1 teaspoon chili powder
1 teaspoon salt
1 teaspoon pepper
1 bay leaf
1 (2-inch) stick cinnamon
1½ pounds tomatoes, peeled and
  quartered
1 (1½-pound) eggplant, cut into
  1-inch cubes
1 (6-ounce) can tomato paste
¼ cup water

Sauté onions in butter in large, heavy saucepan until tender. Add garlic, coriander, chili powder, salt, pepper, bay leaf and cinnamon; stir well. Add tomatoes, eggplant, tomato paste and water, stirring well. Cover and simmer 25 to 30 minutes or until eggplant is tender, stirring occasionally. Serve hot.
Makes 4 servings.

William H. Presnar
Franklin, Pennsylvania

Stuffed Green Peppers

4 large green peppers
1 pound ground beef
¼ cup chopped celery
2 tablespoons chopped onion
1 cup cooked rice
1 medium tomato, peeled and
    chopped
¼ cup catsup
½ teaspoon salt
Dash of pepper
1 (8-ounce) can tomato sauce
1 teaspoon sugar
¼ teaspoon basil leaves
¼ cup (1 ounce) shredded Cheddar
    cheese

Cut tops from peppers; remove seeds and membrane. Cook in boiling water to cover for 5 minutes. Drain and set aside. Brown ground beef, celery and onion in large skillet, stirring to crumble meat; drain. Add rice, tomato, catsup, salt and pepper; stir well. Spoon mixture into reserved peppers. Place peppers in 9-inch square baking dish. Combine tomato sauce, sugar and basil, stirring well; spoon half the sauce over peppers. Bake at 350°F. for 25 to 35 minutes or until peppers are tender. Spoon remaining sauce over peppers and sprinkle with cheese. Bake an additional 5 minutes to melt cheese.
Makes 4 servings.

Sharon Yaney
Celina, Ohio

Zucchini Casserole

2 zucchini, sliced
1 egg, slightly beaten
1 cup all-purpose flour
¼ cup vegetable oil
½ cup grated Parmesan cheese
1 (15½-ounce) jar spaghetti or
    pizza sauce
1 cup (4 ounces) shredded
    Mozzarella cheese

Dip zucchini slices in egg and then in flour. Fry in oil until tender. Place in shallow casserole. Sprinkle with Parmesan cheese and top with spaghetti sauce. Bake at 350°F. for 20 minutes. Remove from oven and sprinkle with Mozzarella cheese. Return to oven and bake until cheese melts.
Makes 4 servings.

Debra Holder
Saline, Michigan

Eggplant Parmigiana

1 large eggplant, peeled and cut
    into ¼ inch slices
3 eggs, beaten
Seasoned dry bread crumbs
Olive oil
1 (24-ounce) carton ricotta cheese
2 eggs, beaten
2 tablespoons chopped fresh parsley
½ teaspoon basil leaves
½ teaspoon dried whole oregano
1 (32-ounce) jar home-style
    spaghetti sauce
6 cups (1½ pounds) shredded
    Mozzarella cheese

Dip eggplant slices into 3 beaten eggs; coat with bread crumbs. Fry in olive oil until golden brown on both sides; drain on paper towels. Combine ricotta cheese, 2 beaten eggs, parsley, basil and oregano; stir well. Layer ⅓ of the eggplant slices in greased 13x9x2-inch baking dish. Top with ⅓ of the spaghetti sauce, ricotta cheese mixture and Mozzarella cheese. Repeat layers, using remaining ingredients. Bake at 350°F. for 45 minutes to 1 hour or until hot and bubbly.
Makes 12 servings.

Lily Ernst
Dallas, Texas

Beef and Veal

Beef Bourguignon

¾ pound small mushrooms
3 tablespoons butter or margarine
3 tablespoons shortening
12 to 18 very small onions
3 pounds lean boneless chuck steak,
  cut into 2-inch cubes
3 tablespoons flour
1 cup beef broth or stock
2 cups dry red wine
1 tablespoon tomato paste or catsup
1 to 4 cloves garlic, crushed
1 teaspoon thyme
1 teaspoon salt
Freshly ground pepper to taste
4 sprigs parsley
1 bay leaf

In a large skillet, sauté mushrooms lightly in butter. Remove mushrooms from skillet and set aside. Add shortening to skillet; brown onions over medium heat. Remove onions from skillet and set aside with mushrooms. Add beef cubes to skillet, a few at a time, browning well on all sides. Add extra shortening as necessary. Remove beef to heavy 4 to 5-quart casserole. To drippings remaining in skillet, stir in flour then beef stock, wine and tomato paste. Bring to a boil, whisking constantly as sauce thickens. Add garlic, thyme, salt, pepper, parsley and bay leaf. Pour sauce over beef in casserole to almost cover beef. Bake, covered, at 350°F. for 2 to 3 hours or until beef is tender. Add more wine or stock as necessary. Gently stir in onions and mushrooms. Bake for 20 to 30 minutes longer. Remove bay leaf and skim off fat. Sprinkle beef with additional chopped parsley. Serve directly from casserole.
Makes 8 to 10 servings.

Good served over noodles accompanied by French bread, salad and red wine.

Linda Ondusky
Brighton, Michigan

Barbecue Beef Brisket

1   (5 to 7-pound) beef brisket
2 teaspoons onion salt
2 teaspoons garlic salt
2 teaspoons celery salt
½   (3½-ounce) bottle liquid smoke
⅓ cup Worcestershire sauce
Black pepper to taste
½   (16-ounce) bottle barbecue sauce

Line baking dish with aluminum foil; place brisket in foil. Sprinkle with onion, garlic and celery salt to taste. Pour ½ bottle liquid smoke over brisket. Close foil; marinate in refrigerator overnight. Add Worcestershire sauce and sprinkle with pepper. Close foil tightly and bake at 250°F. for 5 hours. During last hour of cooking time, test for doneness and baste with barbecue sauce. Fold foil back and cook, uncovered, for 1 hour longer. Slice brisket against grain in ¼-inch slices.
Makes 6 to 8 servings.

Janet M. Bradley
Lilburn, Georgia

Beef Scallopine

½ cup chopped onion
¾ cup olive oil
½ cup chopped prosciutto
½ pound mushrooms, thinly sliced
2 tablespoons butter
1 cup Marsala or other red wine
⅓ cup canned brown gravy
2 tablespoons chopped parsley
8 slices filet of beef, ½ inch thick
Flour for dredging
Oil for frying
8 slices Mozzarella cheese

Preheat oven to 500°F. Cook onion in olive oil in skillet until wilted. Add prosciutto and mushrooms. Cook slowly for about 10 minutes. Pour into sieve and drain, pressing down gently to extract oil. Heat butter in same skillet. Add mushroom mixture, wine and gravy; mix well. Sprinkle with parsley. Simmer for 20 minutes. Dredge beef in flour; shake off excess. Cook beef quickly in oil in skillet until golden on both sides, turning once, 2 to 3 minutes. Drain in colander. Spoon half the mushroom mixture into baking dish. Arrange beef on top. Spoon remaining mushroom mixture over beef. Top with cheese. Bake for 10 to 15 minutes or until cheese melts.
Makes 4 to 8 servings.

Sheila Lipschutz
Hermosa Beach, California

Beef Burgundy

3 pounds stew beef
2   (1¼-ounce) envelopes onion soup mix
2   (10¾-ounce) cans cream of mushroom soup
½ cup Brandy
1   (4-ounce) can mushrooms

Place beef in Dutch oven or large casserole with lid. Combine soup mix, mushroom soup and Brandy; pour over beef. Add mushrooms. Bake, covered, in preheated 325°F. oven for 3 hours.
Makes 6 servings.

Good served with wild or brown rice.

Helen McNulty
Ann Arbor, Michigan

Boliche

1 (3-pound) eye of round roast
1 cup chopped ham or Spanish
   sausage
½ cup chopped green pepper
½ cup chopped onion
1 garlic clove, minced
2 tablespoons olive oil
½ cup white wine
1 bay leaf

Cut pocket in center of roast (not all the way through). Combine ham, green pepper, onion and garlic, mixing well; place stuffing in pocket. Close end with string or skewers. In Dutch oven, brown roast on all sides in olive oil. Add wine and bay leaf; simmer, covered, until tender, about 2 to 2½ hours. Check occasionally; add more wine if necessary. Remove roast from heat; let stand for 5 minutes before slicing. May add wine or water to drippings for gravy.
Makes 4 to 6 servings.

Barb and Dave Board
Ann Arbor, Michigan

Bul-Go-Gi (Korean Sweet Beef)

1½ cups green onions, cut into
   1-inch pieces
5 cloves garlic, crushed
3 tablespoons soy sauce
1 tablespoon sesame seed oil
¼ teaspoon salt
⅛ teaspoon pepper
1¼ cups sugar
½ teaspoon MSG
1 pound lean beef, sliced very thin
1 tablespoon oil

In medium bowl, combine onions, garlic, soy sauce, sesame seed oil, salt, pepper, sugar and MSG; add beef. Marinate in refrigerator for at least 1 hour. In 12-inch skillet, heat oil over high heat until hot. Brown beef, stirring constantly. Serve over steamed rice.
Makes 4 servings.

Robert B. Brock
Medford, Oregon

Grilled Marinated Chuck Roast

1 large onion, peeled and chopped
1 cup cooking oil
¼ cup tarragon vinegar
½ cup Burgundy wine
¼ cup lemon juice
1 teaspoon dry mustard
1 teaspoon salt
3 cloves garlic, minced
1 whole bay leaf
6 peppercorns
Boneless chuck roast, 2 inches thick

Combine all ingredients except roast. Place roast in shallow dish; cover with marinade. Pierce roast in several places. Cover and refrigerate overnight. Grill roast to desired doneness. Slice diagonally.
Makes 4 to 6 servings.

Marinade is ideal for flank steak.

Tala Arnowitz
Trotwood, Ohio

Mexican Steak

1¼ pounds boneless round steak
2 tablespoons butter or margarine
1 (4-ounce) can chopped green
    chilies, drained
1 (8-ounce) jar taco sauce
½ cup (2 ounces) shredded
    Monterey Jack cheese

Trim excess fat from steak. Cut into 4 pieces; pound to ¼ inch thickness. Sauté steak in butter until browned. Place in lightly greased 2-quart casserole. Pour chilies and taco sauce over steak; cover. Bake in preheated 350°F. oven for 40 minutes. Sprinkle steak with cheese. Bake, uncovered, for 5 minutes longer.
Makes 4 servings.

Beckie Hibdon
Nashville, Tennessee

Roladen (Pigs-In-A-Blanket)

2 (3 to 5-pounds each) round
    steaks, cut thin
3 tablespoons prepared mustard
1 teaspoon salt
1 teaspoon pepper
½ pound bacon, cut in thirds
1 onion, sliced in quarters
1 cup flour
3 tablespoons shortening
2 cups water
¼ cup red wine
Cornstarch

Cut each steak into 6 strips. Spread each strip with thin coat of mustard. Sprinkle with salt and pepper. Place bacon on strip. Place onion on top of bacon; roll up and secure with toothpicks or string. Dredge in flour. Brown steak rolls in shortening. Add water and wine and simmer, covered, for 1 to 1½ hours or until steak rolls are tender. Remove from pan. Thicken pan drippings with cornstarch and enough water for desired gravy consistency. Serve with egg noodles.
Makes 6 servings.

A man-size "stick-to-your-ribs" meal. Leftovers taste great. Reheat in pan with extra gravy until warmed through.

Eileen B. Fiedler
Ann Arbor, Michigan

Homemade Spaghetti Sauce With Meatballs

5 cups water
1 large onion, sliced
2 cloves garlic, minced
4 pounds beef short ribs, bone in
2 pounds lamb neck bones (optional)
2 (30-ounce) cans tomato sauce
2 (30-ounce) cans whole peeled
    tomatoes
1 (30-ounce) can tomato purée
2 teaspoons salt
3 pounds lean ground beef
½ cup soft bread crumbs
1 clove garlic, minced
1 egg
¼ teaspoon salt
¾ teaspoon pepper
2 tablespoons Parmesan cheese
3 pounds linguine

In large deep stockpot, combine water, onion and 2 cloves garlic; bring to a boil. Add beef ribs and lamb; stir. Reduce to medium-high heat; cook for about 20 minutes or until water has almost evaporated. Add tomato sauce, tomatoes, tomato purée and salt. Bring to a boil, stirring frequently; reduce heat to medium. Simmer for 2 hours. Remove bones from sauce. In large bowl, combine ground beef, bread crumbs, 1 clove garlic, egg, salt, pepper and Parmesan cheese, mixing thoroughly. Shape mixture into 2-inch meatballs. Fry on medium-high heat or bake meatballs in preheated 300°F. oven for 20 to 30 minutes or until done. Add meatballs to sauce. Cook linguine according to package directions; drain. Add 2 cups sauce to linguine; place in serving bowl. Serve meatballs with remaining sauce in separate serving bowl.
Makes 12 to 15 servings.

Valerie Mueller
Gulfport, Michigan

Marinated Flank Steak

¼ cup soy sauce
2 tablespoons salad oil
2 tablespoons honey
1 tablespoon wine vinegar
⅛ teaspoon garlic powder
½ teaspoon ginger
1½ to 2 pounds flank steak

Combine all ingredients except steak in shallow baking dish, mixing well. Add steak. Marinate in refrigerator overnight. Next day, turn meat and marinate for 6 hours longer. Broil steak to desired degree of doneness. Thinly slice steak across grain.
Makes 4 servings.

Peggy Fine
Ann Arbor, Michigan

Stuffed Steak And Parsley Potatoes

3 large potatoes, cut into ¼-inch
  slices
¾ cup water
3 tablespoons butter or margarine
1 medium onion, chopped
1¼ cups chopped mushrooms
1 cup soft bread crumbs
2 tablespoons chopped fresh parsley
½ teaspoon salt
¼ teaspoon pepper
1 (2-pound) beef top round steak,
  about ½ inch thick
Salt and pepper to taste
Instant unflavored meat tenderizer
2 tablespoons vegetable oil
5 tablespoons butter
1 clove garlic
2 tablespoons chopped fresh parsley
¼ teaspoon salt

In shallow roasting pan, place sliced potatoes in single layer; add water. Bake in preheated 375°F. oven on lower oven shelf until tender. In 10-inch skillet over medium heat, melt 3 tablespoons butter; add onion. Cook for 5 minutes, stirring occasionally. Add mushrooms; cook for 5 minutes longer. Stir in bread crumbs, 2 tablespoons parsley, ½ teaspoon salt and ¼ teaspoon pepper. With potatoes still in oven, increase oven heat to broil. Cut long horizontal slit in side of steak (almost through the other side) to form pocket. With spoon, place bread mixture in pocket; secure with wooden picks. Sprinkle steak with salt and pepper to taste. Add tenderizer as label directs. Brush both sides steak with vegetable oil. Place steak on rack in pan. Broil for 8 to 10 minutes per side, turning once. In small saucepan over medium heat, melt 5 tablespoons butter. Add garlic; cook for 2 minutes, stirring constantly, until golden. Pour over potatoes. Add 2 tablespoons parsley and ¼ teaspoon salt; toss to coat. To serve, remove wooden picks from steak. Place on platter with potatoes. Garnish with parsley sprigs.
Makes 6 servings.

Wanda Swanton
Augusta, Georgia

American Chop Suey

6 pounds ground beef
6 onions, chopped
2 green peppers, chopped
2 tablespoons salt
5 cups uncooked long grain rice
10 cups canned tomatoes
2 (4-ounce) cans mushrooms,
  undrained
6 cups chopped celery

In Dutch oven or large saucepan, brown ground beef, breaking apart as it cooks; drain thoroughly. Add remaining ingredients, except celery, mixing thoroughly. Bake, covered, in preheated 350°F. oven for 1½ hours or until rice is tender. If mixture gets too dry, add extra tomatoes or tomato juice. Add celery and bake for 20 minutes.
Makes 50 servings.

Great as a side dish for buffet.

Gail LaButte
Lakeland, Michigan

Stuffed Flank Steak

2½ to 3 pounds flank steak
5 slices bread, cubed
¼ cup vegetable oil or butter
1 pound ground round
2 eggs
¾ cup finely chopped onion
½ cup finely chopped celery
2 tablespoons finely chopped parsley
2 cloves garlic, minced
1½ teaspoons salt
½ teaspoon pepper
¼ teaspoon thyme
1 tablespoon oil or butter
¾ cup finely chopped carrot
¾ cup finely chopped onion
1 tomato, coarsely chopped
2 bay leaves
1 tablespoon thyme
1 cup beef broth
1 cup dry red wine
2 tablespoons arrowroot or
  cornstarch
¼ cup water

Cut flank steak horizontally with sharp knife, making pocket for stuffing; lift upper portion as you cut. Be careful not to cut through either end or the pocket will be lost; set aside. Brown bread cubes in ¼ cup oil in large skillet. In large bowl, combine bread cubes, ground round, eggs, ¾ cup onion, celery, parsley, garlic, salt, pepper and ¼ teaspoon thyme; mix thoroughly. Place stuffing in center of prepared steak, making sure pocket is filled to corners. Bring lower and upper lips of steak together to form round loaf. Tie securely with string every 2 inches then bring string around lengthwise to secure ends. Heat 1 tablespoon oil in Dutch oven or large pan. Brown rolled steak slowly and evenly on all sides. Combine carrot, ¾ cup onion, tomato, bay leaves and 1 tablespoon thyme; add to steak. Cook, uncovered, for 5 minutes, stirring occasionally. Add beef broth and wine. Bring to a boil; cover. Cook over medium heat on top of stove or in preheated 350°F. oven for 2 hours, turning steak once. Cool slightly. Lift steak from pan to serving platter; remove strings. Keep steak warm. Mix arrowroot with water; stir into vegetable-broth-wine mixture. Bring to a boil, stirring constantly until thickened. Season to taste. Serve sauce with flank steak.
Makes 8 to 10 servings.

Kimberly Breeding Lake
Winchester, Kentucky

Cincinnati Pie

2 pounds ground beef, cooked and
  drained
1 large potato, diced
1 (16-ounce) can peas, drained
1 (16-ounce) can corn, drained
1 cup cauliflower, cut in small
  pieces
2 carrots, diced
1 large onion, chopped
1 (10¾-ounce) can cream of
  mushroom soup
2 cups corn bread batter

Combine ground beef, potato, peas, corn, cauliflower, carrots and onion in large cast-iron skillet. Add mushroom soup, spreading evenly over the vegetable-beef mixture. Pour batter over all to create topping or "icing". Place skillet in preheated 350°F. oven for approximately 45 minutes. Test cornbread topping with toothpick for doneness. Remove skillet from oven; let stand for about 10 minutes. Cut into 6 pie wedges and serve.
Makes 6 to 8 servings.

Enjoy!

Sue Dixon
Marietta, Ohio

Chop Chop Chow Mein

1 pound ground beef
1 small onion, chopped
3 stalks celery, sliced
¼ cup flour
2 tablespoons soy sauce
2 cups tomato juice
1 (16-ounce) can bean sprouts, drained
1 (4-ounce) can mushroom pieces with stems, undrained

In large skillet, sauté ground beef until browned; drain thoroughly. Add onion and celery; cook until onion is tender. Stir in flour. Add soy sauce, tomato juice, bean sprouts and mushrooms; heat to boiling point, stirring constantly. Simmer for 10 to 15 minutes on medium to low heat.
Makes 6 servings.

Serve with rice, if desired.

Sue Dawson
Ann Arbor, Michigan

Ground Beef-Cabbage Casserole

1 medium head cabbage, shredded
2 tablespoons butter or margarine, melted
2 teaspoons salt
1 cup cooked rice
¼ cup chopped onion
1 egg, beaten
1 pound ground beef, cooked

In large saucepan, cook cabbage in boiling salted water for 5 minutes; drain, reserving liquid. Add butter, salt, rice, onion and egg to cabbage; mix thoroughly. Place layer of cabbage in casserole then layer of ground beef. Repeat layers ending with cabbage. Pour ½ cup reserved liquid over cabbage. Bake in preheated 350°F. oven for 1 hour.
Makes 4 to 6 servings.

JoAnn Godwin
Adrian, Michigan

Ground Beef Casserole

3 large potatoes, pared and sliced
3 large carrots, pared and sliced
1 pound lean ground beef
2 medium onions, chopped
1 tablespoon catsup
1 (10¾-ounce) can condensed cream of mushroom soup
1 (4-ounce) can mushrooms, drained
2 slices buttered bread, cubed

Place potatoes and carrots in large saucepan; cover with water. Bring to a boil. Cook for 20 minutes; drain. In large skillet, sauté ground beef and onions until browned; drain thoroughly. In 2-quart casserole, alternate potatoes and beef. Combine catsup and soup; pour over potatoes-beef mixture. Top casserole with mushrooms then bread cubes. Bake in preheated 350°F. oven for 45 minutes.
Makes 4 servings.

Touby Witzky
Hermitage, Tenneseee

Hamburger And Bean Casserole

1 pound ground beef
4 strips bacon, chopped
1 medium onion, chopped
1 (19-ounce) can baked beans
½ cup molasses
½ cup catsup
1 teaspoon dry mustard
1 teaspoon Worcestershire sauce

In large skillet, cook ground beef, bacon and onion until browned; drain thoroughly. Add remaining ingredients, mixing well. Place mixture in greased 2-quart casserole. Bake, covered, in preheated 350°F. oven for 30 minutes.
Makes 4 servings.

Excellent when served with fresh, hot biscuits.

Randy King
Kingston, Ontario, Canada

Meatballs In Onion Gravy

1 pound ground beef
¾ cup rolled oats
1 egg
½ cup milk
1 teaspoon salt
⅛ teaspoon pepper
¼ teaspoon thyme
¼ teaspoon marjoram
⅓ cup flour
2 tablespoons oil
1 (1.25-ounce) package onion
   soup mix
2 cups hot water
¼ cup water

Combine ground beef, oats, egg, milk, salt, pepper, thyme and marjoram; shape into about 25 meatballs. Roll meatballs in flour, reserving excess flour. In large skillet, brown meatballs in hot oil. Combine soup mix with hot water; pour over meatballs. Cover and cook over low heat for 20 to 25 minutes. Remove meatballs from liquid; keep warm. Combine remaining flour and water; blend until smooth. Stir flour mixture into liquid in pan. Stir until mixture comes to a boil. Reheat meatballs in gravy. Serve over noodles or rice.
Makes 5 to 6 servings.

Mary Anne Kane
Ypsilanti, Michigan

Polish Meatballs

1½ pounds ground pork
1½ pounds ground veal
10 to 12 crackers, crushed
1 small onion, diced
1 teaspoon crushed marjoram
¼ cup evaporated milk
Salt and pepper to taste
1 (10¾-ounce) can chicken broth
½ cup water
½ cup sliced celery
½ cup chopped onion

Combine meats, crackers, onion, marjoram, evaporated milk and seasonings; mix thoroughly. Shape into 1½-inch meatballs; brown in large skillet. With slotted spoon, transfer meatballs to large greased baking dish. Combine broth and water. Add broth mixture, celery and onion to meatballs. Bake in preheated 350°F. oven for 1½ hours.
Makes 6 to 8 servings.

Barbara K. Grabbe
Ann Arbor, Michigan

Sculer Meatballs

1 cup barbecue sauce
3½ cups canned tomatoes,
   undrained
½ cup strawberry jelly or jam
¼ cup chili sauce
3 tablespoons molasses
3 pounds ground round steak
2 (1¼-ounce) envelopes dry onion
   soup mix
½ cup sweet relish
½ cup catsup
½ teaspoon garlic salt
1 teaspoon pepper
1 tablespoon soy sauce
1 teaspoon steak sauce
3 tablespoons Parmesan cheese
4 eggs, well beaten
1 (13-ounce) can evaporated milk
3 tablespoons brown sugar
6 cups fine bread crumbs

Combine barbecue sauce, tomatoes, jelly, chili sauce and molasses with enough water to form medium to thin consistency. Mix thoroughly; set aside. Thoroughly combine remaining ingredients. Shape into ½ to ¾-inch meatballs. Place on ungreased cookie sheet. Bake in preheated 425°F. oven for 15 minutes, turning once to brown. Drain and place in deep casserole. Cover with sauce and bake in preheated 325°F. oven for 1 hour.
Makes 25 to 30 meatballs.

Joan M. Cromer
Milan, Michigan

Meat Loaf With Rice Wafers

1½ pounds ground beef
½ to ¾ cup crumbled rice wafers
2 eggs, beaten
¼ cup chopped onion
1 tablespoon chopped green pepper
½ teaspoon salt
¼ teaspoon pepper
¾ cup tomato soup
¼ cup water

Combine all ingredients thoroughly; pack firmly into loaf pan. Bake in preheated 350°F. oven for 1 hour. Let stand for 5 minutes before slicing.
Makes 6 servings.

May be served with mushroom sauce, if desired.

Rhea Y. Fetzer
Kalamazoo, Michigan

Seven-Layer Beef And Rice

1½ cups uncooked rice
1 pound ground beef
Salt and pepper to taste
Onion salt to taste
¼ cup catsup
1 (16-ounce) can green beans,
   drained
1 (10¾-ounce) can cream of
   mushroom soup
1 (14½-ounce) can stewed tomatoes
Garlic salt

Cook rice according to package directions. In skillet, brown ground beef, breaking apart as it cooks; drain thoroughly. Place cooked rice in bottom of 1½-quart casserole. Place ground beef over rice; sprinkle with salt, pepper and onion salt. Spread catsup on beef. Add green beans, soup and tomatoes; sprinkle with garlic salt. Bake, covered, in preheated 350°F. oven for 1 hour.
Makes 6 servings.

Roger L. Rommelfaenger
Sheboygan, Wisconsin

Sloppy Joes

2 pounds ground beef
1 large onion, chopped
Salt to taste
¼ teaspoon pepper
3 cups water
1 tablespoon Worcestershire sauce
1½ cups catsup
½ cup flour
¼ cup sugar

In large skillet over medium heat, brown ground beef and onion; drain thoroughly. Add remaining ingredients, stirring to combine. Simmer for 20 minutes or until thickened. Serve on buttered toasted buns. Makes 6 to 8 servings.

Katherine Gephart
Pinckney, Michigan

Sweet And Sour Casserole (Diet)

1½ pounds lean ground beef or veal
1 small head cabbage, chopped
1 (16-ounce) can sauerkraut
1 (6-ounce) can tomato sauce
1 (6-ounce) can diet tomato juice
1 (1.7 ounce) package brown sugar substitute

In large skillet, cook ground beef until brown; drain thoroughly. Cook cabbage in water until tender; drain. Layer cabbage, sauerkraut, ground beef and tomato sauce in 2-quart casserole. Pour tomato juice over all. Sprinkle brown sugar on top; cover. Bake in preheated 350°F. oven for 45 minutes. Uncover; bake for 15 minutes longer. Makes 6 servings.

Brenda K. Smith
Miamisburg, Ohio

Calf Liver With Red Wine Sauce

4 slices bacon
1 pound sliced calf liver
1 tablespoon flour
1 (10¾-ounce) can French onion soup
½ cup dry red wine
1 cup sliced mushrooms, cooked
Salt and pepper to taste

Fry bacon until crisp; set aside. Drain most of the drippings from skillet. Brown liver on both sides in remaining bacon drippings. Remove from skillet; set aside. Add flour to bacon drippings in skillet, stirring until well blended. Slowly blend in onion soup; add wine and mushrooms, stirring until well blended. Add liver to sauce; season to taste with salt and pepper. Simmer for 10 minutes over low heat. Makes 4 servings.

Barbara Caputo
Durham, North Carolina

Veal Crêpes With Mornay Sauce

2 eggs, beaten
1½ cups milk
4 tablespoons vegetable oil
1¼ cups flour
½ teaspoon salt
1¼ tablespoons chopped parsley
1 tablespoon chopped chives
1 tablespoon thyme
1 tablespoon tarragon
Oil

Combine eggs, milk and 4 tablespoons vegetable oil; beat well. Sift flour and salt together; add to egg mixture, mixing well. Stir in parsley, chives, thyme and tarragon. Set aside for at least 1 hour. If batter is too thick, add a small amount of milk. Brush small frying pan with a few drops of oil and heat. Spoon about 2 tablespoons batter into pan. Tilt pan to spread batter over entire bottom surface. Cook until top is dry; turn over and cook about 15 seconds longer. Repeat with remaining batter. Set aside.

Mornay Sauce

½ cup butter
½ cup flour
2 cups chicken broth
1 cup cream
3 egg yolks
¾ cup Parmesan cheese
1 teaspoon salt
½ teaspoon pepper

Melt butter. Add flour; stir until smooth. Cook for 5 minutes. Add chicken broth, stirring constantly; remove from heat. Add cream; stir in egg yolks, one at a time, beating well after each addition. Return to heat. Add Parmesan cheese, salt and pepper; cook until thick and creamy. Set aside and keep warm.

Filling

2 pounds stewing veal, cut into
   small pieces
1¼ cups chicken broth
½ cup white wine
2 small onions, chopped
⅓ cup butter
¼ cup chopped parsley
1 tablespoon chopped chives
1 teaspoon salt
¼ teaspoon pepper

In saucepan, simmer veal in chicken broth and wine until tender; set aside. Sauté onions in ⅓ cup butter until transparent. Add veal; simmer for 5 minutes. Remove from heat. Stir in parsley, chives, salt, pepper and half the sauce.
To make Crêpes: Fill each crêpe with veal filling. Place in buttered shallow baking dish. Dot with ⅓ cup butter; pour remaining sauce over crêpes. Bake in preheated 350°F. oven for 30 minutes.
Makes 6 servings.

When making crêpes, it is easier to use a nonstick frying pan.

Mary Kogelschatz
Belleville, Michigan

Veal Parmigiana

2 pounds thin veal steaks
¼ cup butter
⅛ teaspoon thyme
⅛ teaspoon garlic powder
¼ teaspoon oregano
1 (8-ounce) can tomato sauce
¼ pound Mozzarella cheese, thinly
   sliced
Grated Parmesan cheese

Pound steaks to tenderize. Melt butter in large skillet; brown steaks. Season with thyme, garlic powder and oregano. Add tomato sauce and simmer over low heat for 15 to 20 minutes. Top with Mozzarella cheese. Heat only until cheese is melted; remove from heat. Place steaks on warmed serving platter. Spoon sauce over steaks and cheese. Sprinkle with Parmesan cheese.
Makes 2 servings.

Jennifer Menges
Dunkirk, New York

Trail Chili Soup

3 pounds ground beef
4 medium yellow onions,
   chopped
3 green peppers, chopped
Chili powder to taste
2 (16-ounce) cans pork and beans

In large skillet, sauté ground beef until lightly browned. Add onions, green peppers and chili powder. Cook until vegetables are soft. Drain thoroughly. Add pork and beans. Cook until mixture is thickened and hot.
Makes 4 to 5 servings.

Michael D. David
Marion, Indiana

Tigress II-Black Bean Chili

3 pounds ground beef
2 tablespoons crushed garlic
½ cup vegetable oil
3 tablespoons flour, dissolved in
   4 tablespoons water
6 tablespoons chili powder
1 teaspoon oregano
1 teaspoon cumin
2 cups Burgundy wine
2 (14-ounce) cans beef broth
4 (16-ounce) cans black beans
1 (17-ounce) can niblet corn
Hot white or brown rice
Sour cream
Grated Cheddar cheese

In large stock pot, brown ground beef and garlic in oil. Add flour mixture, chili powder, oregano and cumin; mix well. Add wine, beef broth, black beans and corn. Simmer for 4 to 6 hours. When you are almost ready to serve, prepare rice according to package directions. Prepare same number servings as people to serve. Serve chili over rice with a generous dollop of sour cream and sprinkle with Cheddar cheese.
Makes 15 to 20 servings.

This recipe is not only very simple to make but is a real crowd pleaser. Over the years exact amounts have faded from memory so you may adjust amounts to suit yourself. You may prefer less beans or more beef or if you prefer a thicker chili, more flour can be added. The beauty of it is it really doesn't matter—it always comes out great. A really hard recipe to ruin! (My kind of cooking).

Joyce DeGaeta
Harbour Heights, Florida

Taco Casserole

1 to 1½ pounds ground beef
2 tablespoons chopped onion
½ package Lawry's taco seasoning
   mix
1 package (12-count) flour tortillas
1½ cups shredded Cheddar cheese

Brown ground beef and onion; drain. Add taco seasoning; mix well. Layer tortillas, meat mixture and cheese in round casserole, ending with tortilla and shredded cheese. Bake in 350°F. oven for 15 minutes or for 5 minutes in microwave. Serve with chopped tomato, shredded lettuce and sour cream.
Makes 4 to 6 servings.

Patricia Sutton
Ypsilanti, Michigan

Chicken

Poppy Seed Chicken

2 pounds chicken breasts
1 can cream of chicken soup
8 ounces sour cream
Ritz crackers (1½ cups)
1 stick margarine
3 tablespoons poppy seed

Boil or pressure cook chicken until tender. Pull chicken from bones. Place in a 13x8½x2-inch casserole. Mix 1 can cream of chicken soup with 8 ounces sour cream. Spread on top chicken. Top with Ritz cracker crumbs. Slice 1 stick margarine on top. Sprinkle with 3 tablespoons poppy seed. Cook at 350°F. for 30 minutes.
Makes 8 to 10 servings.

Cindy Carpenter
Lawrenceville, Georgia

Lemon Chicken

3½ cups peanut oil
1 cup flour
1 teaspoon baking powder
¼ cup cornstarch
1 egg
¼ teaspoon salt
1 teaspoon peanut oil
2 cups water
¾ pound chicken breasts,
   cut into 4 pieces
½ cup lemonade
1 teaspoon lemon extract
½ cup sugar
5 tablespoons white vinegar
3 tablespoons cornstarch
3 tablespoons peanut oil
Lemon slices

Heat 3½ cups peanut oil to 350°F. in wok. Mix flour, baking powder, ¼ cup cornstarch, egg, salt, 1 teaspoon peanut oil and 1 cup water in bowl; mix until smooth. Dip chicken in batter and place gently in hot oil. Deep-fry for 7 minutes or until golden brown. Mix lemonade, lemon extract, sugar, vinegar, 3 tablespoons cornstarch and 1 cup water in saucepan. Bring to a boil, stirring constantly until thickened. Reduce heat and add 3 tablespoons peanut oil. Drain chicken and place on serving plate. Pour sauce over chicken. Garnish with lemon slices.
Makes 4 servings.

Sheila Lipschutz
Hermosa Beach, California

Arroz Con Pollo

1   (3 to 3½-pound) chicken, cut up
¼ cup olive oil
1 medium onion, chopped
1 green pepper, chopped
1 teaspoon minced garlic
1   (8-ounce) can tomato sauce
2   (4-ounce) jars diced pimento,
    drained
1 ounce saffron
2 teaspoons salt
¼ teaspoon pepper
3 cups uncooked rice
¾ cup cooking wine
1   (15-ounce) can asparagus spears,
    drained and heated

Cook chicken in boiling water to cover for 1 hour or until tender. Remove chicken, reserving 6 cups broth. Brown chicken in olive oil in large Dutch oven; remove chicken and set aside. Add onion, green pepper and garlic to Dutch oven; sauté until tender. Add reserved broth, tomato sauce, pimento, saffron, salt and pepper. Bring to a boil, stirring constantly. Add rice, wine and chicken; cover. Simmer for 20 to 30 minutes or until rice is tender. Transfer mixture to large serving dish; garnish with asparagus. Serve immediately.
Makes 8 servings.

Susana Hernandez McHale
Marietta, Georgia

Broccoli-Chicken-Cheese Casserole

1   (10¾-ounce) can cream of
    chicken soup
1   (10-ounce) package broccoli,
    cooked and cut up
4 cups diced cooked chicken
1 cup (4 ounces) shredded Cheddar
    cheese
French fried onion rings

Layer soup, broccoli, chicken and cheese in 1½-quart casserole. Repeat layers. Bake at 350°F. for 25 minutes. Top with onion rings. Bake for 5 minutes longer.
Makes 6 servings.

Diane Black
Ann Arbor, Michigan

Chicken Continental

4 to 6 chicken pieces
2 tablespoons butter
1   (10¾-ounce) can cream of
    chicken soup
2 tablespoons onion flakes
1 teaspoon parsley flakes
½ teaspoon celery flakes
1 teaspoon salt
1⅓ cups water
1⅓ cups uncooked minute rice

Rinse and dry chicken. Sauté chicken in butter; set aside. Mix soup, onion, parsley, celery flakes and salt in saucepan; gradually stir in water. Bring to a boil, stirring constantly. Pour minute rice into 2-quart casserole dish. Stir in soup mixture, reserving ⅓ cup. Top with chicken; pour on remaining ⅓ cup of soup mixture. Bake, covered, at 375°F. for 30 minutes.
Makes 4 to 6 servings.

Ann Borchert
Ann Arbor, Michigan

Chicken Crescents

2 cans boned chicken
¼ cup shredded Cheddar or
  American cheese
1 8-count can crescent rolls
1 (10¾-ounce) can cream of
  chicken soup
1 cup milk
½ cup shredded Cheddar or
  American cheese

Combine chicken and ¼ cup cheese. Separate roll dough into 8 triangles. Place 2 tablespoons chicken mixture on wide end of each triangle. Roll to pointed end. Combine soup, milk and ¼ cup cheese. Heat until cheese melts. Pour half the soup mixture into ungreased 8 or 9-inch pan. Arrange crescents over mixture. Bake at 375°F. for 20 to 25 minutes, or until golden brown. Sprinkle with remaining cheese. Return to oven for 5 minutes until cheese melts. Serve with remaining sauce.
Makes 4 servings.

Lorie Lykins
Ann Arbor, Michigan

Chicken Divan

2 (10-ounce) packages frozen
  broccoli or 2 bunches fresh
  broccoli
2 cups sliced cooked chicken or
  3 chicken breasts, cooked and
  boned
4 tablespoons butter
3 tablespoons whole wheat flour
1½ cups cream
1 cup mayonnaise
1 tablespoon lemon juice
½ teaspoon curry powder
1 cup (4 ounces) shredded sharp
  Cheddar cheese
2 slices whole wheat bread
2 tablespoons butter or margarine

Steam broccoli for 3 or 4 minutes. Arrange in greased 12x8-inch baking dish. Arrange chicken over broccoli. Melt butter; add flour, then slowly add cream, stirring well. Cook over low heat until mixture thickens, stirring constantly. Add mayonnaise, lemon juice and curry powder. Pour over chicken. Sprinkle cheese over chicken and sauce. Spread whole wheat bread with 2 tablespoons butter. Cut into cubes and sprinkle bread cubes over mixture. Bake at 350°F. for 20 to 30 minutes or until thoroughly heated.
Makes 8 servings.

Annastasia Hanna
Stone Mountain, Georgia

Chicken And Dumplings

1 (2½-pound) chicken, disjointed
  and skinned
Water
Salt and pepper to taste
2 cups all-purpose flour
½ cup milk
½ cup water
1½ cups milk

Place chicken in saucepan. Cover with water and sprinkle with salt and pepper. Simmer over medium heat for 30 minutes. Remove chicken, reserving broth for dumplings. Mix flour, ½ cup milk and ½ cup water in small bowl. Stir well, adding more flour if necessary for stiff dough. Press flat on floured surface; let stand for about 10 minutes. Roll dough to ⅛ inch thickness. Cut into 2-inch squares. Bring broth to a boil; add dumplings. Cook for about 10 minutes on high heat. Reduce heat to low and add chicken. Stir in 1½ cups milk; remove from heat. Season with salt and pepper if desired.
Makes 5 servings.

Anne Stover
Lilburn, Georgia

Chicken Drumstick Ragoût

16 chicken drumsticks, about
    4 pounds
1 cup all-purpose flour
4 tablespoons unsalted butter
1 teaspoon salt
½ teaspoon freshly ground pepper
2 tablespoons unsalted butter
2 medium onions, chopped
4 cloves garlic, minced
1 teaspoon thyme
1 teaspoon basil
1 bay leaf
2 cups chicken stock or canned
    broth
1 cup dry white wine
2 tablespoons unsalted butter
1 each red, yellow and green peppers,
    sliced
1   (10-ounce) package frozen
    artichoke hearts, thawed and
    drained
1 cup whipping cream

Dredge chicken drumsticks in flour; shake off excess. In large skillet or flameproof casserole, melt 4 tablespoons butter over moderate heat. Working in batches, season chicken with salt and black pepper. Cook in skillet, turning, until lightly browned, about 10 minutes for each batch. Transfer each batch to a dish and set aside. Add 2 tablespoons butter to pan. Stir in onions, garlic, thyme, basil and bay leaf. Reduce heat to moderately low; cover. Cook, stirring occasionally, for 10 to 15 minutes or until onions are tender. Return chicken to skillet. Add stock and wine: bring to a boil. Reduce heat to moderately low; cover. Simmer, turning legs occasionally, until very tender, about 40 minutes. In medium skillet, melt 2 tablespoons butter over moderately high heat. Add peppers; season with a pinch of salt and pepper. Cook, tossing frequently, until lightly browned, about 5 minutes. Add artichoke hearts; cook for 2 minutes. Transfer chicken, peppers and artichokes to bowl. Strain cooking liquid and return to skillet. Place over high heat; stir in cream. Bring to a boil; boil until liquid is reduced by one-third, about 15 minutes. Season with salt and pepper to taste. Return chicken, peppers and artichokes to skillet. Simmer gently until heated through, about 5 minutes.
Makes 4 to 6 servings.

Mary Johnson
Hayward, California

Chicken Enchilada Pie

1   (3-pound) chicken
1   (10¾-ounce) can cream of
    mushroom soup, undiluted
1   (10¾-ounce) can cream of
    chicken soup, undiluted
1   (4-ounce) can diced green chilies
1 tablespoon minced onion
1 teaspoon chili powder
¼ teaspoon pepper
⅛ teaspoon garlic powder
¼ teaspoon hot sauce
4 cups corn chips or broken corn
    tortillas
2 cups (8 ounces) shredded Cheddar
    cheese

Cook chicken in boiling water to cover until tender; remove chicken from bones, discarding bones and skin. Reserve 1 cup broth. Chop chicken and set aside. Combine reserved broth, soups, green chilies, onion, chili powder, pepper, garlic powder and hot sauce; stir well. Place 3 cups corn chips in 2½ to 3-quart casserole. Top with half the chicken, half the sauce, and half the cheese. Repeat layers, using remaining ingredients. Bake at 350°F. for 30 minutes.
Makes 8 to 10 servings.

Ramona Scarlett
Houston, Texas

Jalapeño Chicken

2½ pounds chicken
Water
6 medium jalapeño peppers
1 medium onion, chopped
1 clove garlic, minced
2 tablespoons salad oil
¼ teaspoon ground cumin
1 (10½-ounce) can cream of
   chicken soup
1 (10-ounce) package frozen
   chopped spinach
½ teaspoon salt
1 pint sour cream
1 (8-ounce) package corn chips
½ pound Monterey Jack cheese,
   shredded
Paprika

In stockpot, cook chicken in 2 inches water until fork tender. Discard skin and bones from chicken; cut meat into bite-sized pieces. Set aside. Reserve one jalapeño pepper for garnish; remove stems and seeds from remaining jalapeño peppers and dice. In 10-inch skillet, sauté jalapeño peppers, onion and garlic in oil over medium heat until tender. Stir in cumin; cook for 1 minute. Add soup, spinach and salt. Heat to boiling, breaking up spinach with fork. Cover and simmer until spinach is cooked. Stir in chicken and sour cream and heat thoroughly. In 2-quart casserole, layer ⅓ of the corn chips and cheese and ½ of the chicken mixture. Repeat layers, ending with cheese on top. Bake in 350°F. oven for 30 minutes or until heated. Sprinkle with paprika and garnish with jalapeño pepper.
Makes 8 servings.

Jerry and Nancy Graf
Ann Arbor, Michigan

Grilled Lemon Chicken

¾ cup butter
½ cup lemon juice
⅓ cup water
1 teaspoon paprika
⅛ teaspoon cayenne pepper
2 tablespoons soy sauce
1 teaspoon honey
1 teaspoon Dijon mustard
2 cloves garlic, minced
½ teaspoon salt
2 whole frying chickens, quartered

Combine all ingredients except the chicken in small saucepan. Heat until butter melts; stir well. Place chicken on greased barbecue grill 5 to 6 inches from coals. Brush with marinade; grill for 25 to 30 minutes or until chicken is done, turning and basting frequently.
Makes 6 to 8 servings.

Gene McAteer
Thousand Oaks, California

Golden Oven-Fried Chicken

1 cup bread crumbs
¼ cup grated Parmesan cheese
2 tablespoons minced parsley
1 teaspoon salt
¼ teaspoon crushed dried thyme
⅛ teaspoon pepper
½ cup butter
1 (2½ to 3-pound) frying chicken,
   cut in pieces

Combine bread crumbs, cheese, parsley, salt, thyme and pepper. Melt butter in shallow baking pan. Dip chicken pieces in butter, then in crumb mixture. Place in baking pan. Bake at 350°F. for about 1 hour or until tender; basting occasionally. Do not turn chicken pieces.
Makes 4 servings.

Sue Donze
Carrollton, Georgia

Leftover Chicken Casserole

1½ cups spaghetti (broken in 2-inch
    pieces)
1½ cups cubed cooked chicken or
    turkey
½ cup chopped onion
1   (10¾-ounce) can cream of
    mushroom soup
½ cup chicken broth or water
½ teaspoon salt
⅛ teaspoon pepper
1¾ cups shredded Cheddar cheese

Cook spaghetti according to package directions. Drain and place in 2-quart casserole. Place chicken, onion, soup, broth, salt, pepper and 1¼ cups cheese in bowl; mix well. Pour over spaghetti; top with remaining cheese. Bake at 350°F. for 45 minutes.
Makes 8 servings.

Mary Kogelschatz
Belleville, Michigan

Mexican Chicken (Chicken Sopa)

1 dozen tortillas, quartered
1 fryer, cooked, boned, diced
2   (10¾-ounce) cans cream of
    chicken soup
3   (5⅓-ounce) cans evaporated
    milk
½ cup chicken broth or water
1 medium onion, chopped
1   (7-ounce) can green chilies
1   (8-ounce) package sliced Swiss
    cheese

Place tortillas in 13x9x2-inch baking dish. Place half the chicken on tortillas. Combine soup, evaporated milk, broth, onion and chilies; stir well. Spoon half the mixture over chicken. Repeat with remaining chicken and sauce. Top with cheese. Bake at 350°F. for 35 to 45 minutes or until bubbly. Let stand for 10 minutes.
Makes 6 to 8 servings.

Leftover turkey can also be used.

Rhonda Brown
Yukon, Oklahoma

One-Cup Chicken Casserole

1 cup cooked noodles
1 cup diced cooked chicken
1 cup mixed frozen or canned
    vegetables
1   (10¾-ounce) can condensed
    cream of chicken soup
1 cup water

Cook and drain noodles according to package directions. Combine chicken, vegetables, soup and water in saucepan. Bring to a boil. Add noodles. Pour into 2½-quart casserole. Place biscuits on top of casserole. Bake at 425°F. for 20 minutes or until biscuits are golden brown.
Makes 6 to 8 servings.

Biscuits

2 cups sifted all-purpose flour
4 teaspoons baking powder
½ teaspoon salt
¼ cup shortening
⅔ to ¾ cup milk

Sift flour, baking powder and salt into bowl. Cut in shortening with pastry blender until mixture resembles coarse crumbs. Add milk all at once. Stir with fork until flour is mixed; do not overmix. Turn dough onto floured surface. Knead 10 to 12 strokes. Roll or pat dough ¾ inch thick. Cut into round biscuits with cutter.

Linda Mueller
Long Beach, Mississippi

Puerto Rican Chicken

1 large chicken, cut into pieces
3 potatoes, peeled and cubed
1 medium onion, chopped
½ green pepper, sliced
2 cups water
1   (8-ounce) can tomato sauce
7 pimento-stuffed olives
1 tablespoon olive juice
1 tablespoon dried whole oregano
1 tablespoon parsley flakes
1 teaspoon garlic powder
1 small bay leaf
Salt and pepper to taste

Combine all ingredients in large saucepan. Cook over medium heat for approximately 45 minutes or until done. Serve over white rice or noodles. Leftover sauce may be combined with mixed vegetables the following day.
Makes 4 servings.

Naomi Funkhouser
San Antonio, Texas

Dad's Swiss Chicken

4 cups diced cooked chicken
2 cups diced celery
2 cups toasted bread cubes
1 cup mayonnaise
½ cup milk
1 onion, chopped
1 teaspoon salt
1 teaspoon pepper
1   (8-ounce) package shredded
   Swiss cheese

Combine all ingredients. Pour into greased 2-quart casserole. Cover and bake at 350°F. for 30 to 40 minutes. This can be made ahead and refrigerated before baking, requiring a little more baking time. This is also a good recipe for leftover turkey.
Makes 4 to 6 servings.

Cheryl L. McCormick
Hendersonville, Tennessee

Baked Chicken With Sherry

8 chicken breasts, skinned and boned
2   (10¾-ounce) cans cream of
   mushroom soup
1   (10¾-ounce) cans cream of celery
   soup
½ cup dry Sherry
Slivered almonds, toasted

Place chicken breasts in greased 13x9x2-inch baking pan. Mix soups and Sherry; pour over top. Bake at 325°F. for about 2 hours. Sprinkle with toasted almonds.
Makes 8 servings.

Lois Govaere
Ann Arbor, Michigan

Chicken Breasts With Tarragon

3 whole chicken breasts, skinned,
  boned and halved
Salt and pepper to taste
¼ cup flour
3 tablespoons butter
1 tablespoon chopped shallots
¼ cup dry white wine
1 teaspoon fresh chopped tarragon
  or ½ teaspoon dried tarragon
½ cup chicken broth
1 tablespoon butter
¼ cup whipping cream

Sprinkle chicken with salt and pepper; dredge with flour. Reserve remaining flour. In large skillet, heat 3 tablespoons butter; add chicken and brown on both sides. Transfer to heated platter. Add shallots to skillet and sauté briefly. Add wine. Cook liquid over high heat until nearly evaporated, scraping loose all brown particles. Add reserved flour and stir to make thick paste. Sprinkle with tarragon and stir in chicken broth. Return chicken to skillet; cover and cook until tender, about 25 minutes. May need a small amount more broth. Transfer chicken to platter; keep hot. Add 1 tablespoon butter and cream to skillet; heat, stirring constantly. Pour sauce over chicken. Serve with wild rice.
Makes 6 servings.

Patricia A. Tovo
Chicago, Illinois

Chicken-Broccoli Casserole

2 medium bunches fresh broccoli
  flowerets
4 chicken breasts
1½ cups condensed cream of
  mushroom soup
¾ cup mayonnaise
10 to 12 medium fresh mushrooms,
  sliced
1½ tablespoons lemon juice
Salt and pepper to taste
¼ pound slivered almonds
1 (Number-2) can French-fried
  onions

Arrange broccoli in ungreased 13x9x2-inch baking dish. Place chicken over broccoli. Mix soup, mayonnaise, mushrooms, lemon juice, salt and pepper to taste; spoon over chicken. Bake, covered, at 350°F. for 45 minutes. Remove cover and sprinkle with almonds and onions.
Makes 6 to 8 servings.

Barbara Eckel
Ann Arbor, Michigan

Chicken Cordon Bleu

4 boneless chicken breast halves
2 cups all-purpose flour
Salt and pepper to taste
2 slices baked ham
2 slices Mozzarella cheese
3 eggs, beaten
Butter

Place chicken breasts between 2 sheets waxed paper; pound to ⅛-inch thickness, using meat mallet or rolling pin. Combine flour, salt and pepper; set aside. Place 1 slice ham and 1 slice cheese on 2 chicken breast halves; top with remaining chicken. Dip chicken in beaten egg; dredge in reserved flour mixture, coating well. Sauté chicken in butter until golden brown.
Makes 2 servings.

Suzanne Stewart
Windsor, Ontario, Canada

Chicken Cordon Bleu

4 egg yolks
1 cup flour
1 cup bread crumbs
8 to 10 boneless chicken breasts
Salt and pepper to taste
1 tablespoon tarragon
¼ pound Swiss cheese, thinly sliced
¼ pound sliced ham, sliced thin

Beat egg yolks; set aside. Place flour and bread crumbs in separate bowls; set aside. Pound chicken breasts flat. Sprinkle with salt, pepper and tarragon. Cut cheese and ham into ¼-inch wide strips slightly shorter than length of chicken breasts. Place strips lengthwise on chicken breasts. Carefully roll to enclose cheese and ham; secure with wooden picks. Coat rolls first in flour, then egg yolks, then bread crumbs. Fry in heated oil (350°) for 8 minutes or until golden brown. (If oil is hotter than 350°, chicken will brown too quickly on outside but still be raw inside.) When cut, makes beautiful dinner. Serve with wild rice, green beans, dinner rolls and salad.
Makes 4 to 5 servings.

Lisa G. Harvey
Hammond, Indiana

Chicken In Sour Cream Sauce

Flour, salt and pepper for coating
    chicken
4 chicken breasts, boned and skinned
3 tablespoons butter
4 green onions, minced
1   (10¾-ounce) can cream of
    mushroom soup
1   (8-ounce) carton sour cream
½ cup white wine

Flour and season chicken breasts. Melt 2 tablespoons butter in skillet. Brown chicken in butter. Place in casserole and set aside. Place 1 tablespoon butter in skillet; sauté green onions. Add mushroom soup, sour cream and wine, mixing well until thick. (May add 1 teaspoon flour to thicken.) Pour over chicken. Bake, covered, in 350°F. oven for 45 minutes.
Makes 3 to 4 servings.

Tracey E. Yost
Hattiesburg, Mississippi

Chicken Juliet

4 whole boneless chicken breasts
    or 8 fillets
¼ cup butter or margarine
8 ounces fresh mushrooms, sliced
2   (10¾-ounce) cans cream of
    mushroom soup
1 clove garlic, minced
Pinch of thyme
Pinch of rosemary
⅔ cup half and half
Hot cooked rice or noodles

Brown chicken in butter in large skillet. Remove chicken and add mushrooms; cook until tender. Add next 4 ingredients; stir well. Add chicken; cover. Simmer for 30 to 45 minutes or until done. Stir in half and half. Serve over hot cooked rice or noodles.
Makes 4 servings.

Barbara Ashley
Ann Arbor, Michigan

Chicken La Scala

3   (16-ounce) cans tomato sauce
2 stalks celery, diced
1 small onion, diced
1 teaspoon each garlic powder, salt,
    pepper, basil leaves, dried whole
    oregano, Italian seasoning and
    crushed red pepper
1 bay leaf
1 egg
1 cup milk
Salt and pepper to taste
4 boneless chicken breast halves,
    skinned
2 cups seasoned bread crumbs
1   (8-ounce) package linguine
½ cup grated Parmesan cheese
1   (12-ounce) package shredded
    Mozzarella cheese
1 teaspoon chopped fresh parsley

Combine tomato sauce, celery, onion, garlic powder, 1 teaspoon salt, 1 teaspoon pepper, basil, oregano, Italian seasoning, crushed red pepper and bay leaf in large saucepan; stir well. Simmer for 30 to 45 minutes or until celery is tender. Combine egg, milk and salt and pepper to taste. Dip chicken in egg mixture; roll in bread crumbs, coating well. Arrange chicken in shallow roasting pan. Bake at 350°F. for 30 minutes or until done. Cut chicken into 1-inch strips. Partially cook linguine according to package directions; drain. Place linguine in 9-inch square baking dish. Spoon half the sauce mixture over linguine. Arrange chicken over sauce; spoon remaining sauce over chicken. Sprinkle with Parmesan cheese and Mozzarella cheese. Bake at 350°F. for 30 minutes or until cheese is lightly browned. Sprinkle with parsley and serve immediately.
Makes 8 servings.

Billie Jo Sims
Tyler, Texas

Chicken With Rosemary Cream Sauce

6 boneless chicken breasts, skinned
1 cup all-purpose flour
2 teaspoons freshly ground pepper
1 teaspoon salt
1 bunch green onions
Clarified butter
2½ cups chicken stock
2 tablespoons dried rosemary leaves
1 tablespoon basil leaves
½ cup dry white wine
¼ cup cream
1 tablespoon lemon juice
Roux
Fresh parsley sprigs

Cut chicken breasts lengthwise into 1-inch strips. Combine flour, pepper and salt; stir well. Dredge chicken in flour mixture, coating well; set aside. Sauté green onions in clarified butter in small saucepan. Combine chicken stock, rosemary and basil; simmer for 5 minutes. Strain, discarding herbs. Add stock to onion mixture. Add wine, cream and lemon juice, stirring well. Cook over low heat, stirring constantly, until thoroughly heated; do not boil. Add roux to thicken. Sauté chicken in clarified butter until golden brown; drain on paper towels. Arrange chicken in serving dish; spoon sauce over. Garnish with parsley and serve immediately.
Makes 3 to 4 servings.

To make roux: Combine equal parts flour and clarified butter. Cook over low heat, stirring constantly, until mixture thickens and becomes the color of copper penny.

Jolene Kemppainen
Drummond Isle, Michigan

Chicken Supreme

3 (10¾-ounce) cans cream of
   mushroom soup
1 (8-ounce) carton sour cream
1 (5-ounce) jar dried beef
4 boneless chicken breasts
4 slices lean bacon

Mix soup and sour cream; set aside. Do not salt chicken. Line bottom of 2½-quart casserole with dried beef. Wrap chicken breasts with bacon; place over dried beef. Spread sauce over chicken pieces. Top with second layer dried beef and remaining sauce. Bake at 350°F. for 45 minutes to 1 hour.
Makes 4 servings.

Hope Heitger
South Lake Tahoe, California

Crab-Stuffed Chicken Breasts

3 large chicken breasts, halved,
   boned and skinned
Salt and pepper to taste
½ cup chopped onion
½ cup chopped celery
3 tablespoons butter, melted
5 tablespoons white wine
1 cup flaked crab meat
½ cup herb-seasoned stuffing
2 tablespoons flour
½ teaspoon paprika
6 tablespoons melted butter
¾ cup Hollandaise Sauce

Pound chicken breasts to flatten. Sprinkle with salt and pepper. Sauté onion and celery in 3 tablespoons butter until tender. Remove from heat and add wine, crab meat and stuffing. Toss to blend. Place 2 tablespoons stuffing mixture on each chicken breast. Roll up and secure with toothpicks. Combine flour and paprika and coat chicken. Place chicken in baking dish and drizzle with 6 tablespoons melted butter. Bake in 375°F. oven for 45 minutes. Spoon Hollandaise Sauce over chicken to serve.
Makes 6 servings.

Hollandaise Sauce

3 egg yolks
2 tablespoons lemon juice
¼ teaspoon salt
⅛ teaspoon Tabasco sauce
½ cup butter, melted
2 tablespoons white wine

Place egg yolks, lemon juice, salt and Tabasco sauce in blender container. Blend for 2 minutes, adding melted butter slowly. Add wine just before serving.

Roileen Domingues
West Sacto, California

French Chicken In Sherry Sauce

3 whole chicken breasts, split
½ teaspoon salt
1 medium onion, sliced
1 cup sliced mushrooms
¼ cup chopped green pepper
1 cup orange juice
½ cup water
¼ cup dry Sherry
1 tablespoon all-purpose flour
1 tablespoon brown sugar
1 teaspoon grated orange rind
1 teaspoon salt
¼ teaspoon pepper
2 teaspoons chopped parsley
Paprika (optional)
1 orange, peeled and sliced
   (optional)

Place chicken breasts, skin-side up, on broiler 2 inches from heat. Broil for 10 minutes or until skin is browned. Place chicken in casserole. Sprinkle with salt, onion, mushrooms and green pepper. Combine orange juice, water, Sherry, flour, brown sugar, orange rind, salt and pepper in saucepan; blend well. Cook over medium heat, stirring constantly, until sauce thickens and bubbles. Add parsley; pour over chicken. Bake at 375°F. for 45 to 60 minutes. Baste several times during baking. Sprinkle with paprika; garnish with orange slices, if desired.
Makes 6 servings.

Barbara Press
Santa Monica, California

Pam's Chicken

6 whole chicken breasts
2 tablespoons butter
2 (10¾-ounce) cans cream of
   mushroom soup
2 cups sour cream
1 (8-ounce) can water chestnuts,
   sliced
2 (4-ounce) cans sliced mushrooms,
   drained
4 ounces almonds, sliced

Brown chicken breasts in butter in skillet. Combine remaining ingredients except almonds. Place chicken breasts in shallow 2-quart baking dish. Cover with soup mixture. Sprinkle almonds over top. Bake, covered, in 350°F. oven for 1 hour.
Makes 6 large or 12 small servings.

Diane Lyon Laughlin
Peoria, Illinois

Peking Imperial Chicken

3 tablespoons cornstarch
1 cup chicken bouillon
½ cup light corn syrup
6 tablespoons soy sauce
¼ cup dry Sherry
¼ teaspoon ground red pepper
3 tablespoons oil
1 to 2 pounds boneless chicken
   breasts, cut into small cubes
2 to 3 (10-ounce) packages frozen
   Chinese vegetables

In small bowl, combine first 6 ingredients and set aside. In large skillet or electric frypan, heat oil over medium heat. Add chicken. Stir-fry until chicken is tender. Add cornstarch mixture to chicken, stirring constantly. Cover and simmer for 10 to 15 minutes. Add frozen vegetables. Simmer for 10 to 15 minutes longer or until thoroughly heated.
Makes 4 to 6 servings.

Jennifer LeClair
Elmwood Park, New Jersey

Quick 'N' Easy Chicken Gourmet

1½ cups sour cream
1 (10¾-ounce) can cream of
  mushroom soup
4 boneless chicken breasts
1 tablespoon paprika
1½ cups small mushroom caps
1 large onion, cut in strips
⅓ cup dry Sherry
1 large green pepper, cut in strips
1 tablespoon fresh ground pepper

Combine sour cream and soup in small bowl; set aside. Place chicken in casserole; sprinkle with paprika. Add mushrooms, onion and wine. Bake at 350°F. for 30 minutes. Remove from oven; add soup mixture and green pepper. Return to oven and continue to cook for 1 hour. Makes 4 servings.

Jackie Herz
Bradenton, Florida

Smothered Hawaiian Chicken

1 (15-ounce) can pineapple chunks
  in own juice, undrained
¾ cup water
¼ cup teriyaki marinade and sauce
4 boneless chicken breasts
8 ounces fresh mushrooms, sliced
1 medium green pepper, chopped
1 small onion, chopped
4 slices provolone cheese
1 (8-ounce) can pineapple rings
  (optional)

Drain pineapple, reserving juice; set pineapple aside. Combine reserved juice, water and teriyaki marinade in 9-inch square baking dish; stir well. Add chicken; cover. Refrigerate for 2 to 3 hours. Remove chicken from marinade, reserving marinade. Combine ½ cup reserved marinade, mushrooms, green pepper and onion in medium skillet; cook over medium heat until tender. Spoon mixture into small bowl; set aside. Combine ½ cup remaining marinade and chicken in skillet; cook over medium heat until chicken is lightly browned. Place chicken in baking dish with remaining marinade; discard marinade used to cook chicken. Spoon sautéed vegetables over chicken; spoon reserved pineapple chunks over vegetables. Cover and bake at 350°F. for 30 minutes. Place cheese over pineapple and bake for 5 minutes longer or until cheese melts. Garnish with pineapple rings if desired. Makes 2 to 4 servings.

Donna Sassano
Tokyo, Japan

Chicken Spaghetti

1 large hen (or 4 to 6 breasts)
2 onions, chopped
3 cloves garlic
4 ribs celery, chopped
1 bell pepper, chopped
1 bunch green onions, chopped
½ bunch fresh parsley
2 tablespoons bacon fat
2 cups chicken broth
1 (16-ounce) can tomatoes
1 (10-ounce) can tomato soup
1 (6-ounce) can tomato paste
2 bay leaves
3 tablespoons Worcestershire sauce
Salt and pepper to taste
6 dashes of hot sauce

Boil chicken in seasoned water. Reserve broth; bone chicken. Add tomatoes, soup, paste and seasonings. Thin mixture to desired taste with chicken broth. Add boned chicken. Simmer, covered, for at least 1 hour. Serve over spaghetti with French bread and salad. Also good over rice.
Makes 6 to 8 servings.

Judie Allen
Norcross, Georgia

Phil's Swiss Chick

2 boneless chicken breasts
2 tablespoons butter
¼ pound Swiss cheese, cut thick
1 (4-ounce) can mushrooms, drained
½ to ¾ cup white wine

Slice chicken into strips. Melt butter in frying pan; sauté chicken until tender but not brown. Place chicken strips in greased casserole. Top with Swiss cheese and mushrooms. Pour white wine on top. Bake at 350°F., covered, for 15 to 20 minutes.
Makes 2 to 4 servings.

Philip James Nagle
Lancaster, Pennsylvania

Chicken Breast Casserole

1 package dried beef
8 slices bacon
8 chicken breast halves, skinned (boneless)
1 cup sour cream
1 can cream of chicken or mushroom soup
Paprika

Tear dried beef into pieces. Place in bottom of 11x7-inch baking dish. Wrap 1 slice bacon around each chicken breast; place in dish on top of beef. Combine sour cream and soup; spoon over top of chicken. Sprinkle lightly with paprika. Bake at 275°F. for 3 hours.
Makes 8 servings.

Susan Burgerhoudt
Plymouth, Michigan

Great Chicken And Spinach Quiche

1 cup cooked, diced chicken
1 cup (4 ounces) shredded Swiss cheese
1 (10-ounce) package frozen chopped spinach, cooked and drained
¼ cup chopped onion
1 unbaked (9-inch) pastry shell (recipe follows)
2 eggs
¾ cup mayonnaise
¾ cup milk
½ teaspoon basil leaves
⅛ teaspoon pepper

Combine chicken, cheese, spinach and onion; mix well. Spoon mixture into pastry shell. Combine remaining ingredients; beat well. Pour over chicken mixture. Bake at 350°F. for 40 minutes or until golden brown and set.
Makes 8 servings.

Pâté Brisée

2 cups all-purpose flour
½ teaspoon salt
½ cup chilled butter
3 tablespoons shortening
5 to 6 tablespoons cold water

Combine flour and salt; cut in butter and shortening until crumbly. Sprinkle water evenly over surface; stir with fork just until moistened. Shape dough into ball. Cover and refrigerate for 2 to 36 hours. Roll dough to ⅛ inch thickness; fit into 9-inch pie plate.
Makes one 9-inch pastry shell.

Judith A. Nelson
Ann Arbor, Michigan

Cornish Game Hens In Flaming Cherry Sauce

2 (16 to 20-ounce) Cornish game
  hens
Seasoned salt
Pepper
2 tablespoons butter or margarine,
  melted
½ teaspoon seasoned salt
½ teaspoon ground ginger
½ teaspoon paprika
1 (8-ounce) can pitted dark sweet
  cherries
⅔ cup water
1 chicken bouillon cube
1 small onion, quartered
8 whole cloves
¼ teaspoon ground cinnamon
1 tablespoon cornstarch
1 tablespoon cold water
¼ teaspoon grated lemon rind
1 tablespoon lemon juice
Orange slices (optional)
2 tablespoons Brandy

Rinse game hens and pat dry. Sprinkle cavities with seasoned salt and pepper. Place game hens, breast-side up, in shallow roasting pan. Add ¼ inch water. Combine butter, ½ teaspoon seasoned salt, ginger and paprika; stir well. Brush over surface of game hens. Bake at 350°F. for 1 hour, basting with pan drippings every 15 minutes. Arrange game hens on serving plates and keep warm. Skim fat from pan drippings; reserve drippings. Drain cherries, reserving ⅓ cup syrup. Combine syrup, water, bouillon cube, onion, cloves and cinnamon in small saucepan; stir well. Bring to a boil; reduce heat, and simmer for 10 minutes. Strain, discarding onion and cloves; reserve sauce in pan. Dissolve cornstarch in 1 tablespoon cold water; add to sauce, stirring until smooth. Cook, stirring constantly, until mixture thickens and boils. Stir in reserved pan drippings, cherries, lemon rind and lemon juice. Garnish game hens with orange slices. Place Brandy in small saucepan. Cook over low heat just until warm. Ignite with long match and pour into cherry sauce. Spoon flaming sauce over game hens; serve immediately.
Makes 2 servings.

John Ricketts
Charlotte, North Carolina

Pheasant Jubilee

4 pheasants, quartered (or chicken)
Flour
½ cup butter or margarine
1 onion, chopped
½ cup seedless raisins
1 cup chili sauce
½ cup water
½ cup firmly packed brown sugar
2 tablespoons Worcestershire sauce
¼ teaspoon garlic powder
1 cup Sherry
1 (16-ounce) can pitted dark sweet
  cherries, drained

Dust pheasants with flour. Melt butter in heavy skillet; brown pheasants thoroughly. Place pheasants in deep casserole. In same skillet, combine onion, raisins, chili sauce, water, brown sugar, Worcestershire sauce and garlic; boil briefly, scraping particles from bottom and sides of pan. Pour over pheasants. Bake, covered, at 325°F. for 1½ hours. Remove cover; add Sherry and cherries. Bake for 20 minutes longer. To serve, transfer to deep chafing or warming dish.
Makes 8 servings.

Karo Schlemmer
Bloomington, Minnesota

Turkey-Pecan Waffles

¼ cup butter
3 chicken bouillon cubes
½ cup flour
4 teaspoons poultry seasoning
2½ cups milk
1 teaspoon lemon juice
2 cups turkey
½ cup celery, chopped
2 tablespoons chopped pimentos
½ cup pecans, chopped
Hot waffles

In medium saucepan, melt butter. Add bouillon cubes. Stir in flour and poultry seasoning. Add milk and lemon juice. Stir slowly, over medium heat, until mixture thickens and bubbles. Stir in turkey and celery; add pimentos and pecans. Heat until warm. Serve over waffles.
Makes 2½ cups.

Chicken can be substituted for turkey. If you don't like pecans, it tastes just as great without them.

Elberta Smoak
Hobbs, New Mexico

Spanish Turkey (Pabo Español)

1 pound ground chuck
1 medium onion, chopped
2 cloves garlic, minced
1   (15-ounce) can tomato paste
8 ounces bacon, cooked and
    crumbled
8 ounces chopped cooked ham
1½ cups chopped mixed nuts
1 cup raisins
2 bay leaves
1 teaspoon dried whole oregano
1 teaspoon dried whole thyme
1   (8 to 12-pound) turkey

Brown ground chuck, onion and garlic in large skillet, stirring to crumble meat; drain. Add ½ can tomato paste, bacon, ham, nuts, raisins, bay leaves, oregano and thyme; stir well. Simmer over low heat for 30 minutes, stirring occasionally. Rinse turkey under cold running water; pat dry. Cut ½ inch slits in fleshy areas of turkey; stuff with ground chuck mixture. Place remaining ground chuck mixture in cavity of bird. Brush turkey with remaining tomato sauce. Place turkey in shallow roasting pan; cover with aluminum foil. Bake at 450°F. for 2½ to 3½ hours or until meat thermometer registers 180° to 185°.
Makes 12 to 16 servings.

Salvador Santamaria
North Charleston, South Carolina

Vlcek's Wild Fowl Recipe

½ stick butter
3 tablespoons diced onion
4 boneless breasts from duck, goose,
    pheasant, quail, grouse, partridge
    or domestic duck
Adolph's meat tenderizer (optional)
2 cups flour
Pinch of salt and pepper (optional)
1   (10¾-ounce) can cream of
    chicken soup
¼ cup sour cream (optional)
2 teaspoons Worcestershire sauce

Melt 2 tablespoons butter in skillet; add onion. Sauté until tender. Tenderize breast fillets by sprinkling with tenderizer and pounding with wooden mallet. Let stand for 2 to 3 minutes. Place flour, salt and pepper in bag. Drop fillets, one at a time, into bag and shake until well coated. Melt 2 tablespoons butter in skillet. Sauté fillets until browned, approximately 5 minutes on each side. In bowl, mix soup, onion and ¼ can water, ¼ cup sour cream and Worcestershire sauce, if desired; mix well. Pour over fillets in skillet. Simmer, covered, for approximately 45 minutes.
Makes 4 servings.

Recipe also good for chicken.

Don Vlcek
Plymouth, Michigan

Pork

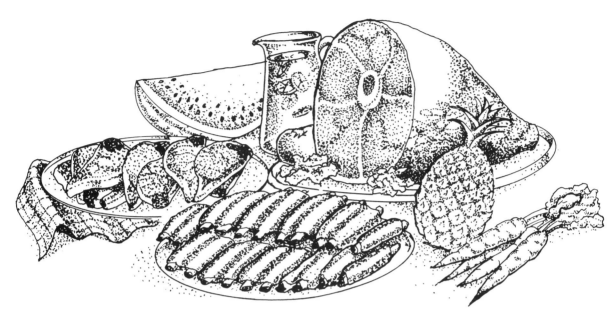

Spanish Pork with Olives

1 (2-pound) pork shoulder, trimmed
    and cut into 1-inch cubes
2 tablespoons olive oil
2 medium onions, sliced
1 tablespoon all-purpose flour
1 pound tomatoes, peeled and chopped
¾ cup red wine
2 cloves garlic, crushed
1 teaspoon basil leaves
Salt and pepper to taste
1 green pepper, chopped
⅓ cup sliced pimento-stuffed olives

Brown pork in oil in large skillet; remove from skillet, using a slotted spoon. Set aside. Sauté onions in skillet until tender; add flour, stirring until smooth. Add reserved pork, tomatoes, wine, garlic, basil, salt and pepper; stir well. Bring to a boil. Transfer mixture to a 2-quart casserole. Cover and bake at 275°F. for 1½ hours. Stir in green pepper and olives. Cover and bake for 30 minutes longer. Serve with hot cooked rice.
Makes 8 servings.

Diane Allan
England

Sweet Pork-Colli

2 tablespoons vegetable oil
1 pound lean pork, cut into
    1-inch cubes
1 cup water
1 envelope gravy mix
    for pork
3 tablespoons vinegar
2 tablespoons brown sugar
1 tablespoon soy sauce
1½ cups broccoli flowerets

Heat oil in wok or large skillet; add pork. Stir-fry for 10 minutes, or until thoroughly cooked. Remove pork and set aside. Add water, gravy mix, vinegar, brown sugar and soy sauce to wok. Bring to a boil, stirring constantly. Add broccoli and cook for 5 minutes. Add reserved pork and cook for 5 minutes longer, stirring constantly. Serve over hot rice.
Makes 4 servings.

Suzanne Gibson
Hamden, Connecticut

Company Pork Chops

2 tablespoons vegetable oil
4 center cut loin pork chops,
    ¾-inch thick
1 small onion, sliced and
    separated into rings
1 clove garlic, minced
½ cup orange juice
1½ tablespoons cider vinegar
1 teaspoon paprika
1 teaspoon honey
Salt and pepper to taste
½ cup chicken broth
2 tablespoons all-purpose flour
½ cup chicken broth
Parsley, chopped (optional)
Orange wedges (optional)

Heat oil in large heavy skillet or electric frying pan; brown pork chops on both sides. Add onion, garlic, orange juice, vinegar, paprika, honey, salt, pepper and ½ cup chicken broth. Bring to a boil. Cover; reduce heat. Simmer for 1 hour. Remove pork chops to platter and keep warm. Gradually stir flour into remaining ½ cup chicken broth. Stir mixture into drippings in skillet; cook, stirring constantly, until thickened. Serve with pork chops. Garnish with parsley and orange wedges, if desired.
Makes 4 servings.

Sherri Seiber
Arlington Heights, Illinois

Haole Lau Lau

3 bunches spinach, cleaned
6 pork chops, ¾ inch thick
1½ teaspoons salt
½ teaspoon pepper
6 medium yams, peeled and sliced
4 tablespoons butter

Place half the spinach in 15x11x2-inch baking pan. Arrange pork chops over spinach; sprinkle with salt and pepper. Arrange yams over pork chops. Top with remaining spinach; dot with butter. Bake, covered, at 350°F. for 2 hours.
Makes 6 servings.

Serge Krivatsy
Honolulu, Hawaii

Pork Chops With Paprika

6 loin pork chops, ¾ inch thick
1 clove garlic, finely chopped
2 teaspoons paprika
1 teaspoon caraway seed
Salt and pepper to taste
1 cup dry white wine
Buttered noodles

Place pork chops in 13x9x2-inch baking dish. Sprinkle with garlic, paprika, caraway seed, salt and pepper. Pour wine over chops. Cover, and refrigerate for 2 to 3 hours. Bake uncovered, at 300°F. for 1 hour or until tender, adding more wine if necessary. Serve with hot buttered noodles.
Makes 6 servings.

Mary Rowley
Columbia, South Carolina

Pork Chop 'N' Potato Bake

6 pork chops
Vegetable oil
Seasoned salt
1   (10¾-ounce) can condensed
    cream of celery soup
½ cup milk
½ cup sour cream
¼ teaspoon black pepper
1   (24-ounce) package frozen hash
    brown potatoes, thawed
1 cup (4 ounces) shredded Cheddar
    cheese
1   (2.8-ounce) can French-fried
    onions

Brown pork chops in a small amount of oil in skillet. Sprinkle with seasoned salt and set aside. Combine soup, milk, sour cream, pepper and ½ teaspoon seasoned salt. Stir in potatoes, ½ cup cheese and ½ can French-fried onions. Spoon mixture into 13x9x2-inch baking dish. Arrange pork chops over potatoes. Bake, uncovered at 350°F. for 40 minutes. Top with remaining cheese and onions; bake, uncovered, for 5 minutes longer.
Makes 6 servings.

Eleanor Hansen
Seattle, Washington

Pork Chop-Sausage Jambalaya

4 to 6 pork chops
1   (1-pound) package sausage
    (hot or mild)
1½ cups long grain rice
1 bunch green onions, chopped
1 small green pepper, chopped
4 pork-flavored bouillon cubes
3 cups hot water

Cut pork chops and sausage into bite-sized pieces. Brown in medium frying pan; drain grease. Set pork chops and sausage aside. In same frying pan, brown rice slowly. Add onions and green pepper and allow to brown. Pour rice mixture into 12x6-inch baking dish. Top with pork chops and sausage. Combine bouillon cubes and hot water. Pour over rice and meat. Cover with foil. Bake in preheated 350°F. oven for 30 minutes.
Makes 4 to 6 servings.

Tammy Jo Hardin
Pacifica, California

Saucy Baked Pork Chops

2 tablespoons shortening
6 pork chops
1 medium onion, sliced
1   (10¾-ounce) can cream of
    chicken soup
3 tablespoons catsup
2 teaspoons Worcestershire sauce

Melt shortening in skillet. Cook pork chops over medium-high heat until brown on both sides. Remove and place in casserole. Layer onion slices over pork chops. Combine remaining ingredients and pour over chops. Bake, covered, at 350°F. for 1 hour.
Makes 6 servings.

Ann Lovernick Litzler
Ann Arbor, Michigan

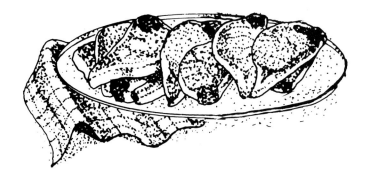

Korean Pork Pagogie

1½ pounds lean pork, cut into thin
  strips
2 carrots, cleaned, pared and cut
  into strips
1 medium onion, cut into medium
  pieces
¼ pound small fresh mushrooms,
  cleaned
½ cup catsup
1 teaspoon soy sauce
½ teaspoon Accent
½ teaspoon salt
½ teaspoon cayenne pepper
¼ teaspoon garlic powder
Dash of ginger
Dash of paprika
2 tablespoons vegetable oil

Combine pork, carrots, onion and mushrooms in large bowl. Combine next 8 ingredients; pour over pork mixture. Let stand for 10 to 15 minutes. Heat oil in wok or large skillet. Stir-fry mixture for 5 minutes or until pork is done. Serve with hot cooked rice.
Makes 6 servings.

Pam Waleri
Norwalk, Ohio

Mandarin Pork And Vegetables

2 tablespoons cornstarch
1¼ cups cold water
⅓ cup soy sauce
⅓ cup corn syrup
¼ to ½ teaspoon crushed red
  pepper
2 tablespoons vegetable oil
1 pound boneless pork, cut into
  thin strips
2 cloves garlic, minced
2 tablespoons vegetable oil
2 cups broccoli flowerets
2 small onions, cut into wedges
1 medium carrot, julienned
8 ounces fresh mushrooms, sliced

Combine cornstarch and water, stirring until smooth. Add soy sauce, corn syrup and red pepper; set aside. Heat 2 tablespoons oil in wok or large skillet. Add pork and garlic; stir-fry for 5 minutes or until tender. Remove from wok. Heat remaining oil in wok. Add broccoli, onions and carrot; stir-fry for 2 minutes. Add mushrooms; stir-fry for 1 minute or until vegetables are crisp-tender. Add reserved pork mixture. Stir reserved cornstarch mixture; add to wok. Bring to a boil, stirring constantly; boil for 1 minute. Serve immediately over hot cooked rice.
Makes 4 servings.

Claudia Miller
Ypsilanti, Michigan

Pork Roast

1 (3 to 4½-pound) pork roast
1 (10¾-ounce) can cream of
  mushroom soup
1 (10¾-ounce) can cream of
  celery soup
½ cup water
2 medium onions, quartered

Place pork in roasting pan, fat-side up. Combine soups and water, mixing thoroughly; pour over roast. Place onions around roast. Bake at 350°F. until tender, 30 to 35 minutes per pound. The internal temperature should be 185°F. on meat thermometer.
Makes 6 to 8 servings.

Annastasia Hanna
Stone Mountain, Georgia

Moo Shu Pork

1 pound pork tenderloin, cut into
   thin strips
¼ cup soy sauce
2 tablespoons dry Sherry
1 tablespoon cornstarch
1½ teaspoons sugar
1 clove garlic, minced
1 teaspoon ground ginger
¼ cup vegetable oil
8 ounces mushrooms, sliced
1½ cups shredded cabbage
1 (8-ounce) can bamboo shoots,
   drained
4 green onions, sliced
2 eggs, scrambled dry
1 (16-ounce) can bean sprouts,
   drained
Hot cooked rice

Combine first 7 ingredients and marinate at least ½ hour. In large skillet, heat oil until very hot. Cook pork mixture, stirring rapidly and constantly, for 2 to 3 minutes. Add mushrooms, cabbage, bamboo shoots and green onions. Cook until cabbage begins to wilt. Add eggs and bean sprouts. Cook and stir until heated through. Serve over hot cooked rice.
Makes 4 servings.

Traditionally this dish is served over wheat pancakes.

Susan Peterson
Diamond Bar, California

Pineapple Chow Mein

1½ to 2 pounds pork steak, cut
   into bite-sized pieces
½ cup chopped onion
1 cup boiling water
1 beef-flavored bouillon cube
1 cup chopped celery
1 (8-ounce) can pineapple chunks,
   undrained
4 ounces fresh mushrooms, sliced
1 (2-ounce) jar diced pimento
Salt and pepper to taste
1 (16-ounce) can chop suey mixed
   vegetables, drained
1 tablespoon cornstarch
2 tablespoons cold water
Soy sauce to taste
Hot cooked rice or chow mein
   noodles

Brown pork and onion in wok or large skillet. Combine water and bouillon cube, stirring until bouillon dissolves. Add bouillon, celery, pineapple, mushrooms, pimento, salt and pepper to taste. Simmer for 5 minutes, stirring frequently. Stir in chop suey vegetables. Dissolve cornstarch in cold water. Add to pork mixture. Bring to a boil, stirring constantly. Cook until mixture thickens; stir in soy sauce. Serve immediately over hot cooked rice or chow mein noodles.
Makes 6 to 8 servings.

Vicki Dean
Chattanooga, Tennessee

Sweet And Sour Pork

2⅔ pounds pork shoulder, cut into
    ½-inch cubes
3 tablespoons cooking Sherry
1½ teaspoons MSG
½ teaspoon ground ginger
3 eggs, beaten
¾ cup all-purpose flour
3 tablespoons cornstarch
Vegetable oil
1 (13½-ounce) can pineapple
    chunks
1 cup sugar
1 cup vinegar
2 green peppers, cut into ½-inch
    strips
½ cup sliced gherkins
2 tablespoons cornstarch
¼ cup water
2 tablespoons soy sauce
2 tomatoes, cut into eighths
½ cup slivered crystallized ginger

Combine pork, Sherry, MSG and ginger; let stand for 10 minutes. Drain well. Combine eggs, flour and cornstarch; beat until smooth. Pour over pork, stirring well. Heat oil to 375°F. in deep-fryer. Fry pork in hot oil for 5 minutes or until golden brown; drain on paper towels. Set aside and keep warm. Drain pineapple, reserving juice; set pineapple aside. Add water to reserved pineapple juice to measure 1 cup. Combine pineapple juice mixture, sugar and vinegar in large saucepan. Bring to a boil, stirring constantly. Add green peppers and gherkins. Boil for 2 minutes. Combine cornstarch and water, stirring until smooth. Add cornstarch mixture, soy sauce, tomatoes, reserved pineapple and ginger to juice mixture. Cook over medium heat until thickened and bubbly. Stir in pork. Serve immediately over hot cooked rice.
Makes 6 to 8 servings.

Nancy Adamson
Denton, Texas

Maui Chow-Funn

1 (16-ounce) package chow-funn
½ pound ground pork
2 teaspoons grated fresh ginger
Minced garlic to taste
1 green onion, chopped
2 teaspoons oyster sauce
Salt to taste
Pepper to taste
2 cups bean sprouts

Boil chow-funn until tender; drain. Stir-fry pork, ginger and garlic until browned. Add chow-funn; stir-fry for 3 minutes. Add remaining ingredients; stir-fry an additional 2 minutes.
Makes 4 servings.

Dane Nakamura
Waipahn, Hawaii

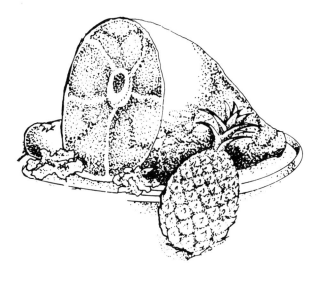

Croissant Sandwiches

1 can Pillsbury crescent rolls
½ stick butter, melted
1 small can mushrooms
½ package Swiss cheese
1 package sliced ham
1 egg, beaten

Place crescent dough on baking sheet and press all perforations to form flat sheet of dough. Brush with melted butter. On ½ of the dough, layer mushrooms, cheese and ham. Fold dough over to form pocket; pinch together edges to seal. Brush with egg and melted butter. Bake in 350°F. oven for 15 minutes or until golden brown. Slice and serve with light salad.
Makes 4 servings.

Carol Ann Riley
Houston, Texas

Ham Loaf

3 to 4 pounds ham loaf mix (ham
  and sausage ground together)
1 egg
½ to 1 cup milk
2 tablespoons teriyaki sauce
Salt, pepper and garlic salt to taste
6 to 8 slices bread, torn into 1-inch
  pieces
1 (16-ounce) can pineapple (rings,
  chunks or crushed)
1 cup brown sugar
2 to 3 tablespoons mustard

Place ham loaf mix in large bowl; add egg, milk, teriyaki sauce, seasonings and bread; mix well using your hands or wooden spoon. Shape into loaf. Place in 13x9x2-inch baking dish. Set aside. Drain pineapple juice into small bowl. Add brown sugar and mustard; blend into a paste. Cover top of loaf with mixture. Arrange pineapple on top. Bake in 350°F. oven for approximately 2 hours.
Makes 10 servings.

Mary Ann Murphy
Zanesville, Ohio

Ham Pie

2 tablespoons butter or margarine
¼ pound fresh mushrooms, sliced
1 small onion, chopped
1 cup milk
4 eggs, beaten
½ teaspoon salt
¼ teaspoon pepper
¾ cup shredded Cheddar cheese
⅓ cup shredded Swiss cheese
1 cup diced cooked ham
1 (9-inch) unbaked pie shell
1 teaspoon parsley flakes

Melt butter in skillet. Add mushrooms and onion. Sauté until tender; drain. Combine sautéed mushrooms and onion, milk, eggs, salt and pepper. Combine cheeses; add to egg mixture, reserving ¼ cup cheese. Add diced ham and pour mixture into pastry shell. Top with ¼ cup cheese. Sprinkle with parsley flakes. Bake at 350°F. for 45 minutes or until set.
Makes 6 servings.

Gail Newsome
Rainbow City, Alabama

Ham Roll-Ups

12 slices Swiss cheese
12 slices ham
1 (16-ounce) package frozen
  broccoli spears, partially
  cooked and drained
1 (10¾-ounce) can cream of
  mushroom soup
1 cup sour cream
Prepared mustard to taste

Place one slice cheese on each ham slice; place 2 broccoli spears in center of each. Roll up tightly and place in 12x8x2-inch baking dish. Combine mushroom soup, sour cream and mustard; spread over rolls. Bake at 375°F. for 30 minutes or until cheese melts.
Makes 4 to 6 servings.

Mark Manders
Ann Arbor, Michigan

Ham Tetrazzini

1 (8-ounce) package spaghetti
3 tablespoons butter or margarine
3 tablespoons all-purpose flour
2 cups milk
2 cups diced lean ham
1 (10¾-ounce) can Cheddar cheese
  soup
½ onion, diced
½ green pepper, diced
1 pimento, diced
1 (2-ounce) can sliced mushrooms,
  drained
Salt and pepper to taste
1 cup (4 ounces) grated Cheddar
  cheese

Prepare spaghetti according to package directions, cooking until not quite done; drain. Melt butter in large saucepan over low heat; add flour, stirring until smooth. Add milk; cook, stirring constantly, until mixture thickens. Remove from heat and stir in ham, soup, onion, green pepper, pimento, mushrooms, salt and pepper. Add spaghetti, mixing well. Spoon mixture into buttered 2-quart casserole; sprinkle with cheese. Bake, covered, at 325°F. for 45 minutes.
Makes 4 servings.

Anne Rowland
Greenville, Texas

Impossible Quiche

1½ cups milk
3 eggs
½ cup buttermilk baking mix
¼ cup butter or margarine, melted
Dash of pepper
Dash of garlic powder
Dash of onion powder
1 cup (4 ounces) shredded Swiss
  cheese
1 cup (4 ounces) shredded Cheddar
  cheese
½ cup chopped cooked ham, chicken
  or mushrooms

Combine milk, eggs, baking mix, butter, pepper, garlic powder and onion powder in blender container; process on High for 15 seconds or until smooth. Pour mixture into greased 9-inch pie plate. Sprinkle with ham and cheese. Bake at 350°F. for 35 to 45 minutes or until a knife inserted in center comes out clean.
Makes 4 to 6 servings.

Anne Rowland
Greenville, Texas

Frittatas

1 medium onion, chopped
½ cup chopped mushrooms
3 tablespoons vegetable oil
7 eggs
⅓ cup milk
2 cloves garlic, minced
2 teaspoons dried oregano or Italian
   seasoning
1 teaspoon parsley flakes
½ teaspoon salt
½ teaspoon pepper
½ cup (2 ounces) shredded
   Mozzarella cheese
¼ cup grated Parmesan cheese
1   (8-ounce) mild Italian sausage,
   cooked and crumbled
1   (10-ounce) package frozen
   chopped spinach, thawed and
   drained
½ cup shredded Mozzarella cheese
¼ cup Parmesan cheese

Sauté onion and mushrooms in oil until tender; set aside. Combine eggs and milk; beat well. Add garlic, oregano, parsley, salt and pepper, beating well. Stir in reserved onion mixture, ½ cup Mozzarella cheese, ¼ cup Parmesan cheese, sausage and spinach. Pour mixture into buttered 9-inch square baking pan; sprinkle with remaining cheeses. Bake at 350°F. for 35 to 40 minutes or until set. Makes 8 servings.

Any type of cheese can be substituted for Mozzarella. One cup cooked diced ham or chicken can be substituted for Italian sausage. Also, either broccoli or zucchini can be substituted for spinach.

Denise Marie Ashford
Ann Arbor, Michigan

Kentucky Country Ham

1 country ham
5-gallon lard can with tight-fitting lid
Cold water
Sunday paper
4 bed blankets or quilts
Aluminum foil

Scrub your newly bought ham in cold water. Place ham in lard can and cover with clean water. Bring to full boil. Continue to boil for 10 minutes per pound. As quickly as possible after boiling, cover and wrap your container with ham inside using all the newspaper and all 4 blankets. Place bundle out of sight for 24 hours. Remove ham from container gently. Wrap in aluminum foil and refrigerate for 1 hour or longer. This will enable you to remove excess fat and bone. Rewrap ham in foil; place in refrigerator until ready for slicing. Cover with aluminum foil and bake at 350°F. for 15 minutes to serve hot.
Tips: Always keep your finished ham covered. They have a tendency to dry quickly when exposed to air.
       Slicing is easy with a cold ham.
       Don't be concerned about overwrapping. It is better to overwrap than not to wrap enough.
A mustard sauce is very good with your country ham, or if you have a craving for real country, use your ham drippings for a "Red-Eye" gravy.

Mary L. Ott
Smyrna, Tennessee

Apple-Sausage Ring

2 pounds bulk sausage
1½ cups cracker crumbs
1 cup finely chopped apple
½ cup milk
¼ cup minced onion
2 eggs, beaten

Combine all ingredients and mix well. Press lightly into greased 6-cup ring mold. Turn out onto shallow pan. Bake at 350°F. for 1 hour. Makes 8 servings.

Lois Govaere
Ann Arbor, Michigan

Sausage-Filled Crêpes

3 eggs, beaten
1 cup milk
1 tablespoon vegetable oil
1 cup all-purpose flour
½ teaspoon salt
1 pound bulk sausage
¼ cup chopped onion
½ cup (2 ounces) shredded American cheese
1 (3-ounce) package cream cheese, softened
½ cup sour cream
½ cup butter or margarine, softened

Combine eggs, milk and oil; beat well. Add flour and salt; beat until smooth. Pour 2 tablespoons batter in greased 6-inch crêpe pan or skillet; tilt pan in all directions to cover pan. Cook for 2 minutes on one side until lightly browned. Remove from skillet and cool on paper towels. Repeat procedure with remaining batter. Brown sausage and onion, stirring to crumble; drain well. Add American cheese and cream cheese, stirring well. Spoon about 2 tablespoons filling in center of each crêpe. Roll tightly and place, seam-side down in 12x8x2-inch baking dish. Bake, covered, at 350°F. for 40 minutes. Combine sour cream and butter; spoon over crêpes spreading evenly. Bake, uncovered, for 5 minutes longer.
Makes 8 servings.

May be prepared a day ahead and baked when ready to serve.

Brian McHale
Marietta, Georgia

Sausage-Stuffing Bake

1½ pounds bulk sausage
1 (8-ounce) package herb-seasoned stuffing mix
1 cup finely chopped cooking apple
½ cup finely chopped celery
¼ cup finely chopped onion
2 tablespoons chopped parsley
2 tablespoons chili sauce
¼ teaspoon dry mustard
¼ teaspoon pepper
Apple slices (optional)

Shape sausage into 12 patties, ¼ inch thick. Prepare stuffing mix according to package directions; add remaining ingredients, mixing well. Arrange 6 patties in 13x9x2-inch dish; spoon stuffing mixture in center of each patty. Top with remaining sausage patties, pinching edges to seal. Bake at 375°F. for 45 minutes. Garnish with apple slices, if desired.
Makes 6 servings.

Regina Goodson
Aurora, Illinois

Country Joe's Ribs

4 to 5 pounds country-style
  pork ribs
1½ cups water
1 cup catsup
¼ cup vinegar
¼ cup vegetable oil
¼ cup firmly packed brown sugar
2 tablespoons onion, finely chopped
2 teaspoons Worcestershire sauce
2 teaspoons Dijon mustard
¼ teaspoon red pepper
½ cup water
1 teaspoon pickling spices

Cook ribs in boiling water to cover for 10 minutes; drain and set aside. Combine 1½ cups water, catsup, vinegar, oil, brown sugar, onion, Worcestershire sauce, mustard and red pepper in large skillet. Bring to a boil. Reduce heat; simmer for 20 to 25 minutes, stirring occasionally. Place ribs on rack in shallow roasting pan. Add remaining water and pickling spices to pan. Bake at 450°F. for 30 minutes; reduce heat to 300°F. and bake 15 minutes longer. Baste frequently with sauce.
Makes 4 servings.

Suzanne Gibson
Hamden, Connecticut

Spareribs With Bourbon Marinade

⅓ cup Bourbon
¼ cup soy sauce
3 tablespoons Dijon mustard
2 tablespoons unsulfured molasses
1 teaspoon Worcestershire sauce
1 large onion, chopped
4 pounds lean spareribs, trimmed of
  fat

Combine Bourbon, soy sauce, Dijon mustard, molasses, Worcestershire sauce and onion in shallow dish. Add spareribs, turning to coat. Refrigerate, covered, for at least 6 hours, overnight if possible. Drain, reserving marinade. Grill for 20 minutes on each side until crisp outside and no longer pink inside. Baste with marinade occasionally.
Makes 4 to 6 servings.

Catherine Rector
Ann Arbor, Michigan

Sausage and Zucchini Casserole

½ pound pork sausage
½ pound Italian sausage
1 cup chopped onion
1 cup chopped green pepper
1 (10¾-ounce) can cream of
  chicken soup, undiluted
½ cup chicken broth
1 teaspoon salt
¼ teaspoon garlic powder
5 cups (1½ pounds) sliced zucchini
3 cups cooked rice
1 cup (4 ounces) shredded Cheddar
  cheese

Brown sausage, onion and green pepper in large skillet, stirring to crumble meat. Drain. Add soup, broth, salt, garlic powder and zucchini, stirring well; cover and simmer for 10 minutes. Stir in rice. Spoon mixture into buttered 2-quart casserole; sprinkle with cheese. Bake at 350°F. for 10 minutes.
Makes 6 servings.

Joyce Edgell
Ypsilanti, Michigan

Spinach Stuffed Manicotti

1 pound ground Italian sausage,
  cooked and drained
  (optional)
½ medium onion, chopped
2 (8-ounce) cans tomato sauce
2 (4-ounce) cans sliced mushrooms,
  drained
1 teaspoon basil leaves
½ teaspoon garlic powder
½ teaspoon dried whole oregano
1 (16-ounce) package manicotti
  (12 to 14 shells)
1 (10-ounce) package frozen
  chopped spinach, thawed
1 (12-ounce) carton ricotta cheese
1¼ cups (5 ounces) shredded
  Mozzarella cheese
½ cup grated Parmesan cheese

Combine sausage, onion, tomato sauce, mushrooms, basil, garlic powder and oregano; stir well. Simmer over low heat for 15 minutes, stirring occasionally. Cook manicotti in boiling water for 8 minutes; drain. Squeeze excess moisture from spinach using paper towels. Combine spinach, ricotta cheese, Mozzarella cheese and ½ cup Parmesan cheese, mixing well. Stuff mixture lightly into manicotti shells. Spoon ⅓ of the sauce mixture into 13x9x2-inch baking dish; arrange stuffed manicotti shells in dish. Spoon remaining sauce over shells. Bake at 375°F. for 45 to 50 minutes. Sprinkle with additional Parmesan cheese and bake for 5 minutes longer.
Makes 6 to 8 servings.

Cheryl A. Riddle
St. Louis Park, Minnesota

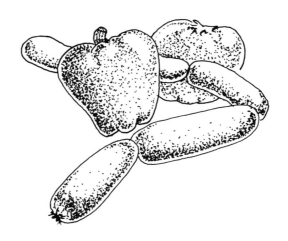

Seafood

Scallops California-Style

2 tablespoons minced onion
1 cup finely chopped, seeded
  fresh tomato
½ cup minced fresh mushrooms
¼ teaspoon thyme
6 tablespoons butter
2 pounds fresh scallops
½ cup flour
2 tablespoons olive oil
½ teaspoon salt
¼ teaspoon white pepper
1½ teaspoons finely chopped garlic
¾ cup dry white wine
1 tablespoon lemon juice
2 tablespoons chopped parsley
1 avocado, cut into ½-inch cubes
Cooked rice for 6 servings

Sauté onion, tomato, mushrooms and thyme in 2 tablespoons butter in skillet for several minutes. Remove from heat and set aside. Cut large scallops into quarters; pat scallops dry. Roll in flour and shake off excess. Sauté scallops in 4 tablespoons butter and olive oil in skillet for about 2 minutes or until light brown on all sides. Season with salt and pepper and garlic; sauté for a few seconds. Add wine, lemon juice and sautéed vegetables; simmer for 2 minutes. Add parsley and avocado just before serving over hot cooked rice. Makes 6 servings.

Tala Arnowitz
Trotwood, Ohio

Grilled Fish With Herbs

1½ to 2 pounds fresh grouper
¼ teaspoon dillweed
¼ teaspoon garlic powder
¼ teaspoon "fine herbs"
Pinch of salt
½ cup butter

Pat fish dry with paper towels. Stir herbs and salt into melted butter. Dip fish pieces into butter. Grill for 5 to 7 minutes on each side. May also be cooked in oven broiler.
Makes 3 to 4 servings.

Laura Ereddia
Marietta, Georgia

Fish Pie

1 medium onion, sliced
1½ to 2 pounds frozen fish
   (sole or halibut)
1 (10¾-ounce) can mushroom
   soup, undiluted
1 (8-ounce) package stove-top
   stuffing
1 cup grated cheese

Arrange onion in bottom of casserole; place frozen fish blocks on top. Spoon soup over fish. Prepare stove-top stuffing according to package directions; spoon over fish. Bake in 350°F. oven for 1 hour. Place cheese on top and presto—fish pie.
Makes 5 to 6 servings.

Dan McIntire
Ann Arbor, Michigan

Fish Sauté

1 cup butter
2 pounds fresh fish fillets
1 teaspoon cayenne pepper
2 medium green peppers, sliced
1 medium onion, sliced
8 ounces fresh mushrooms

Melt butter over low heat in large skillet. Add fish and sprinkle with pepper. Simmer for 20 minutes. Turn fish and add green peppers, onion and mushrooms. Simmer for 20 minutes longer or until vegetables are tender. Serve immediately.
Makes 6 to 8 servings.

Mary E. Gee
Ann Arbor, Michigan

Icelandic Fish Dish (Ysa Dish)

½ cup sour cream
½ cup mayonnaise
½ cup milk
1 medium onion, chopped
1 (4-ounce) can sliced mushrooms,
   drained
1½ cups minute rice
2 to 3 pounds Ysa Fish
   (haddock, etc.)
1 (10-ounce) package frozen
   asparagus
2 cups shrimp, peeled and deveined
½ cup (2 ounces) shredded Cheddar
   cheese (optional)

Mix sour cream, mayonnaise and milk; stir in onion, mushrooms and rice. Cut fish into 2-inch squares; place in 3-quart baking dish. Place frozen asparagus in baking dish. Sprinkle shrimp over fish and asparagus, then pour sour cream mixture over top. Top with Cheddar cheese. Bake in 375°F. oven for 35 to 40 minutes. Serve with rolls or fresh bread.
Makes 6 to 8 servings.

Bobbi Olenski
Long Beach, Mississippi

Flounder With Lemon Broccoli

2 large stalks broccoli
Juice of 1 lemon
Grated lemon rind to taste
1 pound (4) flounder fillets
   (sole or fluke may be used instead)
1 tablespoon vegetable oil
1 tablespoon butter or margarine
2 tablespoons flour
¾ cup skim or low-fat milk
½ cup shredded Cheddar cheese

Cut flowerets of broccoli, leaving about 1-inch stem attached. Separate flowerets. Steam until tender-crisp, about 5 minutes. Cool under cold running water. Sprinkle with lemon juice and rind to taste. Carefully peel skin from fillets. Wrap flounder fillets around broccoli flowerets with stem toward center of fillets. Place flounder, seam-side down, in 8-inch square baking dish. Melt oil and butter in small skillet. Add flour and stir over low heat for 2 or 3 minutes. Add milk and stir over low heat until sauce has thickened. Remove from heat and add cheese, stirring until cheese melts. Pour cheese sauce over flounder. Bake in 350°F. oven for 25 minutes. Serve with lemon wedges.
Makes 4 servings.

Aletha Geisler
Ann Arbor, Michigan

Salmon Loaf

1   (15½-ounce) can salmon
About ½ cup milk
¼ cup chopped onion
¼ cup lemon juice
¼ teaspoon salt
2 cups cracker crumbs
4 eggs, well beaten
¼ cup melted butter

Drain salmon, reserving liquid; add milk to liquid to measure 1 cup. Remove bones from salmon. Mix all ingredients together. Spoon into greased 8x5x3-inch baking dish. Bake in 350°F. oven for 1 hour or until loaf is set in center.
Makes 4 to 6 servings.

Kay Shook
Ypsilanti, Michigan

Fisherman's Curried Cod

2 pounds cod fillets
1 cup sliced celery
½ cup sliced onions
2 tablespoons melted butter
1 teaspoon curry powder
1 teaspoon salt
Dash of pepper
Dash of paprika
¾ cup milk

Place fish in greased 14x9-inch baking dish. Sauté celery and onions in butter for 5 minutes. Add seasonings and milk. Spread celery and onion mixture over fish. Bake at 350°F. for 25 to 30 minutes. Sprinkle with paprika. Garnish with parsley and lemon wedges.
Makes 6 servings.

Susan Swanson
Kent, Washington

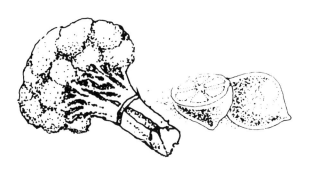

Redfish Court Bouillon

1 (6-pound) redfish, dressed
4 tablespoons butter
4 tablespoons flour
1½ cups chopped onions
2 green onions, chopped
2 tablespoons chopped green pepper
3 cloves garlic, minced
1 (15-ounce) can tomato sauce
3 tablespoons chopped fresh parsley
2 bay leaves
½ teaspoon thyme
2 teaspoons salt
¼ teaspoon pepper
3 to 4 cups hot water
3 cups hot cooked rice

Cut redfish in 2-inch cross sections; set aside. Melt butter in large saucepan over medium heat. Add flour, stirring constantly, until dark brown color is reached. Add onions, green pepper and garlic. Continue cooking, stirring often, until vegetables are soft. Add tomato sauce and cook for 15 minutes. Add parsley, bay leaves, thyme, salt and pepper. Gradually stir in hot water. Cover and cook over low heat for 30 minutes. Place redfish in baking pan and cover with gravy. Bake at 350°F. for 30 to 45 minutes. Serve with rice.
Makes 6 servings.

Mary Beth Soignet
Marietta, Georgia

Sole En Papillote

24 small mushroom caps
12 small sole fillets
¼ cup butter, softened
½ cup (about 8) chopped shallots
1 teaspoon salt
1 teaspoon white pepper
12 slices carrot
1 (6½-ounce) split dry champagne
1 cup skimmed, canned chicken broth
½ cup butter
½ cup flour
¼ cup heavy cream
2 tablespoons lemon juice
2 tablespoons chopped fresh parsley
1 egg white, slightly beaten
Lemon wedges

Set 12 mushroom caps aside. Slice remaining caps; arrange a few slices on center of each fish fillet. Fold ends of fillets over mushrooms. Spread ¼ cup butter in baking pan; sprinkle with shallots, salt and pepper. Place fillets in prepared pan, folded-side down. Place 12 remaining mushroom caps and carrot in pan. Pour in champagne and chicken broth; cover with foil. Bake in 350°F. oven for 20 minutes. Combine ½ cup butter with flour; set aside. Cut oval about 20 inches long and 14 inches wide from 1 large piece butcher's paper or parchment. From second piece paper, cut another oval 1 inch larger all around. Use larger oval for top. Generously butter bottom sheet of paper to within 1 inch of edge and place on ovenproof platter or cookie sheet. Gently lift fillets, mushroom caps and carrot slices from baking pan with slotted spoon; drain. Cover with foil to keep warm. Drain broth from baking pan into saucepan; place over medium heat. Add reserved flour mixture, stirring with whisk until blended. Cook until thickened. (The nice thing about making a sauce by this method is that it is easy to control, just add more or less beurre manié as needed.) Stir in cream, then add lemon juice. Arrange drained fillets on buttered bottom piece of paper. Garnish each with 1 mushroom cap, cutting across top to hold carrot slice. Spoon about 1 cup sauce over fillets; sprinkle with parsley. Set remaining sauce aside to keep warm. Brush edges of both pieces of paper with egg white diluted with a small amount of water. Place second piece of paper on top; fold bottom edge over top edge, rolling together and crimping to get a tight seal. Brush edges and top sheet with egg white. Bake for 10 minutes or until paper gets crisp, puffs up and begins to brown. Serve with lemon wedges and with remaining sauce separately. Serve with boiled potatoes dusted with parsley and steamed broccoli.
Makes 6 servings.

Merle Butterick
Jamesville, Wisconsin

Stuffed Flounder

¼ cup chopped onion
¼ cup butter or margarine
1   (7-ounce) can crab meat,
    drained and flaked
1   (4-ounce) can chopped
    mushrooms, drained
½ cup cracker crumbs
2 tablespoons chopped fresh parsley
½ teaspoon salt
Dash of pepper
2 pounds flounder fillets, fresh or
    frozen
3 tablespoons butter or margarine
3 tablespoons all-purpose flour
¼ teaspoon salt
1½ cups milk
⅓ cup dry white wine
1 cup (4 ounces) shredded Swiss
    cheese
½ teaspoon paprika

Sauté onion in ¼ cup butter until tender. Remove from heat. Stir in crab meat, mushrooms, cracker crumbs, parsley, ½ teaspoon salt and pepper. Spoon mixture over fillets; roll each fillet jelly roll-fashion, beginning at narrow end. Secure with wooden picks. Place rolls, seam-side down, in buttered 13x9x2-inch baking dish. Melt 3 tablespoons butter in small saucepan; stir in flour and ¼ teaspoon salt, stirring until smooth. Add milk and wine; cook, stirring constantly, until mixture thickens. Spoon sauce over fillets. Bake in 400°F. oven for 25 minutes or until fish flakes easily when tested with a fork. Sprinkle with cheese and paprika. Bake for 3 minutes longer or until cheese melts.
Makes 8 servings.

Joan Hocker Miller
Inman, South Carolina

Stuffed Flounder With Cheese Sauce

¼ cup chopped onion
¼ cup butter or margarine
8 ounces fresh mushrooms
2 tablespoons lemon juice
1   (7½-ounce) can crab meat, flaked
½ cup cracker crumbs
2 tablespoons chopped fresh parsley
Pepper to taste
2 pounds flounder fillets
3 tablespoons butter
3 tablespoons all-purpose flour
¼ teaspoon salt
1¼ cups milk
¼ cup whipping cream
⅓ cup dry white wine
6 to 8 ounces Swiss cheese,
    shredded
Parmesan cheese
Paprika

Sauté onion in ¼ cup butter until tender. Cook mushrooms in lemon juice for 5 to 10 minutes; drain, reserving liquid. Combine onion mixture, mushrooms, crab meat, cracker crumbs, parsley and pepper; stir well. Spoon mixture over fillets; roll each fillet jelly roll-fashion, beginning at narrow end. Secure with wooden picks. Place rolls, seam-side down, in buttered 13x9x2-inch baking dish. Melt 3 tablespoons butter in small saucepan; stir in flour and salt, stirring until smooth. Add milk, cream, wine and reserved liquid; cook, stirring constantly, until mixture thickens. Spoon sauce over fillets. Bake at 400°F. for 25 minutes or until fish flakes easily when tested with fork. Sprinkle with cheeses and paprika. Bake for 3 minutes longer or until cheese melts.
Makes 8 servings.

Michael Lombardi
Long Island City, New York

Biscuit-Capped Tuna

½ cup butter or margarine
½ cup chopped celery
1 cup (4 ounces) shredded American
  cheese
1 (6½-ounce) can tuna, drained
1 tablespoon Worcestershire sauce
1½ cups Jiffy Baking Mix
½ cup milk
1 tablespoon instant minced onion

Melt butter in saucepan; add celery and cook until tender. Add cheese and stir until melted. Stir in tuna, breaking up large pieces. Add Worcestershire sauce and stir until blended. Pour tuna mixture into 2-quart casserole and set aside. Stir baking mix, milk and onion with fork to soft dough. Drop by spoonfuls onto tuna mixture. Bake in 425°F. oven for 15 minutes or until lightly browned. Makes 5 or 6 servings.

Howard S. Holmes
Ann Arbor, Michigan

Deluxe Tuna Casserole

1 (14-ounce) package Kraft
  Macaroni and Cheese dinner
1 cup chopped onions
½ cup chopped green pepper
2 tablespoons margarine
2 (10¾-ounce) cans cream of
  celery soup
2 (6½-ounce) cans tuna, drained
  and flaked
½ cup chopped pimento
2 (3-ounce) cans mushrooms,
  drained

Prepare macaroni and cheese dinner according to package directions using ½ of the milk. Sauté onions and green pepper in margarine until tender. Add to macaroni. Add remaining ingredients; mix well. Pour into 3-quart casserole. Bake in 350°F. oven for 35 to 40 minutes. Makes 6 servings.

Brenda K. Smith
Miamisburg, Ohio

Tuna Casserole

1 (8-ounce) package elbow
  macaroni
1 (9¼-ounce) can tuna, drained
12 ounces Colby cheese, cubed
1 (3-ounce) can mushrooms,
  drained
1 (10¾-ounce) can cream of
  mushroom soup
½ cup milk
1 (16-ounce) can French-fried
  onion rings

Prepare macaroni according to package directions; drain. In 6-quart casserole, combine tuna, cheese, mushrooms and macaroni. Combine soup and milk and add to casserole; mix well. Top casserole with ½ can French-fried onions. Bake in 350°F. oven for 45 minutes until top is crisp and brown. Stir casserole and add remaining onions to top. Return to oven; bake for 45 minutes longer. Serve immediately. Makes 6 to 8 servings.

Thomas Monaghan
Ann Arbor, Michigan

Captain Paul's Linguine And Clam Sauce

1 cup olive oil
2 tablepoons butter or margarine
2 tablespoons chopped fresh parsley
2½ cloves garlic, minced
1 teaspoon white pepper
1 teaspoon oregano
4 (6½-ounce) cans chopped clams
   or 1½ pounds fresh clams,
   chopped
1 (8-ounce) bottle clam juice
1 cup white wine
½ cup water
2 teaspoons flour
7½ cups water
1 tablespoon salt
1 (1-pound) package linguine
1 tablespoon butter
2 tablespoons olive oil

Heat olive oil and butter in medium saucepan on medium-high heat. Sauté parsley, garlic, white pepper and oregano until garlic is transparent. Add juice of 4 cans chopped clams and ½ bottle of clam juice. Set clams aside in container. Add wine to sauce and simmer, do not boil, for 30 minutes. Add clams in last 5 minutes. Combine ½ cup cold water and flour, stirring until paste is formed; add to simmering sauce to thicken. Bring 7½ cups water and 1 tablespoon salt to a boil in large stockpot. Add linguine; cook to al dente (firm not soft). Drain in colander and return linguine to stockpot. Add 1 tablespoon butter, 2 tablespoons olive oil and remaining clam juice. Heat over medium-high heat for 1 minute. Add half the sauce mixture and heat for 1 minute. Place on platter. Add sauce and clams from bottom of stockpot, placing in middle of linguine. Garnish with fresh parsley.
Makes 6 servings.

Everyone I've cooked this for likes it except my first mate, Ken. Perhaps because the last time I cooked it on board, we got caught in 12-foot seas 80 miles offshore!

Captain Paul DeGaeta
Harbour Lights, Florida

Chesapeake Bay Crab Cakes

1 cup cracker meal
1 tablespoon celery seed
½ teaspoon salt
½ teaspoon white pepper
Pinch of baking powder
¼ cup mayonnaise
1 sweet red pepper, chopped
1 large green pepper, chopped
¼ cup finely chopped pimento
2 eggs, beaten
1 teaspoon Tabasco sauce
1 pound lump crab meat
Vegetable oil
Sesame seed buns
Tartar sauce

Mix cracker meal, celery seed, salt, pepper and baking powder in large bowl. Mix mayonnaise, peppers, pimento and eggs together. Blend into dry ingredients. Gently but thoroughly fold in crab meat. Make into 6 good-sized patties. (Patties are to hold together on their own. If too loose, add more cracker meal. If too dry, add more mayonnaise.) Place approximately 1-inch cooking oil in frying pan. Heat oil to 350°F. Cook patties for 7 minutes on each side or until golden brown. Remove and drain patties on paper towel. Serve on sesame seed buns with tartar sauce.
Makes 6 servings.

Betty L. Isemann
Beavercreek, Ohio

Crab Soufflés

1½ teaspoons butter
1½ teaspoons all-purpose flour
¾ cup plus 2 tablespoons whipping
  cream
2 eggs, separated
3½ ounces North Sea crabs
Salt and white pepper to taste

Melt butter in saucepan and stir in flour. Add cream; cook, stirring constantly, for 5 minutes. Remove from heat. Stir in egg yolks. Fold in crabs, salt and pepper; let cool. Beat egg whites until very stiff. Fold gently into crab mixture. Spoon batter into greased muffin pans, filling ¾ full. Bake in 325°F. oven for 15 minutes or until puffed and golden. Serve immediately.
Makes 6 servings.

Birgitta Schopen
Federal Republic Germany

Easy Deviled Crab

3 tablespoons butter
2 tablespoons flour
1 cup milk, heated
1 teaspoon salt
1 teaspoon Worcestershire sauce
Dash of cayenne pepper
2 egg yolks, slightly beaten
1 pound lump crab meat
½ teaspoon lemon juice
¼ cup dry white wine
⅔ cup buttered bread crumbs
4 lemon slices
Paprika

Melt butter; stir in flour and milk. Season with salt, Worcestershire sauce and cayenne; cook, stirring constantly, until thick. Add egg yolks and crab meat, stirring constantly. Cook for 3 minutes and stir in lemon juice and wine. Spoon mixture into 4 individual baking shells or ramekins and cover with buttered crumbs. Top each with lemon slice and sprinkle with paprika. Bake in 450°F. oven for about 20 to 25 minutes or until brown.
Makes 4 servings.

Sherri Seiber
Arlington Heights, Illinois

Lobster Seviche

½ cup lime or lemon juice
2 tomatoes, cut into wedges
1 medium onion, sliced
1 green pepper, cut into ½-inch
  pieces
2 tablespoons chopped fresh parsley
1 clove garlic, minced
Salt and pepper to taste
1 pound cubed raw lobster (shrimp
  or fish may be used)

Combine all ingredients except lobster in glass casserole; stir well. Add lobster; stir well. Cover and refrigerate for 1½ to 3 hours or until lobster turns white, stirring every 20 minutes.
Makes 4 servings.

Dave Vincent
Key West, Florida

Scalloped Scallops

2 cups scallops
4 tablespoons butter
4 tablespoons flour
⅛ teaspoon salt
2 cups milk
1   (10¾-ounce) can mushroom
   soup
1 cup bread crumbs
Worcestershire sauce to taste
Ritz crackers
Melted butter

Cover scallops with hot water. Bring to a boil. Allow to cool. Cut scallops into small pieces. Melt butter; add flour, salt and milk, stirring constantly. Add mushroom soup and scallops to white sauce. Add bread crumbs and Worcestershire sauce to taste. Place in casserole. Top with crushed Ritz crackers and drizzle with melted butter. Bake in 350°F. oven for approximately 30 minutes or until topping is brown and casserole is bubbly.
Makes 4 servings.

Monica Reed
Londonderry, New Hampshire

Seafood Alfredo

2 egg yolks
½ cup half and half
¼ cup grated Parmesan cheese
¼ pound fettucini
½ teaspoon minced shallots
¼ teaspoon minced garlic
2 tablespoons butter
½ pound small shrimp, peeled
   and deveined
Salt and pepper
1 teaspoon minced parsley

In bowl, beat egg yolks, half and half and Parmesan cheese; set aside. Prepare fettucini according to package directions, slightly undercooking. In skillet, sauté shallots and garlic in butter; add shrimp. Cook until shrimp turns red. Stir in fettucini; add egg and cheese mixture. Cook for 2 minutes; season with salt and pepper. Add parsley. Serve immediately.
Makes 2 servings.

Sharon Richwine
Bayville, New York

Boiled "Spicy" Shrimp

8 pounds medium shrimp, rinsed
6 medium potatoes, peeled and cut
   into chunks
2 ears corn, cleaned and cut into
   3 pieces each
1 large onion, sliced
3 tablespoons crab boil
3 tablespoons lemon juice
3 bay leaves
2 tablespoons Tony Chachere's
   Creole Seasoning
1 teaspoon salt
1 teaspoon red pepper
1 gallon water

Combine all ingredients in 6-quart stockpot; stir well. Bring to a boil over medium-high heat; boil for 20 minutes. Remove from heat; cover. Let stand for 10 minutes. Drain and serve immediately.
Makes 4 to 6 servings.

Michael J. Villarreal
Belleville, Illinois

California Shrimp Sauté

1 large fresh tomato, diced
1 small yellow onion, chopped
½ large green pepper, chopped
2 tablespoons butter
15 to 20 medium shrimp, cleaned
    and butterflied
¼ cup white wine
½ teaspoon black pepper
½ pint half and half
¼ teaspoon tarragon
¼ teaspoon basil
½ teaspoon parsley, chopped
2 cups cooked white rice

Sauté tomato, onion and green pepper in butter in large skillet. Add remaining ingredients except rice and cook until shrimp are pink and tender. Do Not Overcook. Arrange shrimp and vegetables on bed of rice and serve immediately.
Makes 3 to 4 servings.

Anita J. Mitchell
Livermore, California

Shrimp Casserole

1 (10¾-ounce) can cream of
    mushroom soup
½ cup uncooked rice
3 tablespoons butter
2 tablespoons chopped onion
2 tablespoons lemon juice
Salt and pepper to taste
1 pound fresh cooked shrimp
1 tablespoon chopped parsley
Green pepper rings
Pimento
1 cup grated Swiss cheese

Combine soup and rice in saucepan. Add butter, onion, lemon juice, salt and pepper. Cook over low heat, stirring constantly, until bubbly. Add shrimp and parsley. Pour into greased 12x8x2-inch casserole. Garnish with green pepper rings and pimento. Top with Swiss cheese. Bake in 350°F. oven for 40 minutes.
Makes 4 servings.

Janet M. Bradley
Lilburn, Georgia

Shrimp-Cheese-Bread Soufflé

6 slices white bread, torn into
    1-inch pieces
½ pound sharp Cheddar cheese,
    shredded
1 pound shrimp, shelled and deveined
¼ cup butter, melted
3 eggs, beaten
2 cups milk
½ teaspoon dry mustard
Salt to taste

Layer bread, cheese and shrimp in greased 1½-quart casserole. Pour melted butter over shrimp. Combine eggs, milk, dry mustard and salt; mix well. Pour over shrimp. Cover and refrigerate for 3 hours. Bake, covered, in 350°F. oven for 1 hour until set.
Makes 4 to 5 servings.

Jennifer N. Chaparro
Ann Arbor, Michigan

Shrimp de Jonghe

½ cup softened butter
1 teaspoon salt
1 clove garlic, minced
2 tablespoons finely chopped parsley
⅔ cup fine, dry bread crumbs
⅓ cup Sherry
⅛ teaspoon cayenne pepper
2 pounds cooked shrimp, peeled and
    deveined

Combine butter, salt, garlic, parsley, bread crumbs, Sherry and pepper. Arrange shrimp in 3 to 4-quart shallow casserole and top with bread crumb mixture, covering shrimp. Bake in 375°F. oven for 20 to 25 minutes or until topping has melted and is lightly browned. Makes 4 to 6 servings.

Lisa G. Harvey
Hammond, Indiana

Shrimp Etouffée

2 pounds shrimp
2½ to 3 cups water
¼ cup butter or margarine
3 tablespoons all-purpose flour
1 cup chopped onions
½ cup chopped celery
½ cup chopped green pepper
4 cloves garlic, minced
¼ cup chopped green onion tops
¼ cup chopped fresh parsley
¼ teaspoon Worcestershire sauce
Salt, pepper and red pepper to taste

Peel and devein shrimp, reserving shells; set shrimp aside. Combine water and reserved shells; bring to a boil. Reduce heat and simmer for 20 minutes. Strain, reserving 2 cups stock, discarding shells. Melt butter in large heavy saucepan; add flour, stirring until smooth. Cook over medium heat, stirring constantly, for 10 minutes or until mixture reaches a rich brown color. Add onions, celery, green pepper and garlic; cook, stirring constantly, until tender. Add reserved stock, shrimp, green onion tops, parsley and seasonings, stirring well. Simmer for 15 minutes or until shrimp is pink. Serve over hot cooked rice.
Makes 6 servings.

Louise Kaline
Bloomfield Hills, Michigan

Shrimp Marguerite

1 large onion, chopped
1 large green pepper, chopped
½ cup butter or margarine
1½ (16-ounce) cans Rotel Tomatoes
    with Chili Pepper, undrained and
    chopped
1½ (10¾-ounce) cans cream of
    mushroom soup
1 to 2 pounds small or medium
    shrimp, peeled and deveined
2 cups hot cooked rice

Sauté onion and green pepper in butter. Add tomatoes, stirring well. Simmer for 5 to 7 minutes. Stir in soup; cover. Simmer for 5 to 7 minutes. Stir in shrimp. Simmer for 3 to 4 minutes. Serve with hot cooked rice.
Makes 4 to 6 servings.

Connie Collins
New Orleans, Louisiana

Shrimp-Stuffed Eggplant

4 medium eggplant
1 medium onion, chopped
½ green pepper, chopped
2 stalks celery, chopped
¼ cup vegetable oil
8 ounces smoked sausage, coarsely
    chopped
4 ounces smoked ham, chopped
1 pound small shrimp, peeled and
    deveined
1 tablespoon butter or margarine
Salt and pepper to taste
½ cup seasoned dry bread crumbs
1 cup (4 ounces) shredded Cheddar
    cheese

Split 3 eggplant in half lengthwise; scoop out pulp, leaving ¼-inch shell. Dice pulp. Peel and dice remaining eggplant. Combine diced eggplant with salty water to cover; let stand for 15 minutes. Drain and pat dry. Cook eggplant shells in boiling water to cover for 6 minutes. Drain and arrange in greased 13x9x2-inch baking dish. Sauté onion, green pepper and celery in oil until tender. Add sausage, ham and reserved chopped eggplant; cook over low heat for 30 minutes or until eggplant is tender, stirring occasionally. Remove from heat. Sauté shrimp in butter until shrimp turns pink; sprinkle with salt and pepper. Add to eggplant mixture; stir in bread crumbs. Spoon mixture into eggplant shells; sprinkle with cheese. Bake in 350°F. oven for 5 minutes or until cheese melts.
Makes 6 servings.

Karen Sootin
Long Beach, Mississippi

Sweet-Sour Shrimp (Low-Cal)

1 (15½-ounce) can pineapple
    chunks, drained reserving
    liquid
1¼ teaspoons Pillsbury Sweet 10 or
    ¼ cup Pillsbury Sprinkle Sweet
⅓ cup water
¼ cup vinegar
2 cubes or 2 teaspoons chicken
    bouillon
1 teaspoon paprika
½ teaspoon prepared mustard
Dash of pepper
1 (12-ounce) package uncooked or
    cooked shrimp
1 green pepper, cut in 1-inch pieces
1 stalk celery, sliced diagonally
1 medium onion, sliced
2 tablespoons cornstarch
2 to 3 tablespoons soy sauce

Add water to reserved pineapple liquid to measure 1 cup. In large saucepan, combine pineapple, reserved liquid mixture, sweetener, water, vinegar, bouillon, paprika, mustard and pepper. Cook over low heat to dissolve bouillon cubes. Add shrimp, green pepper, celery and onion. Simmer for 10 minutes or until vegetables are tender-crisp. Combine cornstarch and soy sauce. Stir into shrimp mixture. Heat mixture until it boils and thickens, stirring constantly. Serve over rice if desired.
Makes 6 servings.

Sue Dawson
Ann Arbor, Michigan

Vegetables and Side Dishes

Vegetables and Side Dishes

Artichokes

4 artichokes
Lemon wedge
1 clove garlic, quartered
4 teaspoons grated Parmesan cheese
½ teaspoon salt
½ teaspoon pepper
½ teaspoon chopped fresh parsley
4 teaspoons vegetable oil

Wash artichokes by plunging up and down in cold water. Cut off stem end and trim about ½ inch from top of each artichoke. Remove any loose bottom leaves. With scissors, trim away about ¼ of each outer leaf. Rub top and edges of leaves with lemon wedge to prevent discoloration. Spread leaves apart. Stand artichokes upright in small Dutch oven with about 1 inch water. Place garlic in center of each artichoke; sprinkle each with 1 teaspoon Parmesan cheese, salt, pepper and parsley. Drizzle 1 teaspoon oil over each artichoke. Cover and bring to a boil; reduce heat. Simmer for 45 minutes or until leaves pull out easily.

Angela Virgilio
Westbury, New York

Asparagus With Mustard Sauce

1½ pounds asparagus, cleaned and
    cut into pieces
¼ cup water
⅓ cup mayonnaise
1 tablespoon chopped fresh parsley
1 teaspoon prepared mustard
½ teaspoon onion salt
⅛ teaspoon white pepper

Combine asparagus and water in microwave-safe 2-quart casserole. Cover with plastic wrap. Microwave at HIGH (100% power) for 6 to 7 minutes or until tender, stirring once during cooking. Combine remaining ingredients; stir well. Spoon over asparagus; cover. Microwave at HIGH (100% power) for 1 to 2 minutes or until thoroughly heated.
Makes 6 servings.

Broccoli may be substituted for asparagus.

Mary Beth Soignet
Marietta, Georgia

Calico Baked Beans

1 (16-ounce) can butter beans,
    drained
1 (16-ounce) can red kidney beans,
    drained
1 (16-ounce) can pork and beans
½ cup chopped onion
½ cup chopped green pepper
2 tablespoons butter
1½ cups shredded American cheese
½ teaspoon salt
2 large tomatoes, sliced
Cheese slices

Combine butter beans, kidney beans and pork and beans. Place in 1½-quart casserole. Sauté onion and green pepper in butter. Add sautéed vegetables, shredded cheese and salt to beans; stir thoroughly. Bake at 350°F. for 30 minutes. Remove from oven. Top with tomato and cheese slices. Return to oven for 10 minutes.
Makes 6 servings.

Stephen M. Ley
Zionsville, Indiana

◀Recipes for this photograph on pages 133 and 139.

Frijoles Refritos (Refried Beans)

1 pound pinto beans
Water
2 onions, chopped
2 to 4 teaspoons chili powder,
   according to taste
4 cloves garlic, finely chopped
2 teaspoons salt
1 teaspoon pepper
1 teaspoon dried oregano
½ teaspoon cumin seed
1   (6-ounce) can tomato paste
   (optional)
½ cup hot bacon drippings,
   margarine or lard

Soak beans in 5½ cups water in saucepan overnight. Drain. Add water to cover. Add remaining ingredients except bacon drippings. Cook, covered, over low heat for 3 hours or until tender. Mash beans wildly with potato masher. Add hot bacon drippings; mix well. Cook until thickened, stirring frequently. Serve immediately or refrigerate for later use. Use as filling in tortillas or as side dish.
Makes 6 servings.

Don Segrist
Ann Arbor, Michigan

Mother's Home-Baked Beans

2 cups (1 pound) navy beans
2 cups hot bean liquid
1 medium onion, sliced
¼ pound bacon, unsliced
½ cup dark molasses
½ cup chili sauce
1 teaspoon vinegar
2 teaspoons salt
½ teaspoon dry or prepared
   mustard

Cook beans according to package directions for 1 hour. Combine beans and remaining ingredients and place in baking dish. Bake at 300°F. oven for 6 hours. If additional water is needed during baking, add bean liquid or hot water.
Makes 8 servings.

Norma Lee Clise
Romney, West Virginia

Bean Casserole

1   (22-ounce) can pork and beans
1   (15-ounce) can wax beans,
   drained
1   (15-ounce) can butter beans,
   drained
1   (15-ounce) can green beans,
   drained
1   (16-ounce) can hot chili beans
   in sauce
1   (15-ounce) can tomato paste
1   (10¾-ounce) can tomato soup
2 medium onions, chopped
1 cup firmly packed brown sugar
2 tablespoons mustard
1 pound Bob Evans Hot Pork
   Sausage, cooked and drained

Combine all ingredients in bowl and mix thoroughly. Place in 4-quart casserole. Bake at 325°F. for 90 minutes. For the best flavor, refrigerate overnight before baking.
Makes 16 servings.

Great for potluck dinners.

Ann Krueger
Canton, Michigan

Green Beans and New Potatoes

2 to 3 pounds fresh green beans
½ pound ham, cut into bite-sized
  pieces
10 new potatoes
½ large onion, chopped
1 tablespoon sugar
1½ teaspoons salt
¾ teaspoon pepper
2 beef bouillon cubes
Water
2 tablespoons butter or margarine

Clean and break beans into 1-inch pieces, removing ends. Place green beans, ham pieces, potatoes, onion, sugar, salt, pepper, bouillon cubes and water to cover in large saucepan. Cook over low heat for 45 minutes. Place in serving bowl and dot with butter.
Makes 10 to 15 servings.

Ann M. Holliday
Gulfport, Mississippi

Sweet and Sour Green Beans

1 (16-ounce) can French-cut
   green beans
1 small onion, chopped
4 slices bacon
2 tablespoons butter
½ cup water
½ cup vinegar
½ cup firmly packed brown sugar

Combine all ingredients in saucepan and simmer for 90 minutes. Makes 2 servings.

Great vegetable accompaniment for game hens.

John Ricketts
Charlotte, North Carolina

Broccoli Casserole

1 pound broccoli, chopped
1 (10¾-ounce) can cream of
   mushroom soup
2 eggs, beaten
1 cup shredded sharp Cheddar
  cheese
¾ cup mayonnaise
1 small onion, chopped
Salt and pepper to taste
20 Cheddar cheese Ritz crackers,
   crushed
½ cup melted butter

Steam broccoli for 10 minutes or until tender; drain. Combine broccoli, soup, eggs, cheese, mayonnaise, onion, salt and pepper. Pour into lightly greased 2-quart casserole. Toss cracker crumbs with melted butter. Sprinkle over top of casserole. Bake in 350°F. oven for 45 minutes.
Makes 8 servings.

Cyndie Roberson
Boulder, Colorado

Broccoli-Cheese Casserole

2 (10-ounce) packages frozen
  broccoli spears
1 (10¾-ounce) can cream of
   mushroom soup
1 (10-ounce) stick Kraft Cheddar
   cheese, shredded
1 cup cracker crumbs
3 hard-cooked eggs, sliced

Boil broccoli spears according to package directions. Arrange cooked spears in casserole. Spoon soup over spears. Sprinkle shredded cheese over soup and spears. Top with cracker crumbs and sliced hard-cooked eggs. Bake at 375°F. for 20 to 25 minutes.

Ron Hingst
Ann Arbor, Michigan

Broccoli Soufflé

¼ cup chopped onion
6 tablespoons margarine
2 tablespoons all-purpose flour
½ cup water
8 ounces Velveeta cheese, grated
2 (10-ounce) packages frozen broccoli, slightly cooked and drained
3 eggs, well beaten
Buttered bread crumbs

Sauté onion in margarine. Add flour, stirring until smooth. Stir in water. Cook, stirring constantly, until mixture thickens. Remove from heat. Stir in cheese, stirring until cheese melts. Add broccoli and eggs. Spoon mixture into greased 12x6x2-inch baking pan. Sprinkle with bread crumbs. Bake at 325°F. for 30 minutes.
Makes 6 servings.

You can also use a 20-ounce package of broccoli and cauliflower. It's great either way.

Debra Bores
Mankato, Minnesota

Red Cabbage

⅓ cup water
⅓ cup vinegar
¼ cup butter or margarine
1 tablespoon sugar
1 teaspoon salt
1 (2 to 3-pound) head red cabbage, thinly sliced
¼ cup red currant jelly
2 tablespoons grated apple

Combine water, vinegar, butter, sugar and salt in small Dutch oven. Bring to a boil. Add cabbage; stir well. Bring to a boil; reduce heat. Simmer, covered, for 2 hours, adding water as necessary. Stir in jelly and apple; simmer for 10 minutes longer.
Makes 6 servings.

Esther Swanson
Kent, Washington

Carrots Olé

½ cup water
1 teaspoon salt
6 medium carrots, shredded
2 tablespoons chopped chives or green onion
6 slices bacon, fried, drained and crumbled or 2 tablespoons imitation bacon bits

Combine water, salt and carrots in medium saucepan. Simmer, covered, for 10 to 12 minutes or until tender. Drain. Stir in chives and bacon.
Makes 4 servings.

Sue Dawson
Ann Arbor, Michigan

Glazed Carrots

4 cups cooked carrots
1 tablespoon butter or margarine
1 tablespoon firmly packed brown sugar
1 teaspoon grated orange rind
Dash of coarsely ground pepper

Combine all ingredients in medium skillet. Cook over medium heat, stirring constantly, until sugar melts and carrots are glazed.
Makes 6 to 8 servings.

Erica Noreen Ryan
Ann Arbor, Michigan

Sweet And Tangy Carrots

5 cups cooked sliced carrots
½ cup chopped green pepper
⅓ cup chopped onion
⅔ cup sugar
1   (10¾-ounce) can tomato soup
½ cup apple cider vinegar
⅓ cup oil
1 teaspoon prepared mustard
1 teaspoon Worcestershire sauce

Combine carrots, green pepper and onion in large bowl. Combine remaining ingredients in medium saucepan. Bring to a boil over medium heat, stirring occasionally. Pour over vegetables. Chill thoroughly. Serve cold.
Makes 12 servings.

Susan Webb
Long Beach, Mississippi

Gulliver's Creamed Corn

2   (16-ounce) cans yellow corn,
    drained
1 cup whipping cream
1 teaspoon sugar
½ teaspoon salt
½ teaspoon MSG, optional
2 teaspoons butter or margarine
2 teaspoons flour
Grated Parmesan cheese
Additional butter

Combine corn and cream in large saucepan. Bring to a boil; reduce heat and simmer for 5 minutes. Stir in sugar, salt and MSG. Melt 2 teaspoons butter in small saucepan and stir in flour. Stir into corn and cook until slightly thickened. Spoon corn into 1-quart casserole. Sprinkle with Parmesan cheese and dot with additional butter. Brown under broiling unit.
Makes 8 to 10 servings.

Gail Swisher
Los Angeles, California

Liz's Corn Pudding

1   (16-ounce) can corn, drained
1   (16-ounce) can cream style corn
2 eggs, beaten
1   (8½-ounce) package corn muffin
    mix
½ cup melted margarine
1 cup sour cream
2 cups (8 ounces) shredded Cheddar
    cheese

Mix all ingredients except cheese. Pour into greased 13x9x2-inch baking dish. Bake at 350°F. for 15 minutes. Sprinkle with cheese and bake for 20 minutes longer.
Makes 6 servings.

Maryanne Josefczyk
Dexter, Michigan

Pickled Cucumber With Long Rice

2   (16-ounce) packages long rice
    (glass noodles)
1 cucumber, thinly sliced
1 cup sugar
1 cup vinegar
½ teaspoon grated ginger
Pinch of salt
1 drop of hot sauce

Boil noodles for about 5 minutes or until tender. Drain and rinse with cold water. Combine noodles and cucumbers in large bowl. Mix remaining ingredients and pour over noodles and cucumber, mixing lightly. Let stand in refrigerator for 2 hours.
Makes 4 servings.

Richard Silva
Honolulu, Hawaii

Eggplant À La Italiano

1 medium eggplant, cut into ⅛-inch
  slices
Salt
2 eggs, beaten
1 cup all-purpose flour
Vegetable oil
1 (15-ounce) can tomato sauce or
  spaghetti sauce
¼ cup grated Romano cheese
8 ounces sliced cooked ham
8 ounces sliced Mozzarella cheese
½ cup (2 ounces) shredded
  Mozzarella cheese (optional)

Sprinkle eggplant with salt; let stand for 2 hours. Drain and pat dry. Dip eggplant in egg; dredge in flour. Fry in vegetable oil for 2 minutes on each side or until lightly browned. Drain on paper towels. Spoon about half the tomato sauce into 13x9x2-inch baking dish; sprinkle with 2 tablespoons Romano cheese. Set aside. Cut ham and sliced Mozzarella cheese into 2x1-inch pieces. Place 1 piece ham and cheese in center of each slice of eggplant; roll tightly. Place rolls, seam-side down, in prepared baking dish. Spoon remaining sauce over rolls; sprinkle with remaining Romano cheese and shredded Mozzarella cheese. Bake, covered, at 350°F. for 30 minutes. Serve hot. Makes 6 top 8 servings.

Pat Houseman
Murfreesboro, Tennessee

Mushrooms With Basil Cream

3 tablespoons butter
1 pound large mushrooms, trimmed
  and cut into ¼-inch slices
½ cup heavy cream
¼ cup dry white wine (optional)
3 teaspoons crumbled fresh basil or
  1 teaspoon dried basil
½ teaspoon salt
Freshly ground black pepper

Melt butter in medium skillet over moderately high heat. Add mushrooms and cook, stirring occasionally, about 5 minutes. Remove mushrooms with slotted spoon and set aside. Add cream, wine, basil, salt and pepper to skillet. Simmer over low heat, stirring constantly for 5 minutes or until mixture has thickened slightly. Add mushrooms to cream sauce and toss to coat. Spoon onto serving plates. Makes 4 servings.

Tammy Jewell-Greer
Pasadena, California

Mushroom Puff

½ to 1 pound fresh mushrooms,
  sliced
2 to 3 tablespoons butter or
  margarine
6 slices bread
3 to 4 tablespoons butter, melted
½ cup chopped onion
½ cup chopped celery
½ cup chopped green pepper
½ cup mayonnaise
¾ teaspoon salt
¼ teaspoon pepper
2 eggs, slightly beaten
1½ cups milk
1 cup (4 ounces) shredded sharp
  Cheddar cheese

Sauté mushrooms in butter until slightly browned. Place in buttered 2-quart casserole. Brush 4 bread slices with melted butter. Trim crusts and cut bread into 1-inch cubes. Top mushrooms with half the bread cubes. Combine onion, green pepper, celery, mayonnaise, salt and pepper and spread over bread. Top with remaining bread cubes. Combine eggs and milk; pour over bread. Refrigerate overnight. Brush 2 bread slices with butter; cube and sprinkle over casserole. Bake, uncovered, at 325°F. for 45 minutes. Top with cheese and return to oven for 10 to 15 minutes, or until cheese melts. Makes 4 to 6 servings.

Sherri Seiber
Arlington Heights, Illinois

Baldwin's Onions Au Gratin

2 large onions, thinly sliced
¾ cup boiling water
1 beef or chicken-flavored bouillon
  cube
¼ teaspoon dried whole thyme
Salt and pepper to taste
1 tablespoon butter or margarine
½ cup soft bread crumbs
2 tablespoons butter or margarine,
  melted
¼ cup (1 ounce) shredded sharp
  Cheddar cheese

Arrange onion slices in 10x6x2-inch baking dish. Combine boiling water, bouillon, thyme, salt and pepper; stir until bouillon dissolves. Pour over onions; dot with 1 tablespoon butter; cover. Bake at 400°F. for 20 minutes. Combine bread crumbs and melted butter, stirring well; stir in cheese. Sprinkle over onions. Bake, uncovered, for 10 minutes longer or until golden brown.
Makes 5 to 6 servings.

Jill Noeker
Brighton, Michigan

Vidalia Onion Pie

2 to 4 large Vidalia onions, sliced
2 tablespoons butter
1 (9-inch) unbaked pastry shell
3 eggs, slightly beaten
½ teaspoon salt
½ teaspoon paprika
2 cups milk

Sauté onions in butter until transparent. Place in pastry shell. Mix eggs, salt, paprika and milk; pour over onions. Bake in 375°F. oven for 15 to 20 minutes or until golden brown. Good hot or cold.
Makes 8 servings.

Christi Orcutt
Norcross, Georgia

Giselle's Potatoes

2 (24-ounce) packages frozen
  hashed brown potatoes
1 (10¾-ounce) can Campbell's
  cream of chicken soup
1 (8-ounce) carton sour cream
1 (8-ounce) jar Cheese Whiz

Place potatoes in 13x9x2-inch baking dish. Let thaw for 1 hour. Combine soup, sour cream and Cheese Whiz; pour over potatoes, without stirring. Bake at 300°F. for 1 hour.
Makes 8 to 10 servings.

Nancy Williams
Canton, Michigan

Irish Potatoes

1½ pounds bacon
16 ounces fresh mushrooms, sliced
2 large onions, chopped
6 ounces almonds, slivered
4 to 5 potatoes, sliced
Salt and pepper to taste
Green onions, chopped
Parsley, chopped

Fry bacon until crisp; drain, reserving grease. Sauté mushrooms, onions and almonds in 2 tablespoons reserved grease; remove from skillet. Fry potatoes until crisp in remaining grease. Combine sautéed mushroom mixture, potatoes and remaining ingredients; toss well. Serve immediately.
Makes 8 servings.

Thomas Monaghan
Ann Arbor, Michigan

Make-Ahead Mashed Potatoes

8 large potatoes, peeled and cut
  into thick slices
1 medium onion, chopped
½ cup butter or margarine
1 (8-ounce) package cream cheese,
  softened
½ cup sour cream
1 egg, beaten
Salt and pepper to taste
Additional butter or margarine
Paprika

Combine potatoes and onion in large saucepan with water to cover; bring to a boil. Reduce heat and simmer for 20 minutes or until tender. Drain and add butter, cream cheese, sour cream, egg, salt and pepper. Beat with electric mixer until smooth. Place in greased 2-quart casserole. Dot with butter. Sprinkle with paprika. Bake in 350°F. oven for 30 to 35 minutes.
Makes 8 to 10 servings.

May be made 2 or 3 days ahead. Refrigerate and bake when serving.

Ruth Hendricksen
South Lynn, Michigan

Mashed Potato Casserole

10 to 12 medium potatoes, peeled
1 (8-ounce) package cream cheese,
  softened
2 tablespoons sour cream
½ cup butter or margarine
1 (10-ounce) package extra-sharp
  Cheddar cheese
1 small onion, chopped
2 stalks celery, chopped
Salt and pepper
Additional butter or margarine
Paprika

Cook potatoes in boiling water to cover; drain well. Mash in large bowl with cream cheese and sour cream. Melt butter and Cheddar cheese in saucepan and add onion and celery. Add to potato mixture and mix well. Add salt and pepper to taste. Place in casserole and dot with butter. Sprinkle with paprika. Bake at 350°F. for 45 minutes to 1 hour.
Makes 8 to 10 servings.

This recipe can be made in advance and frozen or kept in refrigerator. Makes Thanksgiving and Christmas dinner a lot easier—elegant.

Barbara A. King
Westerville, Ohio

Potato-Vegetable Soufflé

1 pound potatoes, peeled and sliced
1 (16-ounce) can green peas
¼ cup butter or margarine
2 small onions, chopped
¼ cup all-purpose flour
1 cup chicken broth
1 cup milk
1 teaspoon salt
½ teaspoon sugar
¼ teaspoon white pepper
¼ teaspoon ground nutmeg
2 tablespoons lemon juice
2 tablespoons butter or margarine
1 cup (4 ounces) shredded Holland
  cheese

Cook potatoes in boiling water to cover for 20 minutes until tender; drain. Combine potatoes and peas; set aside. Melt ¼ cup butter in large saucepan. Add onions and cook for 5 minutes or until tender. Add flour, stirring until smooth. Add chicken broth and milk; cook, stirring constantly until mixture thickens. Remove from heat and stir in salt, sugar, pepper, nutmeg and lemon juice. Pour over reserved potato mixture; toss lightly. Spoon mixture into 1½-quart soufflé dish. Dot with butter and sprinkle with cheese. Bake at 325°F. for 15 to 20 minutes.
Makes 4 servings.

Birgitta Shopen
Monchengladbach 1,
Federal Republic of Germany

Scalloped Potatoes

4 cups thinly sliced, pared potatoes
2/3 cup minced onion
2 tablespoons flour
1 teaspoon Nosalt or salt
1/8 teaspoon pepper
2 tablespoons butter or margarine
1 1/2 cups scalded milk
Paprika
1/2 cup (2 ounces) grated Cheddar
   cheese, optional

Place layer of potatoes in greased 2-quart casserole; top with about 2 tablespoons onion. Combine flour, Nosalt and pepper; sprinkle over onion. Dot with butter. Repeat layers, using remaining potatoes, onion, flour mixture and butter. Pour milk over casserole; sprinkle with paprika. Bake, covered, in 375°F. oven for 45 minutes; uncover and bake for 15 minutes longer. Sprinkle with cheese during last 5 minutes of baking, if desired.
Makes 8 servings.

Jennifer Menges
Dunkirk, New York

Stuffed Potatoes

4 medium baking potatoes
3 tablespoons butter or margarine
1/2 cup grated cheese (Muenster,
   Mozzarella or Cheddar)
1/3 cup milk
1 cup diced ham
2 tablespoons finely minced
   onion
Salt and pepper to taste

Bake potatoes at 425°F. for approximately 1 hour, (or 1/2 hour if using metal baking skewers). Cut potatoes in half lengthwise; scoop out pulp, leaving 1/8-inch shells. Combine pulp, butter and cheese; mash with fork. Add milk and mix to consistency slightly stiffer than mashed potatoes. (The amount of milk needed may vary depending on the size of potato). Add ham, onion, salt and pepper. Spoon mixture back into potato shells and place on shallow baking pan. Bake in 375°F. oven for 15 minutes or until cheese is melted and tops are slightly browned.
Makes 8 servings.

Variations: Substitute or combine any of following leftovers for the ham: white tuna, turkey, sautéed mushrooms, corned beef or cooked broccoli.

Joan Curran
Ann Arbor, Michigan

Swedish Baked Potatoes

6 medium potatoes
1/2 cup melted butter
Salt and pepper to taste
4 teaspoons Parmesan cheese

Peel potatoes and place in cold water for a few minutes. Quarter potatoes and place in casserole. Pour half the melted butter over potatoes. Add salt and pepper to taste. Bake in 375°F. oven for 45 minutes. Top with remaining butter and Parmesan cheese. Bake for 15 minutes longer.
Makes 12 servings.

Potato peels may be placed in 400°F. hot oil for 2 to 4 seconds or until lightly browned. Place on paper towels to absorb grease. Salt and serve.

Suzanne Stewart
Windsor, Ontario, Canada

Tennessee Spuds

2½ pounds potatoes, sliced
1½ teaspoons salt
¾ teaspoon pepper
1 medium onion, sliced
1½ cups (6 ounces) shredded
    Swiss cheese
1 tablespoon Dijon mustard
1¼ cups white wine
¼ cup fine dry bread crumbs
¼ cup grated Parmesan cheese

Place ⅓ of the potato slices in greased 12x8x2-inch baking dish; sprinkle with ½ teaspoon salt and ¼ teaspoon pepper. Top with half the onion slices, ¾ cup Swiss cheese and 1½ teaspoons Dijon mustard. Repeat layers once. Top with remaining potato slices; sprinkle with remaining salt and pepper. Pour wine over potatoes; sprinkle with bread crumbs and Parmesan cheese. Bake, covered, in 350°F. oven for 1½ hours; uncover, and bake for 10 minutes longer. Let stand for 10 minutes.
Makes 8 servings.

Sarah L. Bender-Hutmier
Nashville, Tennessee

Twice-Baked Stuffed Potatoes

4 large potatoes
2 cups ground cooked ham or bacon
½ cup mayonnaise
½ cup salad dressing
½ cup (2 ounces) shredded Swiss
    cheese
2 tablespoons chopped green pepper
1 tablespoon chopped onion
4 slices American or Cheddar cheese

Bake potatoes; cut in half lengthwise. Scoop out pulp, leaving ¼-inch shell. Combine potato pulp, ham, mayonnaise, salad dressing, Swiss cheese, green pepper and onion; mix well. Spoon mixture into reserved shells; top with cheese. Bake in 425°F. oven for 15 minutes.
Makes 8 servings.

Ann Krueger
Canton, Michigan

Spinach Casserole

2 (10-ounce) packages frozen
    chopped spinach, thawed
2 (8-ounce) cartons creamed
    cottage cheese
6 eggs, beaten
¼ cup butter or margarine
½ pound Colby cheese, cubed
6 tablespoons flour

Thaw and squeeze excess water from spinach. Combine all ingredients in large mixing bowl; stir well. Spoon mixture into buttered 2½-quart casserole. Bake at 375°F. for 1 hour.
Makes 8 servings.

Vicki Dean
Chattanooga, Tennessee

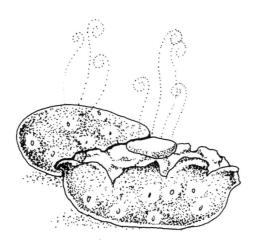

Stuffed Acorn Squash

1 large acorn squash
1 cup boiling water
1 chicken-flavored bouillon cube
1½ cups (6 ounces) shredded
   Cheddar cheese
3 slices white bread, cubed
¼ cup chopped onion
1 egg, beaten
Salt and pepper to taste

Cut squash in half lengthwise; discard seeds and membranes. Place squash, cut-side down, in 9-inch square baking dish. Bake in 375°F. oven for 45 minutes to 1 hour or until tender. Let cool slightly. Scoop out pulp, leaving ¼-inch shell. Combine water and bouillon cube, stirring until bouillon dissolves. Combine squash, bouillon mixture and remaining ingredients; stir well. Spoon mixture into reserved shells. Return shells to baking dish. Bake in 375°F. oven for 30 minutes or until golden brown.
Makes 2 servings.

To cook squash in microwave: microwave at HIGH (100% power) for 20 minutes.

Sue Corbin
Brighton, Michigan

Sweet Potatoes

2 eggs, beaten
1½ cups sugar
½ cup butter or margarine, melted
½ cup evaporated milk
1 teaspoon vanilla extract
½ teaspoon ground cinnamon
½ teaspoon ground nutmeg
3 cups mashed sweet potatoes
1 cup firmly packed brown sugar
1 cup chopped walnuts or pecans
½ cup butter or margarine,
   softened
⅓ cup all-purpose flour

Combine eggs, sugar, melted butter, milk, vanilla, cinnamon and nutmeg; beat well. Stir in sweet potatoes. Spoon mixture into buttered 2-quart casserole. Bake at 350°F. oven for 30 minutes. Combine remaining ingredients; mix well. Sprinkle over sweet potatoes. Bake for 15 minutes longer or until golden brown.
Makes 8 to 10 servings.

Pat Trapnell
Northville, Michigan

Spanakopita (Greek Spinach Pie)

1 medium onion, chopped
¼ to ½ cup olive oil
3 (8-ounce) bags fresh spinach,
   cleaned and torn into small
   pieces
8 ounces Feta cheese, crumbled
2 eggs, beaten
½ cup butter or margarine
1 tablespoon cornstarch
1 cup milk, heated
2 eggs
½ (16-ounce) package phyllo
   pastry
½ cup butter or margarine, melted

Sauté onion in ¼ cup oil until tender. Gradually add spinach and cook for 5 minutes or until spinach wilts. Add more oil if necessary to prevent sticking. Remove from heat and stir in cheese and beaten eggs; set aside. Melt butter in small saucepan over low heat. Gradually add cornstarch, stirring constantly. Stir in milk. Add eggs, one at a time, stirring well after each addition. Cook, stirring constantly, until mixture thickens slightly. Remove from heat. Layer half the phyllo pastry in 13x9x2-inch baking pan, brushing each sheet with melted butter. Spoon spinach mixture over pastry, spreading evenly; spoon sauce over spinach. Layer remaining pastry over sauce, brushing each sheet with melted butter. Bake at 325°F. for 30 minutes or until golden brown.
Makes 12 servings.

Anna M. Chapekis
Ann Arbor, Michigan

Sweet Potato Soufflé

1 cup sugar
½ cup milk
2 eggs, beaten
3 tablespoons butter or margarine,
   softened
1 teaspoon salt
1 teaspoon vanilla extract
3 cups mashed sweet potatoes
1 cup firmly packed brown sugar
1 cup chopped nuts
1   (3½-ounce) can flaked coconut
⅓ cup all-purpose flour
3 tablespooons butter or margarine,
   melted

Combine sugar, milk, eggs, softened butter, salt and vanilla; mix well. Stir in sweet potatoes. Spoon mixture into buttered 9-inch square baking dish. Combine remaining ingredients, mixing well; sprinkle over sweet potatoes. Bake at 350°F. for 35 minutes.
Makes 4 to 6 servings.

Karen Boone
Kent, Ohio

Sweet Potato And Apple Casserole

4 medium sweet potatoes
6 medium baking apples, peeled and
   sliced
½ cup maple syrup
½ cup brown sugar
½ cup butter
Salt to taste
1 cup chopped walnuts

Bake sweet potatoes at 350°F. for 1 hour or until tender. Peel and slice; keep warm. Combine remaining ingredients in large saucepan. Cook over medium heat, stirring frequently for 20 minutes or until apples are tender. Layer ¼ of the potatoes in greased 2-quart casserole; top with ¼ of the apple mixture. Repeat layers, using remaining ingredients. Serve immediately.
Makes 6 servings.

May be made ahead of time and heated in a 350°F. oven until very hot, about 30 to 45 minutes. Always bake sweet potatoes to retain their best flavor.

Karen Lynn Ferns
Rancho Cucamonga, California

Yam And Cranberry Casserole

1   (12-ounce) package fresh whole
   cranberries
1¼ to 1½ cups sugar
½ cup pecan halves
1 small orange, sliced
¼ cup orange juice
¾ teaspoon ground cinnamon
¼ teaspoon ground nutmeg
⅛ teaspoon ground mace
1   (40-ounce) can yams, drained

Combine all ingredients except yams in greased 2-quart casserole. Bake at 375°F. for 30 minutes. Stir in yams. Bake for 15 minutes longer or until thoroughly heated. Serve warm.
Makes 8 servings.

Claudia Miller
Ypsilanti, Michigan

Tomatoes Country-Style

1 (8-ounce) package cream cheese, softened
¼ cup minced parsley
1 teaspoon chopped fresh basil or ½ teaspoon dried basil leaves
1 clove garlic, minced
⅛ teaspoon salt
4 beefsteak or large tomatoes
½ cup all-purpose flour
1 egg, beaten with 1 tablespoon milk
⅔ cup dry bread crumbs
3 tablespoons butter
3 tablespoons olive oil
Fresh basil or parsley, optional

Beat together in mixer, or process in food processor, cream cheese, parsley, basil, garlic and salt. Cut tomatoes into 12 even slices, about ½ inch thick. Spread 6 slices with about 2 tablespoons cream cheese mixture each; top with remaining slices to make 6 sandwiches. Dip each in flour, then in egg mixture and finally in crumbs. Fry on both sides over medium heat in mixture of butter and olive oil until brown. Garnish with fresh basil.
Makes 6 servings.

Mary Johnson
Hayward, California

J. R.'s Zucchini

3 small or 2 large zucchini, unpeeled and sliced
¼ cup olive oil, divided
1 (15-ounce) jar marinara sauce
½ cup red wine
1 clove garlic, minced
¼ teaspoon basil leaves, crushed
⅛ teaspoon dried whole oregano, crushed
1 cup (4 ounces) shredded Monterey Jack cheese

Sauté zucchini in 3 tablespoons olive oil until lightly browned; drain. Place in 1½-quart casserole. Combine marinara sauce, wine, remaining oil, garlic, basil and oregano in small saucepan; stir well. Simmer for 15 minutes, stirring occasionally. Spoon sauce over zucchini; mix well. Sprinkle cheese over sauce; cover. Bake at 325°F. for 30 minutes. Bake, uncovered, for 5 minutes longer. Serve casserole immediately.
Makes 6 servings.

Peggy Romano
Boulder, Colorado

Easy Garden Vegetable Pie

2 cups chopped fresh broccoli
½ cup chopped onion
½ cup chopped green pepper
1 cup (4 ounces) shredded Cheddar cheese
1½ cups milk
¾ cup baking mix
3 eggs
1 teaspoon salt
½ teaspoon pepper

Heat 1-inch salted water to boiling. Add broccoli; cover and return to boil. Cook until almost tender, about 5 minutes; drain thoroughly. Combine broccoli, onion, green pepper and cheese in greased 10-inch deep-dish pie plate. Combine remaining ingredients in blender container; process for 15 seconds or until smooth. Pour over broccoli mixture. Bake at 400°F. for 35 to 40 minutes or until golden brown and a knife inserted halfway between center and edge comes out clean. Let stand for 5 minutes. Garnish as desired.
Makes 8 servings.

Kim Swanson
Whitmere Lake, Michigan

Garden Delight Vegetable Casserole

1½ cups uncooked brown rice
2 large onions, chopped
3 cups water
3 tablespoons soy sauce
2 tablespoons butter or margarine, melted
3 teaspoons instant vegetable-flavored bouillon granules
1 teaspoon salt
½ teaspoon dried whole thyme
1 bunch broccoli, cut into flowerets
1 head cauliflower, cut into flowerets
2 red or green peppers, chopped
2 cloves garlic, minced
3 tablespoons vegetable oil
1 cup chopped cashews
2 cups (8 ounces) shredded Cheddar cheese

Combine rice, half the onions, water, soy sauce, butter and bouillon granules in 2-quart casserole; cover. Bake at 350°F. for 20 minutes. Stir in salt and thyme. Sauté remaining onions, broccoli, cauliflower, peppers and garlic in oil for 5 minutes. Spoon over rice mixture. Cover and bake at 350°F. for 10 minutes. Sprinkle cashews over center of casserole; sprinkle cheese around edges. Bake for 5 minutes longer or until cheese melts.
Makes 6 servings.

Denise Kruer
Middleton, Ohio

Applesauce Dressing

2 medium onions, chopped
4 stalks celery, chopped
2 tablespoons butter or margarine
1 (16-ounce) loaf white bread, cubed
2 (16-ounce) cans applesauce
¼ cup dried parsley flakes
Salt, pepper and garlic powder to taste

Sauté onions and celery in butter until tender. Combine sautéed mixture with bread, applesauce, parsley flakes, salt, pepper and garlic powder; stir well. Spoon into 12x8x2-inch baking dish. Bake at 350°F. for 30 minutes.
Makes 6 to 8 servings.

Can be used as stuffing for turkey or chicken.

Joseph S. Cangialosi
Massillon, Ohio

Curried Baked Fruit

1 (1-pound) can pears
1 (1-pound) can peaches
1 (15¼-ounce) can pineapple chunks
1 (17-ounce) can apricot halves
12 maraschino cherries
¾ cup firmly packed brown sugar
½ teaspoon curry powder
⅓ cup butter or margarine
⅔ cup almond halves (optional)

Drain pears, peaches, pineapple chunks, apricots and cherries in colander overnight in the refrigerator. In large bowl, combine fruit, brown sugar, curry powder, butter and almonds. Place in casserole. Bake in preheated 350°F. oven for 25 to 30 minutes.
Makes 12 servings.

Serve with dinner as you would cranberry sauce.

Ruth Hendricksen
South Lyon, Michigan

Dumplings

2 cups flour
2 eggs
½ teaspoon salt
¾ cup water
5 or 6 slices white bread, dried overnight and cut into ½-inch cubes
¼ cup flour

Place 2 cups flour in bowl; make well in center. Place eggs, salt and water in well. Beat mixture, starting in center working outward, until well combined. Dough will be thick. Add bread cubes and mix well. Roll spoonfuls of dough in ¼ cup flour. Shape with hands into balls; drop gently into boiling water in large saucepan, stirring occasionally. Boil for 20 minutes. Makes 5 or 6 servings.

Can be served with any meat dish which has gravy.

Suzanne Mae Vlcek
Plymouth, Michigan

Grits Casserole

1 cup uncooked grits
½ cup margarine
2 eggs, slightly beaten
1 (6-ounce) package Kraft garlic cheese

Cook grits according to package directions. Stir in margarine, eggs and cheese. Place grits mixture in greased 1-quart casserole. Bake at 350°F. for 25 to 30 minutes.
Makes 8 servings.

Pat Carpenter
Lawrenceville, Georgia

California Macaroni And Cheese

½ pound (8 ounces) elbow macaroni
4 tablespoons butter or margarine
4 tablespoons flour
1½ cups milk
2 cups (½ pound) shredded Cheddar cheese
½ cup California Sherry
½ teaspoon dry mustard
1 teaspoon Worcestershire sauce
Salt and pepper to taste
½ cup buttered bread crumbs

Cook macaroni in boiling salted water until tender; drain. Melt butter and stir in flour. Add milk and cook, stirring constantly, until thick and smooth. Add cheese and stir until melted. Blend in Sherry and seasonings. Mix with macaroni. Place in greased casserole; top with buttered crumbs. Bake at 350°F. for 30 minutes or until brown. Makes 6 servings.

Bruce Binderman
Winston-Salem, North Carolina

Madame's Noodles (Easy Fettucini!)

1 (12-ounce) package noodles
4 teaspooons salt
4 quarts water
¾ cup salted butter
1 cup cream, heated
1 cup shredded Swiss cheese
1 clove garlic, minced
½ cup minced fresh parsley

Cook noodles in salted water according to package directions. Place butter and cream in bowl; set over saucepan containing steaming water until butter melts. Drain noodles and quickly add to bowl with butter and cream. Toss until noodles are creamy. Add cheese, garlic and parsley; toss until cheese melts and strings. Serve immediately. Makes 6 servings.

Ildiko Marcus
Xenia, Ohio

Pasta With Cream Sauce

1 pound spinach noodles
2 tablespoons olive oil
1 teaspoon sweet basil
½ teaspoon garlic powder
¼ teaspoon salt
¼ teaspoon pepper
2 tablespoons sour cream

Cook noodles according to package directions; drain. Combine remaining ingredients and stir into noodles.
Makes 2 to 3 servings.

Can be served as a main dish or a side dish. Fast and easy.

Alison A. Shipman
Boca Raton, Florida

Green Rice

3 cups minute rice
1 cup chopped parsley or ½ cup parsley flakes
½ cup grated Cheddar cheese
½ cup finely chopped onion
¼ cup chopped green pepper
2 eggs, beaten
½ teaspoon each seasoning salt and pepper
¼ teaspoon Accent'
2 tablespoons lemon juice
1 teaspoon grated lemon rind
Paprika

Prepare rice according to package directions. Stir in parsley, cheese, onion, green pepper, eggs, seasoning salt, pepper and Accent'. Spoon mixture into greased 10x8x2-inch baking dish. Sprinkle lemon juice, lemon rind and paprika over mixture; cover. Bake at 350°F. for 45 minutes.
Makes 8 servings.

H. D. Robinson, Jr.
Wichita, Kansas

Wild Rice Casserole

½ pound bulk sausage
1 medium onion, chopped
1 medium green pepper, chopped
1   (6-ounce) package long-grain and wild rice
1   (4-ounce) package wild rice, rinsed
1   (10¾-ounce) can cream of mushroom soup, undiluted
1   (10¾-ounce) can cream of chicken soup, undiluted
1 cup shredded sharp Cheddar cheese
1   (4-ounce) can sliced mushrooms, drained

Brown sausage in skillet; drain and reserve 1 tablespoon drippings. Sauté onion and green pepper in reserved drippings. Combine sautéed vegetables, long grain and wild rice mix, including seasoning package, wild rice, soups, cheese and mushrooms; mix well. Spoon into shallow 2-quart casserole; cover. Bake in 325°F. oven for 1 hour.
Makes 8 servings.

Diane Lyon Laughlin
Peoria, Illinois

Scalloped Rice

3 cups cooked long-grain rice
¼ cup flour
1 teaspoon salt
⅓ cup sliced green onions
½ cup chopped parsley (optional)
2½ cups milk
Grated Cheddar cheese

Place rice in greased 13x9x2-inch casserole. Sprinkle flour, salt, green onions and parsley over rice. Pour milk over all. Cover with grated Cheddar cheese. Bake at 350°F. for 30 to 45 minutes or until set.
Makes 6 servings.

Barbara Schubert
Carmichael, California

Breads

Breads

Angel Biscuits

2 (¼-ounce) packages yeast
¼ cup warm water
5 cups self-rising flour
⅓ cup sugar
1 teaspoon soda
1 cup shortening
2 cups buttermilk
Melted butter

Preheat oven to 400°F. Dissolve yeast in warm water; set aside. Sift dry ingredients into large bowl; cut in shortening. Add buttermilk and yeast mixture. Stir until thoroughly moistened. Turn onto floured board and knead for 1 or 2 minutes. Roll out to desired thickness. Cut into rounds with biscuit cutter. Brush with melted butter. Bake on ungreased baking sheet for 12 to 15 minutes or until lightly browned.
Makes 2 dozen biscuits.

These biscuits freeze well. They are soft even when warmed over. The dough can be kept in a covered bowl for days in refrigerator.

Joyce A. Archenbronn
Ypsilanti, Michigan

Mum's Molasses Biscuits

3 teaspoons soda
1 cup warm water
½ cup shortening
2 cups molasses
6 cups flour
2 teaspoons ginger
Dash of salt

Preheat oven to 350°F. Grease cookie sheets. Mix soda in water. Cream shortening. Add molasses and water mixture; stir well. Combine flour, ginger and salt in mixing bowl. Gradually add dry ingredients to liquid mixture; stir until moistened. Dough will become quite thick and soft. Turn dough onto lightly floured surface and knead until smooth. Lightly flour dough and roll to ½-inch thickness. Cut with 3-inch round biscuit cutter. Place on cookie sheets. Bake for 15 minutes.
Makes 28 biscuits.

Excellent served warm with butter.

Randy King
Kingston, Ontario, Canada

Baked Hush Puppies

1 cup cornmeal
1 cup flour
1 tablespoon baking powder
1 teaspoon sugar
1 teaspoon salt
¼ teaspoon cayenne pepper
¾ cup milk
2 eggs, beaten
½ cup chopped onion
¼ cup melted butter or oil

Preheat oven to 425°F. Grease small muffin cups. Combine cornmeal, flour, baking powder, sugar, salt and cayenne pepper in bowl; mix lightly. Add milk, eggs, onion and butter. Stir only until well blended. Place 1 tablespoon batter into each muffin cup. Place muffin cups on sheets of aluminum foil to prevent over browning. Bake for 15 to 20 minutes or until golden brown.
Makes about 4 dozen.

Christi Orcutt
Norcross, Georgia

◀Recipes for this photograph on pages 154, 157 and 162.

Bread Sticks

3 cups flour
1 teaspoon salt
1 teaspoon sugar
1 (¼-ounce) package dry yeast
1 cup lukewarm water
½ cup butter or margarine

Preheat oven to 350°F. Combine flour, salt and sugar in mixing bowl. Dissolve yeast in 1 cup water. Stir yeast mixture into flour; blend well. Cut butter into flour mixture with pastry blender or 2 knives until mixture resembles coarse crumbs. Turn out on floured surface and knead for a few minutes. Let rise for 2 to 3 hours. Cut dough into 3 portions. Divide each into 14 pieces. Shape each piece with palms of hands into stick by rolling on lightly floured surface. Bake in oven for 30 minutes or until golden brown.
Makes 42 bread sticks.

Sally A. Watson
Adrian, Michigan

Corn Bread (or Johnny Cake)

¾ cup cornmeal
1 cup flour
⅓ cup sugar
2½ teaspoons baking powder
¾ teaspoon salt
1 cup milk or 1 cup heavy cream
1 egg
2 tablespoons melted shortening

Preheat oven to 425°F. Grease an 8-inch square baking pan. Sift together cornmeal, flour, sugar, baking powder and salt in mixing bowl; set aside. Beat together milk, egg and shortening in separate bowl. Add to cornmeal mixture and stir until blended. Pour into prepared pan. Bake for 20 minutes or until golden brown.
Makes 9 servings.

T. R. claims this one is as good as they were in the U. S. Marine Corps!

T. R. Minick
Ann Arbor, Michigan

Mexican Corn Bread

1 cup yellow cornmeal
½ teaspoon salt
½ teaspoon soda
⅓ cup oil or bacon drippings
2 eggs, beaten
1 cup cream-style corn
⅔ cup buttermilk or milk or
   1 (8-ounce) carton sour cream
1 cup grated sharp Cheddar cheese
1 (4-ounce) can green chili
   peppers, drained and finely
   chopped

Preheat oven to 350°F. Grease heavy 12-inch skillet. Combine cornmeal, salt and soda in bowl. Stir in oil. Add eggs, corn and buttermilk; blend thoroughly. Spoon half the mixture into prepared skillet. Sprinkle cheese and chopped peppers over mixture and cover with remaining batter. Bake for 30 to 45 minutes or until golden brown.
Makes one 12-inch skillet corn bread.

Bill Adamson
Denton, Texas

Apple Fritters

1 cup flour
1 teaspoon baking soda
½ teaspoon salt
1 egg, beaten
½ cup milk
1 tablespoon melted butter
3 to 4 apples, peeled and cut up
Oil for deep-frying

Mix dry ingredients together. Mix egg and milk together. Stir in dry ingredients. Add butter and mix well. Fold in apples. Heat deep fryer to 360 or 375°F. Drop tablespoonfuls of batter into hot oil. When they are golden brown, take out of grease, put in a bag full of sugar and shake until coated. Serve.

Lynne L. Martel
Forest Park, Illinois

Old Tavern Fritters

1 cup flour
1 teaspoon baking powder
½ teaspoon salt
2 eggs, lightly beaten
⅔ cup milk
1 teaspoon butter, melted
½ cup Cheddar cheese
Oil for deep frying

Combine flour, baking powder and salt in bowl. Mix together eggs and milk; add to dry ingredients. Beat until smooth. Stir in butter and then cheese; mix well. Drop by tablespoons into hot oil. Fry until light brown. Drain on brown paper and serve hot.
Makes 12 to 14 fritters.

Sara Viers
Antioch, Tennessee

French Toast

3 eggs
2 teaspoons sugar
1 teaspoon cinnamon
1 teaspoon allspice
6 slices cinnamon-raisin bread

Beat eggs in mixing bowl. Add sugar, cinnamon and allspice; mix well. Dip cinnamon-raisin bread slices into mixture and fry until golden brown on medium heat. Serve with maple syrup.
Makes 2 servings.

Susan T. Pope
Martinsville, Virginia

Blender Popovers

1 cup milk
2 eggs
1 cup flour
¼ teaspoon salt
1 tablespoon melted butter

Combine all ingredients in blender container. Process for 30 seconds. Pour into muffin cups. Bake at 400°F. for 20 minutes. Reduce heat to 350°F. Bake for 10 minutes longer. Serve with butter, honey, jam or jelly.
Makes 12 servings.

Susan Sanders
Belgrade, Montana

Golden Cheese Wheel

1 (¼-ounce) package active dry
  yeast
⅔ cup warm water (110°-115°)
2 tablespoons oil
½ teaspoon sugar
½ teaspoon salt
2 cups all-purpose flour
1 egg, beaten
½ cup snipped parsley
½ teaspoon garlic salt
⅛ teaspoon pepper
3 cups shredded Muenster cheese
1 egg, slightly beaten
1 tablespoon water
1½ teaspoons sesame seed
1 teaspoon sugar

Dissolve yeast in warm water in mixing bowl. Stir in oil, ½ teaspoon sugar and salt. Add 1 cup flour and mix thoroughly. Stir in enough remaining flour to make a moderately stiff dough. Turn out onto lightly floured surface. Knead until smooth and elastic, about 5 to 8 minutes. Place in lightly greased bowl, turning to grease top. Cover; let rise in warm place until doubled in bulk, about 1 hour. Punch down; divide in 2 portions. Cover and let rest for 10 minutes. On lightly floured surface, roll 1 portion into 13-inch circle. Place on 12-inch round pan. Combine beaten egg, parsley, garlic salt and pepper. Spread over dough. Sprinkle with cheese. Roll out remaining dough; place on top. Trim and flute edges. Bake in 400°F. oven for 20 minutes. Remove from oven. Brush with mixture of egg and water. Top with sesame seed and 1 teaspoon sugar. Return to oven and continue baking 15 to 20 minutes. Cut into small wedges. Serve hot. Makes one 13-inch wheel.

Lorraine Galloway
St. Louis, Missouri

Scones

2 cups flour
¼ cup sugar
1 teaspoon baking powder
1 teaspoon soda
Pinch of salt
¼ cup shortening
1 egg
½ cup milk

Combine flour, sugar, baking powder, soda and salt; cut in shortening. Add egg and milk; stir until well blended. Roll dough into ½-inch thick round on floured board. Heat greased griddle until very hot. Cook scones on griddle for about 3 minutes and turn, cook about 3 minutes on other side. Cut into wedges. Serve Scones with butter or jam.
Makes 10 servings.

Catherine N. Graham
Ann Arbor, Michigan

Spoon Bread

2 cups milk
2 tablespoons sugar
1 teaspoon salt
¾ cup cornmeal
6 egg whites
6 egg yolks, beaten
½ teaspoon baking powder

Preheat oven to 375°F. Grease 2-quart baking dish; set aside. Combine milk, sugar and salt in saucepan and bring to a boil. Add cornmeal and stir until cooked, almost 2 minutes. Beat egg whites in bowl until soft peaks form. Add egg yolks and baking powder to cornmeal; blend well. Fold egg whites into cornmeal mixture until well blended. Pour into prepared baking dish. Bake for 30 minutes or until golden brown.
Makes 12 servings.

Kimberly Callicotte
Cincinnati, Ohio

Homemade Wheat Germ Herb Bread

5½ to 6½ cups unsifted all-purpose
   flour
2   (¼-ounce) packages dry yeast
⅓ cup sugar
1 teaspoon salt
1 teaspoon thyme leaves, crushed
1 teaspoon marjoram leaves, crushed
1½ cups milk
½ cup water
½ cup butter or margarine
2 eggs
1 egg yolk
1⅓ cups wheat germ (regular or
   sugar & honey)
1 egg white, beaten
1 tablespoon wheat germ

In large mixer bowl, combine 3 cups flour, yeast, sugar, salt and herbs; mix well. In saucepan, heat milk, water and butter until warm (120° to 130°; butter does not need to melt); add to flour mixture. Add eggs and egg yolk. Blend at low speed until moistened; beat for 3 minutes at medium speed. By hand, gradually stir in 1⅓ cups wheat germ and enough remaining flour to make a soft dough. Knead on floured surface until smooth and elastic, about 10 minutes. Place in greased bowl, turning to grease top. Cover; let rise in warm place until light and doubled in bulk, about 1 hour. Punch down dough. Divide into 2 portions. Roll each portion on lightly floured surface and shape into 12x8-inch rectangle. Cut each rectangle into 2 equal 12-inch strips. Pinch edges of each strip together to make a rope. Twist 2 ropes together; seal ends and tuck under loaf. Place in well-greased 8½x4½x2⅛-inch loaf pans. Cover; let rise for 30 to 40 minutes. Lightly brush with egg white; sprinkle with 1 tablespoon wheat germ. Bake at 350°F. for 35 to 45 minutes. Cover loosely with foil the last 5 to 10 minutes of baking. Remove from pans; cool. Makes two 1½-pound loaves bread.

Connie DeVantier
Ann Arbor, Michigan

Whole Wheat-Granola Loaf

2 packages yeast
½ teaspoon malt (optional)—
   available at health food stores
1 cup water
1 cup granola, as is or crushed
1¼ teaspoons salt
2 tablespoons soy flour
1 egg
1 tablespoon oil
2½ to 3 cups whole wheat bread flour

Dissolve yeast and malt in warm water (105-110°F.). In a separate bowl, combine granola, salt and soy flour. Add to dissolved yeast; mix well. Beat in egg, oil, and enough flour to make a medium stiff, kneadable dough. Knead about 8 minutes. Place in oiled bowl, turning once, and cover. Let rise in warm place until doubled, about 40 minutes. Punch down and let rise for 20 minutes. Form 1 loaf and press into 9x4½x2½-inch pan. Let rise until almost doubled. Bake in 400°F. oven for about 40 minutes. To test for doneness, remove loaf from pan and rap with fingers on side or bottom of loaf. It should have a hollow, drum-like sound. If not done, return to oven for 5 or 10 minutes longer, then test again. When done, remove from pan and cool on rack.
Makes 1 loaf.

To get increased volume from whole wheat breads, add 3 teaspoons of a 100 milligram ascorbic acid/flour mixture to this recipe along with the granola. To make, crush a 100 milligram ascorbic acid tablet (vitamin C) and mix with 8 teaspoons flour.

Beverly Switzer
Ann Arbor, Michigan

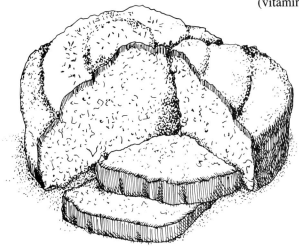

Sausage Bread

2 cups Jiffy baking mix
2/3 cup milk
1 cup shredded Mozzarella cheese
1 cup cooked mild sausage, drained
1 tablespoon butter
1 teaspoon basil

Preheat oven to 450°F. Lightly grease large baking sheet; set aside. Pour baking mix into bowl. Add milk and stir to mix. Roll dough out into 13x9x½-inch sheet. Sprinkle sausage on dough, to within 1 inch of edge; sprinkle Mozzarella cheese over sausage. Roll up; pinch edges to seal ends. Brush butter on top of bread; sprinkle basil over butter. Place seam-side down on prepared baking sheet. Bake for 15 to 20 minutes. Cool slightly; slice and serve.
Makes 6 servings.

Alison A. Shipman
Boca Raton, Florida

Swiss Cheese Onion Bread

1   (16-ounce) package Pillsbury Hot
     Roll Mix
3/4 cup warm water
1 cup shredded Swiss cheese
1/2 cup chopped onion
2 tablespoons oil
1 tablespoon prepared mustard
1 egg
1 egg white
2 teaspoons water
Sesame seed

Dissolve yeast from hot roll mix in warm water. Stir in cheese, onion, oil, mustard and egg. Add flour mixture and blend well. Cover and let rise in warm place for 45 to 60 minutes. Preheat oven to 375°F. Grease cookie sheet. Knead dough on floured surface until no longer sticky. Divide dough into 2 portions. Shape each into long roll, slightly longer than cookie sheet. Twist rolls together about 3 times and seal ends. Beat together egg white and water; brush over loaf. Sprinkle with sesame seed. Let rise, covered, in warm place about 30 minutes. Bake for 20 to 25 minutes or until golden brown. Cool bread in pan for 10 minutes. Turn bread out onto wire rack to cool completely.
Makes 1 loaf.

Mary Kogelschatz
Belleville, Michigan

Parker House Potato Rolls

2   (¼-ounce) packages active dry
     yeast
1½ cups very warm water
2/3 cup sugar
2/3 cup shortening
1 cup warm, unseasoned mashed
     potatoes
7 to 8 cups flour
3 eggs
1½ teaspoons salt
¼ cup melted butter

Dissolve yeast in ½ cup water. Let stand until bubbly. Beat together 1 cup water, sugar, shortening, potatoes and 2 cups flour with mixer until smooth. Add yeast mixture, eggs and salt; beat until smooth. By hand, mix in remaining flour, 1 cup at a time, until dough is soft and not sticky. Knead for 1 to 2 minutes. Shape into ball with greased hands. Place in greased bowl, turning to coat. Cover with damp cloth. Let rise for 1 hour. Punch dough down. Divide dough into 2 portions. Place on floured surface. Knead for 1 minute. Roll out to 3/8-inch thickness. Brush with melted butter. Cut with biscuit cutter. Fold 1/3 over. Place 1 inch apart on ungreased cookie sheet. Let rise until doubled in bulk (about 30 minutes). Repeat procedure with second portion dough. Preheat oven to 400°F. and bake for 15 minutes.
Makes 5½ dozen.

Rhonda Brown
Yukon, Oklahoma

Pull-Apart Breakfast Rolls

18 frozen dinner rolls
½ (3-ounce) package butterscotch
   pudding mix (not instant)
¼ cup cinnamon-sugar
½ cup butter
½ cup firmly packed brown sugar

Place frozen rolls in well-greased bundt pan. Combine dry pudding mix and cinnamon-sugar; sprinkle over rolls. Melt butter and brown sugar in small saucepan over medium heat; stir until blended. Pour over rolls. Cover with foil and let rise until doubled in bulk. Bake at 350°F. for 30 minutes.
Makes 18 servings.

Keith Witte
Richfield, Minnesota

Refrigerator Yeast Rolls

1 cup sugar
1 cup shortening
1 cup boiling water
2 (¼-ounce) packages yeast
1 cup cold water
½ teaspoon salt
2 eggs, beaten
6 to 7 cups unbleached flour
½ cup melted butter or margarine

Mix sugar, shortening and boiling water in large bowl. Dissolve yeast in 1 cup cold water; add to shortening mixture. Stir in salt, eggs and unbleached flour; beat until smooth. Add 1 cup flour if needed to make dough easy to handle. Turn dough onto lightly floured surface and knead for 5 minutes, until dough is smooth and elastic. Place in greased bowl. Lightly grease top of dough and cover. Let rise until doubled in bulk. Punch down; knead. Cover tightly and refrigerate for 8 hours. Remove from refrigerator and knead until warm. Divide dough in half. Roll dough into 10x8-inch rectangle. Cut with round cookie cutter dipped in flour, until all dough has been used. Place rolls in 2 lightly greased 13x9x2-inch pans with sides touching. Brush tops with melted butter. Let rise for 1 hour. Bake in 400°F. oven for 20 to 25 minutes.
Makes 3 to 3½ dozen rolls.

Kimberly Breeding Lake
Winchester, Kentucky

Apple Bread

¾ cup butter or margarine
1½ cups sugar
3 eggs
3 tablespoons sour milk
3 cups flour
1 teaspoon salt
1 teaspoon soda
1 teaspoon vanilla extract
3 cups chopped apples
½ cup chopped walnuts
2 tablespoons brown sugar
2 tablespoons flour
2 tablespoons butter or margarine
½ teaspoon cinnamon

Preheat oven to 350°F. Grease and flour one 9x5x3-inch loaf pan. Cream ¾ cup butter and sugar until light and fluffy. Beat in eggs and milk. In separate bowl, combine 3 cups flour, salt and soda. Add dry ingredients to first mixture. Stir in vanilla. Add apples and walnuts and mix well. Pour into prepared loaf pan. Combine brown sugar, 2 tablespoons flour, 2 tablespoons butter and cinnamon. Sprinkle over top of bread. Bake for 1 hour or until toothpick inserted in center comes out clean. Cool bread in pan for 10 minutes. Turn bread out onto wire rack to cool completely.
Makes 1 loaf.

Marcia L. Johnson
Ionia, Michigan

Banana-Nut Bread

1 cup sugar
1 cup butter
2 eggs
3 ripe bananas, mashed
2 cups flour
1 teaspoon baking powder
½ teaspoon soda
½ teaspoon salt
1 cup nuts
1 teaspoon vanilla extract

Preheat oven to 350°F. Grease and flour one 9x5x3-inch loaf pan. Cream sugar and butter until light and fluffy. Add eggs and bananas. In separate bowl sift together flour, baking powder, soda and salt. Add to banana mixture and blend well. Stir in nuts and vanilla; mix thoroughly. Pour into prepared loaf pan or 1-pound coffee can. Bake in oven for 60 minutes or until toothpick inserted in center comes out clean. Cool in pan for 10 minutes. Turn bread onto wire rack to cool completely.
Makes 1 loaf.

Michelle R. Rogers
Indianapolis, Indiana

Breakfast Bread

1½ cups whole wheat flour
1 cup unbleached flour
½ cup raw wheat germ
1 cup bran
½ cup raisins
2 tablespoons Brewers yeast flakes
½ cup sunflower seed (optional)
2 cups buttermilk
½ cup unprocessed honey
½ cup blackstrap molasses
1 teaspoon salt
2 teaspoons soda

Preheat oven to 400°F.; reduce temperature to 350°F. for baking. Grease and flour 9x5x3-inch loaf pan; set aside. Combine flours, wheat germ, bran, raisins, yeast flakes and sunflower seed in mixing bowl. Pour buttermilk, honey, molasses, salt and soda in 4-cup measuring cup; stir ingredients thoroughly until mixture begins to foam over top of cup. Pour into dry ingredients and mix thoroughly. Pour batter into prepared pan. Bake at 350°F. for 1 hour or until golden brown; cool bread in pan for 10 minutes. Turn bread out onto wire rack to cool completely. Freezes well.
Makes 1 loaf.

Paula K. Porter
Hermitage, Tennessee

Lemon Bread

6 tablespoons shortening
1 cup sugar
2 eggs, beaten
1 tablespoon grated lemon peel
1½ cups flour
1 teaspoon baking powder
½ teaspoon salt
½ cup milk
½ cup chopped walnuts
⅓ cup sugar
3 tablespoons lemon juice

Preheat oven to 350°F. Grease and flour one 8½x4½x2½-inch loaf pan. Cream shortening and 1 cup sugar until light and fluffy. Add eggs and lemon peel. Sift together flour, baking powder and salt; add alternately with milk to first mixture. Fold in walnuts. Pour into prepared loaf pan. Bake in oven for 1 hour or until toothpick inserted in center comes out clean. Remove from oven and let cool in pan for 15 minutes. Dissolve ⅓ cup sugar in lemon juice. Pour over bread. Cool bread in pan for 10 minutes. Turn bread onto wire rack to cool completely.
Makes 1 loaf.

Donna Haley
Columbus, Ohio

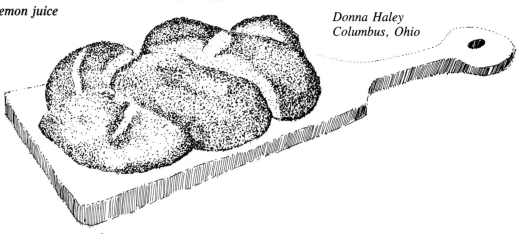

Pumpkin Spice Bread

3 cups flour
1½ cups sugar
1½ teaspoons cinnamon
1 teaspoon soda
1 teaspoon salt
¾ teaspoon nutmeg
¾ teaspoon cloves
½ teaspoon baking powder
3 eggs
1 cup vegetable oil
1 (16-ounce) can pumpkin
1 cup golden or dark seedless
   raisins
½ cup chopped walnuts

Preheat oven to 350°F. Grease and flour two 8½x4½x2½-inch loaf pans. Combine flour, sugar, cinnamon, soda, salt, nutmeg, cloves and baking powder in large bowl and mix. In medium bowl, beat together eggs, oil and pumpkin until blended. Stir pumpkin mixture into flour mixture, just until flour is moistened. Stir in raisins and walnuts. Spoon into prepared loaf pans. Bake for 1 hour and 15 minutes or until toothpick inserted in center comes out clean. Cool in pans for 10 minutes. Turn bread onto wire rack to cool completely. Makes 2 loaves bread.

Barbara Schubert
Carmichael, California

Zucchini Bread

2½ cups shredded zucchini
3 eggs
1 cup vegetable oil
1½ cups sugar
1 teaspoon vanilla extract
3 cups flour
1 tablespoon cinnamon
1 teaspoon soda
½ teaspoon baking powder
1 teaspoon salt
½ cup chopped nuts
½ cup raisins, soaked in hot water
   and drained, or ½ cup chopped
   dates

Preheat oven to 350°F. Grease and flour two 9x6x3-inch loaf pans. Combine zucchini, eggs, oil, sugar and vanilla in mixing bowl; stir to blend. Sift together flour, cinnamon, soda, baking powder and salt. Add to zucchini mixture. Stir only until well moistened. Fold in nuts and raisins. Pour batter into prepared loaf pans. Bake for 50 to 60 minutes or until toothpick inserted in center comes out clean. Cool in pan for 10 minutes. Turn bread onto wire rack to cool completely. Makes 2 loaves.

Pineapple may be added for a delicious change.

Joan M. Cromer
Milan, Michigan

Pineapple-Zucchini Bread

3 eggs
1 cup oil
2 cups sugar
2 teaspoons vanilla extract
2 cups shredded zucchini
   or pumpkin
1 (8¼-ounce) can crushed
   pineapple, well drained
3 cups flour
2 teaspoons soda
1 teaspoon salt
¼ teaspoon baking powder
1½ teaspoons cinnamon
¾ teaspoon nutmeg
1 cup currants or raisins
1 cup chopped walnuts

In mixing bowl, beat eggs, oil, sugar and vanilla until thickened. Stir in zucchini, pineapple, flour, soda, salt, baking powder, cinnamon, nutmeg, currants and walnuts; mix well. Pour into 2 greased 9x5-inch loaf pans or 13x9-inch baking pan. Bake in 350°F. oven for 1 hour or until bread tests done.
Makes 2 loaves.

Virginia Wasczenski
Garden City, Michigan

Cinnamon Bubble Ring

1 box Pillsbury Hot Roll Mix
2 tablespoons margarine, softened
1 egg
2 tablespoons sugar
1 cup hot tap water
2 tablespoons melted margarine
2 cups sugar
2 tablespoons cinnamon

Empty flour mixture and yeast package into large bowl and mix well. Add softened margarine, egg, sugar and hot water. Stir until dough forms a ball. Knead until smooth (you may need to sprinkle flour on hands to reduce sticking). Cover dough and let rise for 5 minutes. While waiting, grease bundt pan, then melt margarine and pour into small bowl. Mix sugar and cinnamon in second small bowl. After the 5-minute rising, begin making small balls with dough. Roll each ball in margarine then in cinnamon-sugar mixture. Place each ball in bundt pan. Heat oven to 375°F., cover bundt pan with towel and place on top of heated oven for 30 minutes. Then bake for 15 to 20 minutes. Makes 4 to 6 servings.

Kathy Germond
Vernon Hills, Illinois

Cherry Coffee Cake

2 cups flour
¾ cup sugar
1 teaspoon baking powder
¼ teaspoon soda
¼ teaspoon salt
10 tablespoons butter or margarine, melted
½ cup milk
1 egg
1 teaspoon vanilla extract
¼ teaspoon lemon extract
1 (21 or 22-ounce) can cherry pie filling

Preheat oven to 350°F. Grease and flour 9x9-inch baking pan. In large bowl, combine 1½ cups flour with ½ cup sugar, baking powder, soda and salt. Add 8 tablespoons butter, milk, egg and vanilla. Beat until well mixed. Pour evenly into pan. In small bowl, combine remaining flour, sugar and butter. Stir until mixture resembles coarse crumbs. Sprinkle half the mixture on batter. Stir lemon extract into cherry pie filling. Spread over batter. Sprinkle with remaining crumb mixture. Bake for 1 hour or until top is lightly golden.
Makes one 9x9-inch cake.

Katherine Gephart
Pinckney, Michigan

Deutsch Kuchen

¾ cup plus 1 tablespoon sugar
¼ cup butter or margarine, softened
4 eggs
2 teaspoons vanilla extract
Pinch of salt
2 cups plus 2 tablespoons all-purpose flour
1 teaspoon baking powder
3 tablespoons milk
Raisins (optional)
Walnuts (optional)
Chocolate chips (optional)

Combine sugar, butter, eggs, vanilla and salt; mix well. Gradually add flour, baking powder and milk, stirring well. Stir in raisins, walnuts and chocolate chips. Pour batter into greased 10-inch bundt pan. Bake at 350°F. for 1 hour. Cool in pan for 10 minutes. Remove from pan and cool completely.
Makes one 10-inch cake.

Petra Oudehengel
West Germany

Crumble Coffee Cake

¾ cup shortening
1½ cups sugar
2 eggs
4 cups flour
5 teaspoons baking powder
1 teaspoon salt
1½ cups milk
1 teaspoon vanilla extract
1 cup sugar
4 teaspoons cinnamon
4 tablespoons flour
2 tablespoons (about) shortening

Preheat oven to 375°F. Grease and flour 13x9x2-inch pan. Cream ¾ cup shortening and 1½ cups sugar until light and fluffy. Add eggs and beat well. Combine 4 cups flour, baking powder and salt; add to creamed mixture alternately with milk, beginning and ending with flour mixture. Stir in vanilla. In separate bowl, combine 1 cup sugar, cinnamon, 4 tablespoons flour and 2 tablespoons shortening. Stir until mixture resembles coarse crumbs. Spread half the batter in prepared pan. Sprinkle half the crumb topping over batter. Pour remaining batter in pan then sprinkle with remaining crumb topping. Bake for 50 minutes.
Makes one 13x9-inch coffee cake.

Marguerite M. Hughes
South Lyon, Michigan

Monkey Bread (Coffee Cake)

1 cup firmly packed brown sugar
3 tablespoons milk
1 cup chopped walnuts
3 (11-ounce) cans biscuits
2 cups butter or margarine
½ cup sugar

Preheat oven to 400°F. Grease and flour 10-inch bundt pan. Mix brown sugar, milk and chopped walnuts together; sprinkle in bottom of prepared pan. Separate biscuits and stand on end around pan (like spokes in a wheel). Melt butter and mix with sugar. Pour mixture over top of biscuits. Bake in oven until golden brown. Invert bundt pan on cake plate and slowly remove pan.
Makes one 10-inch cake.

Linda Doyle
Hamburg, Michigan

Mexican Sweet Bread

3½ to 4 cups plain flour
1 (¼-ounce) package dry yeast
1 cup milk
¼ cup sugar
¼ cup shortening
1 teaspoon salt
2 eggs
⅔ cup flour
½ cup sugar
¼ cup shortening
2 egg yolks, beaten
¼ teaspoon vanilla extract

Combine 2 cups flour and yeast in large mixing bowl. In saucepan, heat milk, sugar, shortening and salt until warm, stirring constantly. Add to dry mixture. Beat in eggs at low speed for 30 seconds. Scrape bowl. Beat for 3 minutes at high speed. Stir in enough remaining flour to make a soft dough. Knead dough on lightly floured surface for 5 minutes or until smooth. Place in greased bowl; let rise in warm place until doubled in bulk. Preheat oven to 375°F. Divide dough into 16 balls. Pat to 3-inch circles. Place on greased baking sheet. Combine remaining ingredients for topping and mix until consistency of cookie dough. If too dry, add a small amount of egg white. Divide into 16 portions. Flatten each with palm of hand to a size a little larger than the 3-inch circles. Place on 3-inch circles, shaping to cover completely. Let rise until doubled in bulk. Bake in oven for 15 to 18 minutes.
Makes 16 servings.

For chocolate topping add 2 tablespoons cocoa to mixture.

Bonnie Villarreal
Belleville, Illinois

Shoo Fly Coffee Cake

¾ cup soft butter
1 cup sugar
3 eggs
1½ teaspoons vanilla extract
½ cup light molasses
1½ teaspoons baking powder
2 teaspoons soda
¼ teaspoon salt
3 cups flour
1⅓ cup sour cream
½ cup packed brown sugar
½ cup chopped nuts
1½ teaspoons cinnamon

Heat oven to 350°F. Grease tube pan, 10x4-inch baking pan, or two 9x5x3-inch loaf pans. Combine butter, sugar, eggs, vanilla and molasses in large mixing bowl. Beat on medium speed for 2 minutes. Stir together baking powder, soda, salt and flour; add to creamed mixture alternately with sour cream. Mix remaining ingredients for filling. For tube pan, pour ⅓ of the batter (about 2 cups) into pan. Sprinkle with 6 tablespoons filling. Repeat. For loaf pans, pour ¼ of the batter (1½ cups) into each pan. Sprinkle each with ¼ of the filling (about 5 tablespoons). Repeat. Bake for 55 to 60 minutes. Cool slightly in pan before removing.

Sara Ann Briggs
Okemos, Michigan

Potato Doughnuts

1 cup hot mashed potatoes
2 tablespoons butter, melted
1⅓ cups sugar
1 cup milk
3 eggs, beaten
½ teaspoon pure vanilla extract
4 cups flour
6 tablespoons baking powder
2 tablespoons nutmeg
½ teaspoon salt
Oil for deep frying
Confectioners' sugar

Combine first 6 ingredients. Sift together flour, baking powder, nutmeg and salt. Add to potato mixture and mix thoroughly. Chill for 2 hours. Pat out on floured board. Cut with doughnut cutter. Fry in hot oil at 375°F. until golden. Drain on paper towels. Sprinkle with confectioners' sugar. Serve either hot or cold.
Makes 1½ to 2 dozen doughnuts.

Marcia L. Johnson
Ionia, Michigan

Southern Doughnuts

2 eggs, separated
1 cup sugar
½ cup melted shortening
1 cup milk
1 tablespoon vanilla extract
4 cups self-rising flour
1 teaspoon cinnamon
Oil for deep frying
Chocolate icing
Coconut or nuts (optional)

Beat egg yolks. Add sugar and shortening; mix well. Add milk and vanilla. Blend in flour and cinnamon. Fold in stiffly beaten egg whites. Roll on floured board ⅛-inch thick. Cut with doughnut cutter. Fry in very hot oil until golden brown. Drain on absorbent paper. Frost with chocolate icing. Sprinkle with coconut or nuts.
Makes 2 dozen.

JoAnn Godwin
Adrian, Michigan

Banana-Oatmeal Muffins

½ cup sugar
½ cup butter or margarine
2 eggs
1 cup mashed bananas
¼ cup honey
1½ cups flour, sifted
1 teaspoon baking powder
1 teaspoon soda
¾ teaspoon salt
1 cup rolled oats

Cream together sugar and butter. Beat in eggs, bananas and honey. Stir in flour, baking powder, soda and salt until well blended. Stir in oats. Fill 16 to 20 muffin cups ⅔ full. Bake at 375°F. for 20 minutes. Cool on wire rack.
Makes 8 to 10 servings.

Delicious warm or cold as a snack, breakfast, luncheon or anytime.

Chris Peters
Denton, Texas

Blueberry-Orange Muffins

1 cup uncooked regular oats
1 cup orange juice
3 cups flour
4 teaspoons baking powder
1 cup sugar
½ teaspoon soda
1 teaspoon salt
1 cup oil
3 eggs, beaten
3 to 4 cups blueberries
¼ cup sugar
1 tablespoon cinnamon

Preheat oven to 400°F. Grease 12 muffin cups or line with paper liners. Combine oats and orange juice; set aside. Mix flour, baking powder, 1 cup sugar, soda and salt in large bowl. In separate bowl, beat together oil and eggs. Add oats/orange juice mixture. Make a hole in center of dry ingredients and pour in liquid mixture. Gently stir until just moistened. Fold in 3 to 4 cups blueberries. Fill prepared muffin cups ⅔ full. Combine ¼ cup sugar and cinnamon. Sprinkle over top of muffins. Bake for 15 to 20 minutes or until golden brown. Makes 30 muffins.

Sally A. Watson
Adrian, Michigan

Lempi's Bran Muffins

3 cups sugar
5 cups flour
9 cups Raisin Bran
1 quart buttermilk
1 cup oil
4 eggs
5 teaspoons soda
2 teaspoons salt
Cinnamon-sugar

Combine first 3 ingredients. In separate bowl, combine buttermilk, oil, eggs, soda and salt. Combine the two mixtures; stir only until mixed. Do not overstir! Grease muffin cups; fill ¾ full. Sprinkle top with cinnamon-sugar. Bake at 350°F. for 15 minutes for small muffins or for 20 minutes for regular muffins. Makes lots!

Mix will keep in refrigerator for several weeks.

Lempi Warner
Gainesville, Florida

Jackie's Six-Week Bran Muffins

4 cups unprocessed coarse bran
2 cups All Bran cereal
2 cups boiling water
2 cups sugar
½ cup firmly packed brown sugar
  or 2 cups honey
2 tablespoons molasses
1 cup shortening
1 quart buttermilk
4 eggs
5 cups unsifted wheat flour
5 teaspoons soda
1½ teaspoons salt
1   (16-ounce) package raisins

Mix bran, cereal, boiling water and sugar. Let stand until water is absorbed. Add brown sugar, molasses, shortening, buttermilk and eggs to bran; mix well. Add to combined dry ingredients. Stir in raisins. Place in covered container in refrigerator. (Keeps in refrigerator for 6 weeks.) Preheat oven to 375°F. Spoon muffin batter into greased muffin cups. Bake for 20 minutes.
Makes 96 muffins.

Ann Krueger
Canton, Michigan

Oatmeal-Coconut Muffins

1 cup rolled oats
1 cup buttermilk
1 cup sifted flour
1½ teaspoons baking powder
½ teaspoon salt
½ teaspoon soda
½ cup melted shortening or oil
½ cup firmly packed brown sugar
1 egg
¾ cup shredded coconut
4 tablespoons strawberry preserves

Preheat oven to 400°F. Grease 12 muffin cups; set aside. Combine oats and buttermilk in bowl; let soak for 30 minutes. Sift flour, baking powder, salt and soda in separate bowl. Blend together shortening, brown sugar, egg and coconut in separate bowl. Add to oatmeal mixture; blend well. Stir in dry ingredients, mixing only enough to moisten. Spoon batter into prepared muffin cups. Place 1 teaspoon preserves in center of each muffin and cover with small amount of batter. Bake for 20 minutes.
Makes 12 muffins.

Christopher McCormick
Hendersonville, Tennessee

Sunshine Muffins

1 stick of margarine
¾ cup sugar
1 large egg
1 teaspoon vanilla extract
3 small or 2 large bananas, mashed
1 small can crushed pineapple, drained
½ cup raisins
1½ cups flour
1 teaspoon soda
½ teaspoon baking powder
1 teaspoon cinnamon

Mix margarine and sugar thoroughly. Add egg, vanilla, bananas, pineapple, raisins; mix well. In separate bowl, mix flour, soda, baking powder and cinnamon. Combine all ingredients together. Spray muffin cups with Pam. Fill ¾ full. Bake at 350°F. for 20 minutes or until golden brown. Cool and enjoy.
Makes 12 to 15 muffins.

Dona Gerstein
Valdosta, Georgia

Baked Apple Pancake

1 cup flour
1 cup milk
4 eggs, slightly beaten
Pinch of nutmeg
6 tablespoons butter
2 large apples, peeled and
    thinly sliced
Cinnamon

Preheat oven to 425°F. Combine flour, milk, eggs and nutmeg. Beat lightly, leaving batter a bit lumpy. Melt butter in two 9-inch pie pans or one 15x9x2-inch pan in oven. Pour hot melted butter in batter. Pour batter into pans and top with apples. Sprinkle generously with cinnamon. Bake in oven for 15 to 20 minutes.

Linda Jenks
Winchester, Massachusetts

English Pancakes

¼ cup oil
1 cup flour
1 teaspoon baking powder
1 cup milk
½ teaspoon salt
1 egg
Sugar
Orange juice

Heat oil in skillet. Combine flour, baking powder, milk, salt and egg in bowl; mix well. Pour about ½ cup of mixture at a time into hot oil. Cook until golden brown around edges then turn and cook until other side is golden brown. Remove from pan and drain on paper towel. Place on plate; sprinkle with sugar and cover with orange juice. Makes 4 to 6 pancakes.

Elaine Allen
Hermitage, Tennessee

Jewish Potato Pancakes

1 pound potatoes
¼ pound onions
1 egg
¾ cup matzo meal
¼ teaspoon salt
¼ teaspoon pepper
Oil for frying
Applesauce or sour cream

Grate potatoes and onions in bowl. Drain all juice. Add egg, matzo meal, salt and pepper; mix well. Shape into flat pancakes. Heat ½ inch oil in skillet. Place 1 or 2 pancakes in skillet; brown well on one side then turn. Repeat with remaining batter. Serve hot with cold applesauce or sour cream.
Makes 4 servings.

Dona Gerstein
Valdosta, Georgia

Pumpkin Pancakes

2 cups flour
2 tablespoons brown sugar
1 tablespoon baking powder
1 teaspoon salt
2 teaspoons ground cinnamon
½ teaspoon ground nutmeg
¼ teaspoon ground ginger
1½ cups milk
½ cup pumpkin
2 tablespoons vegetable oil
Whipped cream or maple syrup

Combine dry ingredients in mixing bowl; set aside. In separate bowl, blend milk, pumpkin and vegetable oil. Slowly stir into dry ingredients and beat until smooth. Pour ¼ cup batter at a time onto hot lightly greased griddle or skillet. Cook, turning once, until lightly browned on both sides. Top with whipped cream or maple syrup. Makes about 20 pancakes.

Margaret Clise
Martinsburg, West Virginia

Strawberry Pancakes

2 cups flour
½ teaspoon salt
2 teaspoons soda
2 tablespoons brown sugar
3 eggs
3 cups buttermilk
¼ cup melted butter
½ teaspoon vanilla extract

Sift together flour, salt, soda and brown sugar. In separate bowl, beat eggs; add buttermilk, melted butter and vanilla. Add liquid ingredients to dry ingredients and beat until just smooth. Bake 5-inch hotcakes on medium griddle. Remove to towel covered baking sheet and keep warm. Spread each pancake with 1 tablespoon Strawberry Creme. Assemble into serving-size stacks. Pour Strawberry Syrup over stacks and serve.
Makes 6 servings for brunch or desserts.

Strawberry Creme

4 ounces whipped cream cheese
2 cups marshmallow creme
½ cup soft butter
½ cup strawberry topping (for ice cream sundaes)

Combine cream cheese, marshmallow creme, butter and strawberry topping; beat until smooth.

Strawberry Syrup

1 cup corn syrup
¼ cup water
½ cup strawberry topping

Bring corn syrup, water and strawberry topping to a boil.

I won $1,000 in a Kraft Recipe Contest with this entry.

Bev Switzer
Ann Arbor, Michigan

German Pretzels

2 cups milk
1 cup sugar
1 cup shortening
2 yeast cakes (or dry yeast)
¼ cup warm water
12 cups flour
2 eggs, beaten
1½ teaspoons baking powder
1½ teaspoons salt
1 quart hot water
1 teaspoon lye

Scald milk. Add sugar and shortening; mix. Cool to lukewarm. Dissolve yeast in warm water and add to cooled milk. Stir in about half of flour. Let rise until bubbly. Add beaten eggs, remaining flour, baking powder and salt. Let rise until double. Punch down dough and shape into pretzels. Let rise until light. Drop each pretzel into a solution of 1-quart hot water and 1 teaspoon lye. Place on a lightly greased cookie sheet. Sprinkle with coarse salt. Bake at 550°F. until brown.
Makes 3 dozen or more.

Sylvia Miller
Colorado Springs, Colorado

Desserts

Desserts

Bavarian Apple Torte

½ cup margarine, softened
⅓ cup sugar
¼ teaspoon vanilla extract
1 cup flour
1 (8-ounce) package cream cheese, softened
¼ cup sugar
1 egg
½ teaspoon vanilla extract
4 cups (5 or 6) peeled apple slices
⅓ cup sugar
½ teaspoon ground cinnamon
¼ cup sliced almonds

Cream together margarine and ⅓ cup sugar until light and fluffy. Blend in ¼ teaspoon vanilla. Add flour and mix well. Spread dough in bottom and 1½ inches up sides of 9-inch square pan. Combine cream cheese and ¼ cup sugar; mix well. Blend in egg and ½ teaspoon vanilla. Pour into pastry-lined pan. Toss apples with remaining ⅓ cup sugar and cinnamon. Spoon over cream cheese layer. Sprinkle with almonds. Bake at 450°F. for 10 minutes. Reduce temperature to 400°F.; bake for 25 minutes longer. Cool completely. Cut into squares.
Makes 12 servings.

Rita Bertram
Norwalk, Ohio

Cinnamon Apples

6 medium apples
6 wooden skewers
1⅓ cups sugar
2 cups light corn syrup
¼ teaspoon red food coloring
10 drops of oil of cinnamon

Wash and dry apples; remove stems. Insert skewers into blossom-end of each apple. Combine sugar, corn syrup and food coloring in top of double boiler. Cook directly over low heat stirring until sugar dissolves, about 4 minutes. Cover and cook slowly for 8 minutes. Uncover; cook, without stirring, to hard-crack stage (300°). Stir in flavoring. Place top of double boiler over boiling water in lower pan. Dip each apple in syrup to coat, twirling apple to coat evenly. Let excess syrup drip back into pan. Place apples on buttered cookie sheet. If syrup thickens, reheat over direct heat.
Makes 6 servings.

Bob Totte
Ann Arbor, Michigan

Campfire Applesauce

4 apples, peeled, cored and chopped
½ cup water
1 (4-ounce) package cinnamon candy

Combine all ingredients in medium saucepan. Bring to a boil. Reduce heat and cook for 20 minutes or until apples are tender and candy melts. Stir frequently to mash apples.
Makes 4 servings.

Ronnie McMichael
Dallas, Texas

◀Recipes for this photograph on pages 171, 179, 193 and 202.

Caramel Bananas With Rum

1⅓ cups firmly packed brown sugar
¼ cup whipping cream
2 tablespoons butter or margarine
⅓ cup rum
1 cup whipping cream
2 tablespoons brown sugar
8 medium bananas
½ cup sliced almonds

Combine 1⅓ cups brown sugar, ¼ cup whipping cream and butter in small saucepan. Cook over low heat, stirring constantly, until sugar dissolves. Remove from heat and stir in rum. Cover and refrigerate for 1 hour. Beat 1 cup whipping cream until soft peaks form; gradually add 2 tablespoons brown sugar, beating until stiff peaks form. Cut each banana in half crosswise; cut each half lengthwise. Place bananas in individual dessert plates; top with sauce. Garnish each serving with a dollop of whipped cream and sliced almonds.
Makes 8 servings.

Norma Serrano
Aurora, Illinois

Blueberry Torte

1½ cups graham cracker crumbs
¼ cup sugar
½ cup butter or margarine, melted
1 (8-ounce) package cream cheese, softened
2 eggs
½ cup sugar
1 tablespoon vanilla extract
¼ teaspoon salt
1 (15-ounce) can blueberries, drained
½ cup sugar
2 tablespoons cornstarch
2 teaspoons lemon juice
¼ teaspoon salt
1 tablespoon butter or margarine

Combine graham cracker crumbs, ¼ cup sugar and ½ cup melted butter in small mixing bowl; stir well. Press mixture into greased 10-inch pie plate. Combine cream cheese, eggs, ½ cup sugar, vanilla and ¼ teaspoon salt in medium mixing bowl; beat until light and fluffy. Spoon mixture into prepared crust. Bake at 375°F. for 25 minutes or until set. Cool to room temperature. Combine blueberries, ½ cup sugar, cornstarch, lemon juice and ¼ teaspoon salt in small saucepan, stirring well. Bring to a boil. Reduce heat and simmer, stirring constantly, for 3 minutes or until mixture thickens. Remove from heat and stir in 1 tablespoon butter. Spoon mixture over cream cheese layer. Refrigerate for 8 hours. Cut into wedges to serve.
Makes 8 servings.

Lucy Kay Gottsche
Lufkin, Texas

Quick Blender Mousse

4 egg whites, at room temperature
1 (6-ounce) package chocolate chips
5 tablespoons boiling water or coffee
4 egg yolks
3 teaspoons vanilla extract or 2 tablespoons rum

Beat egg whites until stiff but not dry. Place chocolate chips in blender container. Process to break pieces up. Add water. Blend until smooth. Add egg yolks and vanilla; blend for 1 minute. Pour slowly over egg whites, folding in gently. Spoon into individual serving dishes or 1-quart serving dish. Refrigerate for about 1 hour or until firm.
Makes 8 to 10 servings.

Becky Belknap
Ann Arbor, Michigan

Broken Glass Dessert

24 graham crackers, crushed
¼ cup sugar
½ cup butter or margarine, melted
1 (3-ounce) package orange gelatin
3 cups boiling water, divided
3 cups cold water, divided
1 (3-ounce) package lime gelatin
1 (3-ounce) package lemon gelatin
1 (3-ounce) package cherry gelatin
1 envelope unflavored gelatin
¼ cup cold water
1 cup pineapple juice
2 cups whipping cream
½ cup sugar
1 teaspoon vanilla extract

Combine graham cracker crumbs, ¼ cup sugar and butter in small mixing bowl; stir well. Press ⅔ of the crumb mixture into bottom of greased 13x9x2-inch baking pan; set pan aside. Reserve remaining crumb mixture for topping. Prepare orange gelatin according to package directions, using ¾ cup boiling water and ¾ cup cold water. Chill until firm. Repeat procedure with lime, lemon and cherry gelatins and remaining 2¼ cups boiling water and cold water. Soften unflavored gelatin in ¼ cup cold water in small saucepan; add pineapple juice. Cook over low heat, stirring constantly, for 1 minute or until gelatin dissolves. Chill until mixture reaches consistency of unbeaten egg white. Beat whipping cream until soft peaks form; gradually add remaining ½ cup sugar and vanilla, beating until stiff peaks form. Fold into pineapple mixture. Cut gelatins into 1-inch cubes; fold into whipped cream mixture. Spoon mixture into prepared pan. Sprinkle with reserved crumb mixture. Chill for 6 to 8 hours. Cut into squares to serve.
Makes 15 servings.

Donna Calta
Bowling Green, Kentucky

Chocolate Paté

2 (4-ounce) packages German's sweet chocolate
⅓ cup butter or margarine
2 tablespoons dark rum or 1 teaspoon vanilla extract
1 tablespoon instant coffee granules
2 eggs, beaten
1½ cups finely ground walnuts
2 cups whipping cream, whipped

Line 8x4x3-inch loaf pan with plastic wrap; set aside. Combine chocolate and butter in small saucepan. Cook over low heat, stirring constantly, until mixture melts. Add rum and coffee granules, stirring until coffee dissolves. Stir ¼ of the hot mixture into beaten eggs; add to remaining hot mixture, stirring constantly. Cook over low heat until thickened. Transfer mixture to large mixing bowl; cool to room temperature. Stir in walnuts; fold in whipped cream. Spoon mixture into prepared pan. Chill overnight. Turn paté onto serving platter. Garnish with additional whipped cream and chocolate curls.
Makes 16 servings.

Barbara Caputo
Durham, North Carolina

Chocolate-Peanut Butter Pizza

½ cup sugar
½ cup brown sugar
½ cup margarine
½ cup peanut butter
½ teaspoon vanilla extract
1 egg
1½ cups all-purpose flour
2 cups miniature marshmallows
1 (6-ounce) package chocolate chips

Preheat oven to 375°F. Cream together first 6 ingredients. Stir in flour and mix well. Press dough evenly over bottom of 12-inch or 14-inch ungreased pizza pan. Be sure to form a rim along outside edge. Bake in 375°F. oven for 10 minutes. Remove from oven and sprinkle with marshmallows and chocolate chips. Return to oven and continue to bake for 5 to 8 minutes longer or until lightly browned. Cool, then cut into wedges with sharp knife.
Makes 12 servings.

Brenadette A. Schaub
Spokane, Washington

Chocolatissimo

10 (1-ounce) squares semisweet
    chocolate, broken up
1 teaspoon instant coffee granules
1¼ cups unsalted butter or
    margarine, softened
1¼ cups sugar
10 eggs, separated
Confectioners' sugar

Melt chocolate with coffee in top of double boiler or bowl set over hot, not boiling, water. Stir until smooth; cool. In very large bowl, cream butter and sugar. Add cooled chocolate; blend well. Add egg yolks, 1 at a time, beating well after each addition, beating for 15 minutes in all. Beat egg whites until stiff, but not dry. Fold gently into chocolate mixture. Refrigerate ½ cup mixture. Pour remaining mixture into greased (bottom only) 9-inch springform pan. Bake in preheated 350°F. oven for 50 minutes. Cool completely in pan on wire rack. (The cake will sink in middle.) Spread reserved chocolate mixture over top. Cover and chill overnight. Garnish with confectioners' sugar.
Makes 12 servings.

Joanne Cone
Elkridge, Maryland

Heavenly Surprise

1½ cups graham cracker crumbs
1 (2-ounce) package walnuts,
    finely chopped
½ cup butter or margarine, melted
1 (8-ounce) package cream cheese,
    softened
2 tablespoons milk
1 (8-ounce) carton frozen whipped
    topping, thawed
2 (4-ounce) packages instant
    chocolate pudding
3 cups milk

Combine graham cracker crumbs, walnuts and butter; stir well. Press mixture evenly into greased 13x9x2-inch baking pan, reserving 1 tablespoon for garnish. Bake at 350°F. for 5 minutes; cool completely. Beat cream cheese and 2 tablespoons milk until light and fluffy; fold in half the whipped topping. Spoon mixture evenly over crust. Prepare pudding according to package directions, using 3 cups milk. Spoon evenly over cream cheese mixture. Spread remaining whipped topping over pudding. Sprinkle with reserved crumb mixture. Refrigerate for 4 to 6 hours. Cut into squares to serve.
Makes 12 to 16 servings.

Any flavor pudding may be used.

Terri Romyananda
Worthington, Ohio

Oreo Cake

2 (6-ounce) packages chocolate
    pudding
1 (1½-pound) package Oreo cookies,
    crumbled
1 cup confectioners' sugar
1 (12-ounce) carton Cool Whip
1 (8-ounce) package cream cheese,
    softened

Prepare pudding according to package directions. Reserve ⅓ of the crumbled Oreo cookies. Line bottom of 9x13-inch pan with ⅔ of the cookie crumbs. Mix confectioners' sugar, ⅔ of the Cool Whip and cream cheese until smooth. Spread over Oreo crumb crust in cake pan. Spread chocolate pudding over Cool Whip mixture. Spread remaining ⅓ of the Cool Whip over top of pudding. Sprinkle remaining cookie crumbs across the top and it is ready to serve or chill until serving.
Makes 12 to 15 servings.

Peg Henerdine
Champaign, Illinois

Ice Cream Cookie Sandwiches

2 cups butter or margarine,
  softened
1 cup firmly packed brown sugar
½ cup sugar
2 eggs
1 teaspoon vanilla extract
2¾ cups all-purpose flour
1 teaspoon soda
1 teaspoon salt
1 (12-ounce) package semisweet
  chocolate chips
1 (6-ounce) package Heath Bits of
  Brickle (optional)
1 cup pecans or walnuts (optional)
½ gallon ice cream, softened
  (any flavor)

Cream butter in large mixing bowl; add sugars, eggs and vanilla, beating until light and fluffy. Combine flour, soda and salt; fold into creamed mixture. Stir in chocolate chips, Bits of Brickle and pecans. Spoon batter onto ungreased cookie sheets, using about ⅓ cup batter for each cookie. Bake at 275°F. for 20 to 25 minutes or until lightly browned but still soft. Remove from cookie sheets and cool completely on wire racks. Spoon about 1 cup ice cream on half the cookies; top with remaining cookies. Wrap each cookie individually with plastic wrap. Store in freezer.
Makes 6 sandwich cookies.

Barbie Monaghan
Ann Arbor, Michigan

Lorna Doone Dessert

1 (16-ounce) package Lorna Doone
  cookies, crushed
½ cup butter or margarine, melted
2 (3¼-ounce) packages instant
  vanilla pudding
3 cups milk
1 quart vanilla ice cream, softened
1 (8-ounce) carton frozen whipped
  topping, thawed
4 chocolate-covered toffee bars,
  crushed

Combine crushed cookies and butter; mix well. Press evenly into greased 13x9x2-inch baking dish. Set aside. Prepare pudding according to package directions, using 3 cups milk. Add ice cream, beating just until blended. Spoon mixture into prepared pan. Spread whipped topping over pudding; sprinkle with crushed toffee bars. Chill for 3 hours to overnight.
Makes 12 to 16 servings.

Cindy Janis
Ferndale, Michigan

Orange Refrigerator Dessert

½ (16-ounce) angel food cake,
  broken into 1-inch pieces
1 envelope unflavored gelatin
¼ cup cold water
¼ cup boiling water
1 cup orange juice
1 cup sugar
2 cups whipping cream, whipped
Grated orange rind

Place cake in 13x9x2-inch baking pan; set aside. Soften gelatin in cold water. Add boiling water, stirring until gelatin dissolves. Combine orange juice and sugar; add to gelatin mixture, stirring well. Chill until mixture reaches consistency of unbeaten egg white. Beat at high speed of electric mixer until foamy. Fold in whipped cream. Pour mixture evenly over reserved cake. Sprinkle with orange rind. Chill until set.
Makes 12 servings.

John P. Keith
Sacramento, California

Fruit Spectacular Platter Pizza

1 (18-ounce) package refrigerated
sugar cookie dough
1 (8-ounce) package cream cheese,
softened
1 (4-ounce) carton frozen whipped
topping, thawed
2 cups fresh strawberries, halved
2 to 3 medium bananas, peeled and
sliced
1 (16-ounce) can sliced peaches,
drained
1 (8-ounce) can pineapple chunks,
drained
1 cup fresh blueberries
½ cup sugar
1 tablespoon cornstarch
Dash of salt
½ cup orange juice
¼ cup water
2 tablespoons lemon juice
½ teaspoon grated orange rind

Cut cookie dough into ⅛-inch slices. Arrange slices on greased 14-inch pizza pan; press together to seal. Bake at 350°F. for 10 to 12 minutes or until edges are lightly browned. Cool completely. Beat cream cheese until light and fluffy; stir in whipped topping. Spread mixture evenly over crust. Arrange fruit over cream cheese mixture. Combine sugar, cornstarch and salt in small saucepan; stir well. Add orange juice, water and lemon juice. Cook over medium heat, stirring constantly, until mixture is thickened and bubbly. Boil for 1 minute longer. Remove from heat and stir in orange rind. Cool. Pour mixture over fruit. Cut into wedges to serve.
Makes 10 servings.

Nancy Holtz
Virginia Beach, Virginia

Raspberry Delight

40 vanilla wafers, crushed
¾ cup butter or margarine, softened
1 (3-ounce) package cream cheese,
softened
2 cups confectioners' sugar
1 (3-ounce) package chopped
pecans
1 (3-ounce) package raspberry
gelatin
1 cup boiling water
2 (10-ounce) packages frozen
raspberries
1½ cups whipping cream, whipped

Sprinkle crushed vanilla wafers in greased 13x9x2-inch baking pan, reserving ¼ cup crumbs for topping. Beat butter and cream cheese until light and fluffy; add confectioners' sugar, beating well. Spread mixture over vanilla wafer crumbs; sprinkle with pecans. Dissolve gelatin in boiling water; add frozen raspberries, stirring well. Chill until thickened. Spoon mixture evenly over pecans. Spread whipped cream over raspberry mixture; sprinkle with reserved vanilla wafer crumbs. Refrigerate overnight.
Makes 12 to 15 servings.

Nancy Adamson
Denton, Texas

Strawberries Susan

4 bananas, sliced
2 tablespoons currant jelly, melted
Sugar to taste
1 quart strawberries
1 cup heavy cream
4 tablespoons sugar
6 almond macaroons
Slivered almonds (optional)

Slice bananas and place in bottom of 9x13-inch glass dish. Melt currant jelly and add sugar to taste. Spread over bananas. Crush strawberries and layer over banana mixture. Whip heavy cream, adding 4 tablespoons sugar. Spread over strawberries. Crumble almond macaroons and sprinkle over whipped cream. Top with slivered almonds.
Makes 12 servings.

Sandra Gast-Kolecki
Whitmore Lake, Michigan

Sunshine Pine

1 whole fresh pineapple
½ cup orange liqueur, Brandy or rum
¼ cup lemon juice
2 egg whites
2 tablespoons sugar
Whipped cream
8 strawberries, halved
1 kiwi, peeled and sliced

Slice pineapple in half lengthwise. Scoop out pulp, leaving ½-inch shell; cut pulp into 1-inch cubes. Combine pulp, liqueur and lemon juice; cover and refrigerate for 2 hours. Drain. Spoon pineapple back into shells. Beat egg whites until foamy; gradually add sugar, beating until stiff peaks form. Spoon meringue over pineapple, sealing to edge of pineapple shell. Bake at 400°F. for 2 minutes or until meringue is lightly browned. Place on individual dessert plates. Garnish each with whipped cream, strawberry halves and sliced kiwi.
Makes 2 servings.

David and Sallyanne Robin
Sydney, Australia

Blender Cheesecake

15 graham cracker sections
½ cup sugar
½ teaspoon cinnamon
¼ cup melted butter
2 eggs
½ cup sugar
2 teaspoons vanilla extract
1½ cups sour cream
2 (8-ounce) packages cream cheese, sliced
2 tablespoons melted butter

Break graham crackers into blender, 5 at a time. Blend for 6 minutes. Place in bowl; add sugar, cinnamon and melted butter. Stir until completely moistened. Press into buttered 9-inch springform pan. Make sure crust goes up side of pan a bit, to prevent filling from seeping through. Bake in preheated 400°F. oven for 6 minutes. Meanwhile, put eggs, sugar, vanilla and sour cream in blender; blend. With motor running, remove lid and add cream cheese by slices, then add butter. Pour slowly into baked crust and bake at 350°F. for 35 minutes. Center of cake should be firm. Remove and allow to cool. Chill thoroughly before serving. Cake may be served with strawberries or blueberries.
Makes one 9-inch cheesecake.

For a larger cake, double recipe making a single batch at a time. Bake for 1 hour and 15 minutes.

Chris Seufert
Ypsilanti, Michigan

Chocolate Cheesecake

1 cup graham cracker crumbs
½ cup ground walnuts
¼ cup plus 2 tablespoons butter or
 margarine, melted
2 tablespoons sugar
3 (8-ounce) packages cream cheese,
 softened
1 cup sour cream
1 cup sugar
3 eggs
1 (6-ounce) package semisweet
 chocolate chips, melted
4 (1-ounce) squares semisweet
 chocolate
¼ cup sour cream

Combine graham cracker crumbs, walnuts, butter and 2 tablespoons sugar; mix well. Press mixture onto bottom and sides of 9-inch springform pan. Bake at 325°F. for 10 minutes. Beat cream cheese, 1 cup sour cream and 1 cup sugar until light and fluffy. Add eggs, 1 at a time, beating well after each addition. Stir in melted chocolate chips. Spoon into prepared crust. Bake at 325°F. for 1 hour. Turn oven off and let cheesecake cool completely in oven, leaving oven door open. Loosen side of pan and remove. Melt semisweet chocolate; add ¼ cup sour cream, stirring well. Spread over cooled cheesecake. Makes one 9-inch cheesecake.

Nancy deJolsvay
Hopkins, Minnesota

Frozen Mocha Cheesecake

1¼ cups chocolate wafer cookie
 crumbs
¼ cup sugar
¼ cup butter or margarine, melted
1 (8-ounce) package cream cheese,
 softened
1 (14-ounce) can sweetened
 condensed milk
⅔ cup chocolate syrup
2 tablespoons instant coffee granules
1 teaspoon hot water
1 cup whipping cream, whipped
Chocolate curls (optional)

Combine cookie crumbs, sugar and butter in small mixing bowl; stir well. Press mixture onto bottom and sides of 9-inch springform pan. Chill. Beat cream cheese until light and fluffy in large mixing bowl; add condensed milk and syrup, beating well. Dissolve coffee in hot water. Add to cream cheese mixture, stirring well. Fold in whipped cream. Spoon mixture into prepared pan. Cover and freeze for 6 hours or overnight. Garnish with chocolate curls.
Makes 12 to 16 servings.

Polly Minick
Ann Arbor, Michigan

Old-Fashioned Cheesecake

1⅓ cups graham cracker crumbs
¼ cup sugar
¼ cup plus 2 tablespoons butter or
 margarine, melted
2 (8-ounce) packages cream cheese,
 softened
1 cup sugar
1 teaspoon grated lemon rind
3 eggs
1 cup sour cream
2 tablespoons sugar
1 teaspoon vanilla extract

Combine graham cracker crumbs, ¼ cup sugar and butter; mix well. Press mixture into bottom and halfway up sides of 9-inch springform pan. Set aside. Beat cream cheese until light and fluffy; gradually add 1 cup sugar and lemon rind, beating well. Add eggs, 1 at a time, beating well after each addition. Pour into prepared pan. Bake at 300°F. for 1 hour. Turn oven off and let cheesecake cool in oven for 30 minutes, leaving oven door open. Combine sour cream, sugar and vanilla; stir well. Spread over cheesecake. Let cheesecake cool in oven for 30 minutes longer, leaving oven door open. Chill thoroughly. Makes one 9-inch cheesecake.

Mary Butterfield
St. Cloud, Minnesota

Baked Custard (Low-Cal)

2 teaspoons Pillsbury Sweet-10
  or ⅓ cup Sprinkle Sweet
¼ teaspoon salt
1 teaspoon vanilla extract
3 eggs, slightly beaten
2½ cups skim milk
Dash of nutmeg

In large bowl, blend sweetener, salt, vanilla and eggs. Gradually stir in milk. Pour into six 6-ounce custard cups. Sprinkle with nutmeg. Place custard cups in 13x9-inch pan with about 1-inch hot water. Bake at 350°F. for 45 to 50 minutes or until knife inserted near center comes out clean. Serve warm or chilled.
Makes 6 servings.

Sue Dawson
Ann Arbor, Michigan

Blintz Soufflé

6 tablespoons butter or margarine
12 frozen cheese blintzes
6 eggs
1½ cups sour cream
1½ teaspoons vanilla extract
½ cup sugar
3 tablespoons orange juice
1 teaspoon salt

Melt butter in 13x9x2-inch baking dish. Roll blintzes in melted butter and arrange in baking dish. Beat remaining ingredients together; pour over blintzes. Bake at 350°F. for 1 hour and 10 minutes or until set, puffy and golden brown.
Makes 8 servings.

Lois Kane
Tucson, Arizona

Lemon Soufflé

4 eggs, separated
½ cup sugar
½ cup lemon juice
2 tablespoons all-purpose flour
1 teaspoon baking powder
Pinch of salt

Lightly butter 1½-quart soufflé dish; sprinkle with sugar. Cut a piece of aluminum foil long enough to circle dish, allowing a 1-inch overlap. Fold foil lengthwise into thirds and lightly butter one side. Wrap foil around dish, buttered-side against dish, allowing it to extend 2 inches above rim. Secure foil with string. Set prepared dish aside. Combine egg yolks, sugar, lemon juice, flour and baking powder in large mixing bowl; beat well. Combine egg whites and salt in large mixing bowl; beat until stiff but not dry. Stir about ¼ of the beaten egg whites into yolk mixture. Fold remaining egg whites gently into yolk mixture. Spoon mixture into prepared soufflé dish. Bake at 350°F. for 30 to 35 minutes or until puffed and golden brown. Remove collar; serve immediately.
Makes 6 servings.

Polly Minick
Ann Arbor, Michigan

Raisin-Honey Bread Pudding

4 cups white bread cubes
½ cup honey
4 cups milk
5 eggs, beaten
¼ cup sugar
2 teaspoons vanilla extract
¼ teaspoon salt
¾ cup raisins
Ground nutmeg

Combine bread and honey in large saucepan. Cook over low heat, stirring constantly for 2 to 3 minutes or until honey is absorbed. Combine milk, eggs, sugar, vanilla and salt; stir well. Add milk mixture and raisins to bread; stir well. Spoon mixture into greased 1½-quart baking dish. Sprinkle with nutmeg. Place baking dish in larger dish; add hot water to a depth of 1 inch. Bake at 350°F. for 1 hour or until knife inserted in center comes out clean.
Makes 6 to 8 servings.

Jolene Kempphinen
Drummond Island, Michigan

New Orleans Bread Pudding

½ (16-ounce) loaf French or Italian bread, cut into ½-inch cubes
3 cups milk
2 eggs
1 cup sugar
1½ teaspoons vanilla extract
⅛ teaspoon salt
⅔ cup raisins
2 tablespoons butter or margarine, melted
Bourbon sauce (recipe follows)

Combine bread and milk in large mixing bowl; stir well. Set aside for 5 minutes. Combine eggs, sugar, vanilla and salt in medium mixing bowl; beat well. Add to bread mixture; stir well. Stir in raisins. Spoon mixture into greased 8-inch square baking pan. Drizzle butter over top. Bake at 350°F. for 1 hour or until a knife inserted in center comes out clean. Serve warm or at room temperature with Bourbon Sauce.
Makes 8 servings.

Bourbon Sauce

½ cup butter or margarine
1 cup sugar
1 egg
½ cup Bourbon

Melt butter in top of double boiler over simmering water. Add sugar and egg; cook, stirring constantly for 5 minutes or until thickened. Remove from heat and let cool completely. Stir in Bourbon.
Makes about 1½ cups.

Teresa Faeth
Poland, Ohio

Noodle Pudding

1 (16-ounce) package egg noodles
1 cup cottage cheese
1 cup sour cream
½ cup butter or margarine, melted
4 egg yolks, beaten
2 medium apples, peeled, cored and chopped
¼ cup raisins
1 teaspoon vanilla extract
½ teaspoon grated lemon rind
½ teaspoon grated orange rind
Pinch of salt
4 egg whites

Cook noodles according to package directions; drain. Combine noodles, cottage cheese, sour cream, butter, egg yolks, apples, raisins, vanilla, grated rinds and salt; stir well. Beat egg whites until stiff peaks form; fold into noodle mixture. Spoon mixture into greased 13x9x2-inch baking dish. Bake at 350°F. for 1 hour or until set. Serve warm.
Makes 12 servings.

Miriam Shaw
Ann Arbor, Michigan

Hot Fudge

¾ cup water
½ cup sugar
1 (4-ounce) package chocolate
  pudding
1 tablespoon butter or margarine

Combine water, sugar and pudding in small saucepan. Bring to a boil. Cook, stirring constantly, until mixture thickens. Remove from heat and stir in butter. Serve warm over ice cream.
Makes about 1 cup.

Betsy Kanitz
Milan, Michigan

Hot Fudge Ice Cream Sauce

1 cup sugar
3 tablespoons cornstarch
3 tablespoons cocoa
¼ teaspoon salt
1 cup boiling water
3 tablespoons butter or margarine
1 teaspoon vanilla extract
½ cup peanut butter (optional)

Mix sugar, cornstarch, cocoa and salt in small saucepan. Add water; cook over medium heat for 10 minutes or until thick and glossy, stirring constantly. Remove from heat. Add butter, vanilla and peanut butter; stir well. Serve warm over ice cream.
Makes 6 to 8 servings.

Kim Swanson
Whitmore Lake, Michigan

Cranberry Ice

4 cups fresh cranberries
2 cups water
2 cups sugar
2 cups water
¼ cup lemon juice

Combine cranberries and 2 cups water in medium saucepan. Bring to a boil. Cook over medium heat for 10 minutes. Press mixture through sieve, discarding skins. Combine cranberry mixture, sugar, 2 cups water and lemon juice; stir well. Pour mixture into 9-inch square baking dish. Freeze until firm. Remove from freezer; beat at high speed of electric mixer until slushy. Return to freezer and freeze until firm.
Makes about 1½ quarts.

Barbara J. Baum
North Tonawanda, New York

Snow Cream

12 cups snow
¼ to ½ cup evaporated milk
⅓ to ½ cup cocoa
2 teaspoons vanilla extract
Pinch of salt
Sugar to taste

Combine all ingredients; stir well. Serve immediately or freeze.
Makes about 10 servings.

Scrape off top inch of snow and use only clean snow underneath.

Earnestene Findley
Bellefontaine, Ohio

Chocolate-Peanut Butter Cookie Ice Cream

1 (14-ounce) can sweetened
    condensed milk
¾ cup chocolate syrup
¾ cup peanut butter
¾ cup chopped peanuts
2 cups crushed Oreo cookies
2 cups heavy cream, whipped

Combine sweetened condensed milk, chocolate syrup, peanut butter, peanuts and crushed cookies; mix well. Fold in whipped cream. Pour mixture into 2½-quart freezer container. Cover and freeze overnight. Makes about 2 quarts.

Susie Monaghan
Ann Arbor, Michigan

Coffee Ice Cream

2½ cups sugar
3 tablespoons instant coffee granules
2 tablespoons all-purpose flour
¼ teaspoon salt
2½ cups milk
2½ cups strong brewed coffee
6 egg yolks, beaten
5 cups whipping cream
⅓ cup Tia Maria or Kahlua (optional)
2 tablespoons vanilla extract

Combine sugar, coffee granules, flour and salt in small Dutch oven; stir well. Add milk and coffee, stirring well. Cook over low heat, stirring constantly, until slightly thickened. Gradually stir about 1 cup hot mixture into egg yolks; add to remaining hot mixture, stirring constantly. Cook for 1 minute. Chill thoroughly. Stir in cream, liqueur and vanilla. Pour mixture into container of 1-gallon electric or hand-turned ice cream freezer. Freeze according to freezer manufacturer's directions.
Makes about 1 gallon.

Anne Rowland
Greenville, Texas

Mocha Ice Cream Cake

1 (3-ounce) package ladyfingers
½ gallon coffee ice cream, softened
1 quart chocolate ice cream, softened
2 tablespoons instant coffee granules
½ cup coffee-flavored liqueur
6 chocolate-covered toffee bars,
    crushed
Chocolate sauce
1 cup heavy cream, whipped

Line ladyfingers around sides of 9-inch springform pan. Mix softened ice creams together. Add coffee granules, liqueur and crushed toffee bars. Pour into springform pan. Spread thin layer of chocolate sauce over top. Freeze. Before serving, spread cake with whipped cream. Do not let this cake defrost before serving. Serve immediately upon removing from freezer.
Makes one 9-inch cake.

Lorin Frye
Rochester, New York

Fresh Peach Ice Cream

1 cup mashed fresh peaches
½ cup whipping cream
1 (14-ounce) can sweetened
    condensed milk
½ cup confectioners' sugar
1 cup whipping cream
1 teaspoon vanilla extract

Combine peaches, ½ cup whipping cream, sweetened condensed milk and confectioners' sugar; stir well. Chill. Beat 1 cup whipping cream until frothy. Add vanilla, beating until soft peaks form. Fold into peach mixture. Spoon mixture into 9-inch square baking pan. Freeze until slushy. Beat at high speed of electric mixer until smooth. Return mixture to freezer and freeze until firm.
Makes about 1 quart.

Teena Madison
Los Angeles, California

Cakes

Butter Cream Icing

1 egg white
1 cup sugar
¾ cup warm milk
½ cup shortening
½ cup butter
1 teaspoon vanilla extract
1 teaspoon almond extract

Beat egg white until stiff. Slowly add sugar, a small amount at a time. Slowly beat in warm milk. Place in refrigerator to cool for 20 minutes. Blend together shortening and butter. Add cooled egg white mixture a small amount at a time. Beat on high until well blended. Stir in vanilla and almond extracts.
Makes icing for 8-inch cake.

Marge Monaghan
Ann Arbor, Michigan

Butterscotch Cake

1 (18-ounce) package yellow cake mix
1 (4-ounce) can butterscotch pudding
2 tablespoons butter or margarine, melted
2 eggs
1 (6-ounce) package bits of brickle
1 (6-ounce) package butterscotch chips
1 (3-ounce) package pecan pieces
½ cup butter or margarine
1 cup firmly packed brown sugar
¼ cup whipping cream
3½ cups confectioners' sugar

Combine cake mix, pudding and butter in large mixing bowl; beat well. Add eggs, beating well. Fold in bits of brickle. Pour batter into greased and floured 13x9x2-inch baking pan. Sprinkle with butterscotch chips and pecans. Bake at 350°F. for 25 to 30 minutes or until a wooden pick inserted in center comes out clean. Cool slightly. Combine ½ cup butter, brown sugar and cream in large saucepan, stirring well; bring to a boil. Remove from heat and stir in confectioners' sugar. Spread icing over warm cake.
Makes one 13x9-inch cake.

Beverly Griffith
Ann Arbor, Michigan

Carrot Cake

4 eggs
1½ cups oil
2 cups sugar
2 teaspoons vanilla extract
2 cups all-purpose flour
2 teaspoons baking powder
1 teaspoon soda
1 teaspoon salt
1 teaspoon ground cinnamon
2 cups grated carrots
1 cup crushed pineapple, drained
½ cup chopped walnuts
½ cup raisins
Frosting (recipe follows)

Combine eggs, oil, sugar and vanilla in large mixing bowl; beat until smooth. Combine flour, baking powder, soda, salt and cinnamon; add to egg mixture, stirring well. Stir in carrots, pineapple, walnuts and raisins. Pour batter into greased and floured 13x9x2-inch baking pan. Bake at 350°F. for 1 hour or until a wooden pick inserted in center comes out clean. Cool completely. Spread Frosting over cake. Makes one 13x9-inch cake.

Frosting

1 (8-ounce) package cream cheese, softened
½ cup butter or margarine
3½ cups confectioners' sugar
2 teaspoons vanilla extract
1 cup chopped walnuts

Beat cream cheese and butter until light and fluffy; gradually add confectioners' sugar, beating well. Stir in vanilla and walnuts. Makes enough for one 13x9-inch cake.

Donna Owen
Ann Arbor, Michigan

Devil's Food Peanut Layer Cake

1 (18¼-ounce) devil's food cake mix
1 (3½-ounce) package vanilla pudding mix
1½ cups milk
1½ cups (6 ounces) chocolate-covered peanut butter cups, coarsely chopped (10 large or 21 small candies)
6 ounces dark mildly sweet chocolate candy bar, chopped fine
¼ cup whipping cream

Preheat oven to 350°F. Grease and flour two 9-inch fluted tart pans or round layer-cake pans. Prepare and bake cake mix according to package directions. Cool in pans on rack for 15 minutes. Remove from pans. Cool completely on rack.

To make filling: Stir pudding mix and milk in medium saucepan until smooth. Bring to a full boil over medium heat, stirring constantly. Pour into bowl. Cover with plastic wrap directly on surface of pudding. Refrigerate for about 15 minutes to cool slightly. Remove wrap. Stir chopped peanut butter cups into pudding until they melt slightly. Cover surface again with plastic wrap and return to refrigerator to cool completely.

To make icing: Place chocolate bar in small bowl. Heat cream in small saucepan over low heat until it just begins to bubble. Add chocolate in slow steady stream, beating constantly with whisk or electric mixer until chocolate melts, about 4 minutes, and mixture thickens to spreading consistency.

To assemble: Put 1 layer top-side down on serving plate. Spread filling to edges. Cover with remaining cake layer top-side up; press gently. Spread icing on top, smoothing with spatula. Makes 12 servings.

Adam Takessian
San Diego, California

Mahogany Cake

3 squares semisweet chocolate
½ cup water
1 cup sour cream
⅔ cup butter or margarine
1 cup sugar
⅔ cup firmly packed brown sugar
3 eggs
1⅔ cups flour
1½ teaspoons baking powder
1 teaspoon soda
1 teaspoon salt
2 teaspoons vanilla extract
Chocolate-Cream Cheese Frosting
   (recipe follows)

Preheat oven to 350°F. Grease and flour two 9-inch round cake pans. Melt chocolate squares in water over low heat, stirring constantly. Remove from heat and let cool. Add sour cream to chocolate mixture and mix thoroughly. Cream butter until fluffy. Gradually add sugars, mixing until well blended. Add eggs 1 at a time, blending thoroughly after each addition. Add vanilla and mix on medium speed for 1 minute. Pour into prepared pans. Bake in 350°F. oven for 35 to 40 minutes. Remove from oven and cool in pans for 15 minutes. Remove from pans and cool for 20 to 25 minutes then frost.
Makes 12 to 24 servings.

Chocolate-Cream Cheese Frosting

3 squares semisweet chocolate
1 (8-ounce) package cream cheese,
   softened
1¾ cups confectioners' sugar
2 teaspoons milk (optional)

In double boiler, melt chocolate. Beat cream cheese until smooth, then add to melted chocolate. Blend in confectioners' sugar to desired consistency. If frosting is too thick, add milk; if too thin add more confectioners' sugar.

Gracie Merkerson and Nancy Smith
Gainesville, Georgia

Mississippi Mud Cake

1 cup butter or margarine, softened
2 cups sugar
4 eggs
1½ cups all-purpose flour
1 cup flaked coconut
⅓ cup chocolate syrup
1 teaspoon vanilla extract
1 cup chopped nuts
Marshmallow creme
Chocolate Frosting (recipe follows)

Cream butter in large mixing bowl; gradually add sugar, beating well. Add eggs, 1 at a time, beating well after each addition. Stir in flour, coconut, chocolate syrup and vanilla; stir well. Stir in 1 cup nuts. Spoon batter into greased and floured 13x9x2-inch baking pan. Bake at 350°F. for 45 minutes or until wooden pick inserted in center comes out clean. Spread marshmallow creme over hot cake. Let cool for 20 minutes. Spread frosting over marshmallow creme, swirling frosting through marshmallow creme. Sprinkle with ½ cup nuts.
Let cool completely.
Makes one 13x9-inch cake.

Chocolate Frosting

½ cup butter or margarine, softened
¼ cup plus 2 tablespoons milk
⅓ cup chocolate syrup
3 cups confectioners' sugar
½ cup chopped nuts

Combine butter, milk and chocolate syrup; beat well. Add confectioners' sugar, beating until smooth. Stir in nuts.
Makes enough for one 13x9-inch cake.

Darla Montoya
Reedley, California

Tennessee Chocolate Cake

2 cups self-rising flour
2 cups sugar
1 cup water
½ cup butter or margarine
¼ cup cocoa
1 teaspoon soda
½ cup buttermilk
2 eggs
Chocolate Icing (recipe follows)

Sift together flour and sugar in large mixing bowl; set aside. Combine water, butter and cocoa in medium saucepan; bring to a boil. Pour over reserved flour mixture, mixing well. Dissolve soda in buttermilk; add buttermilk and eggs to batter, mixing well. Pour batter into greased and floured 13x9x2-inch baking pan. Bake at 300°F. for 45 minutes or until wooden pick inserted in center comes out clean. Spread Chocolate Icing over warm cake.
Makes one 13x9-inch cake.

Chocolate Icing

½ cup butter or margarine
¼ cup plus 2 tablespoons buttermilk
¼ cup cocoa
3½ cups confectioners' sugar
1 cup chopped pecans
1 teaspoon vanilla extract

Combine butter, buttermilk and cocoa in a large saucepan; bring to a boil. Remove from heat and add confectioners' sugar, beating well. Stir in pecans and vanilla.
Makes enough for one 13x9-inch cake.

Mary Goad
Nashville, Tennessee

Chocolate Sandwich Cookie Cake

2 cups whipping cream
¼ cup almond flavored liqueur
1   (16-ounce) package chocolate
    sandwich cookies, coarsely chopped
Sliced fresh strawberries (optional)
Additional chocolate sandwich cookies
    (optional)

Combine whipping cream and liqueur in large mixing bowl; chill for 30 minutes. Beat at high speed of an electric mixer until stiff peaks form. Combine chopped cookies and ½ cup whipped cream mixture in medium mixing bowl; stir well. Press ⅓ cookie mixture evenly into lightly greased 7 or 8-inch springform pan. Spoon ⅓ whipped cream mixture over cookies, spreading evenly. Repeat layers, ending with whipped cream mixture. Cover and freeze for at least 2 hours (may be frozen for up to 3 days.) Remove sides of pan 1 hour before serving; place cake in refrigerator to thaw slightly. Garnish with strawberries and additional cookies. Cut into wedges to serve.
Makes 12 servings.

Kenneth R. Keuhn
Linthicum, Maryland

Golden Fruitcake

1   (28-ounce) jar maraschino
    cherries, drained
1   (15-ounce) package raisins
1 cup coarsely chopped nuts
½ cup all-purpose flour
½ cup butter or margarine, softened
1 cup sugar
4 eggs
2 cups flour
1 teaspoon vanilla extract
½ teaspoon salt

Quarter cherries; pat dry. Combine cherries, raisins, nuts and ½ cup flour; stir well. Set aside. Cream butter in large mixing bowl; gradually add sugar, beating well. Add eggs, 1 at a time, beating well after each addition. Stir in 2 cups flour, vanilla and salt. Fold in fruit mixture. Pour batter into greased and floured tube pan. Bake at 325°F. for 1 hour or until wooden pick inserted in center comes out clean. Cool in pan for 15 minutes; remove from pan and cool completely.
Makes 30 servings.

This cake will keep for up to 3 weeks if covered tightly.

James J. Mudd
Belleville, Illinois

Turtle Cake

1 (18-ounce) package devil's
   food cake mix
1 (14-ounce) package caramels
¾ cup butter or margarine
½ cup evaporated milk
1 cup semisweet chocolate chips
1 cup chopped nuts
1 (3½-ounce) can flaked coconut
Frosting (recipe follows)

Prepare cake mix according to package directions. Pour half the batter into greased and floured 13x9x2-inch baking pan. Bake at 350°F. for 15 minutes. Place caramels in top of double boiler; cook over boiling water, stirring occasionally, until caramels melt. Add butter and evaporated milk, stirring until butter melts. Spread caramel mixture over cake; sprinkle with chocolate chips, nuts and coconut. Spread remaining batter over coconut. Bake at 350°F. for 30 minutes longer. Spread frosting over warm cake. Cool.
Makes one 13x9-inch cake.

Frosting

½ cup butter or margarine
⅓ cup milk
3 tablespoons plus 1½ teaspoons cocoa
Dash of salt
3½ cups confectioners' sugar
1 cup chopped nuts

Combine butter, milk, cocoa and salt in large saucepan; bring to a boil. Remove from heat, and stir in confectioners' sugar and nuts.
Makes enough for one 13x9-inch cake.

Mary Beth Soignet
Marietta, Georgia

Viennese Chocolate Torte

3 (1-ounce) squares unsweetened
   chocolate
½ cup butter or margarine
⅔ cup firmly packed light brown sugar
⅔ cup firmly packed dark brown sugar
3 eggs
1 teaspoon vanilla extract
1½ cups cake flour
2 tablespoons soda
⅛ teaspoon salt
½ cup buttermilk
½ cup boiling water
Buttercream Frosting (recipe follows)
1 teaspoon instant coffee granules
2 teaspoons boiling water
3 (1-ounce) squares semisweet
   chocolate
Chocolate Glaze (recipe follows)

Melt chocolate in top of double boiler over boiling water; set aside. Cream butter; gradually add brown sugar, beating well. Add eggs, one at a time, beating well after each addition. Stir in reserved chocolate and vanilla. Sift together flour, soda and salt. Add to creamed mixture alternately with buttermilk and boiling water, beating well after each addition. Pour batter into waxed paper-lined greased and floured 9-inch round cake pan. Bake at 350°F. for 35 minutes or until wooden pick inserted in center comes out clean. Cool in pan for 10 minutes. Remove from pan to wire rack and cool completely. Place ¼ of Buttercream Frosting in small bowl. Dissolve coffee granules in 2 teaspoons boiling water; add to frosting, beating well. Melt semisweet chocolate in top of double boiler over boiling water; add to remaining Buttercream Frosting, beating well. Slice cake horizontally into 3 layers. Spread chocolate-flavored frosting between remaining layers and on top and sides of torte, reserving 3 tablespoons for garnish. Place torte in freezer for 10 minutes. Pour Chocolate Glaze over torte; cool completely. Garnish with reserved frosting and grated chocolate.
Makes 1 9-inch torte.

Buttercream Frosting

⅔ cup sugar
3 tablespoons water
4 egg yolks
1 cup butter, softened
1 teaspoon vanilla extract

Combine sugar and water in small heavy saucepan. Bring to a boil. Cook, without stirring, until mixture reaches soft-ball stage (234°). Slowly pour syrup over egg yolks, beating constantly. Continue beating until mixture cools. Add butter, 1 tablespoon at a time, beating until creamy after each addition. Stir in vanilla.
Makes 2 cups.

Chocolate Glaze

8 (1-ounce) squares semisweet
   chocolate
¼ cup butter or margarine

Combine chocolate and butter in top of double boiler. Place over boiling water until mixture melts; stir well. Cool slightly.
Makes 1 cup.

Patricia Topping
Ann Arbor, Michigan

White Chocolate Cake

1 cup butter or margarine, softened
2 cups sugar
4 eggs
8 ounces white chocolate, melted
1 teaspoon vanilla extract
2½ cups all-purpose flour
1 teaspoon baking powder
Dash of salt
1 cup buttermilk
1 cup chopped nuts
1 cup flaked coconut
Frosting (recipe follows)

Cream butter in large mixing bowl; gradually add sugar, beating well. Add eggs, 1 at a time, beating well after each addition. Stir in chocolate and vanilla. Sift together flour, baking powder and salt; add to creamed mixture alternately with buttermilk, beating well after each addition. Stir in nuts and coconut. Pour batter into 2 greased and floured 9-inch round cake pans. Bake at 350°F. for 30 minutes or until wooden pick inserted in center comes out clean. Cool in pans for 10 minutes. Remove from pans and let cool completely. Spread frosting between layers and on top and sides of cake.
Makes one 2-layer cake.

If tube pan is used, bake at 350°F. for 1 hour and 10 minutes or until a wooden pick inserted in center comes out clean.

Frosting

2 cups sugar
1 (14-ounce) can evaporated milk
½ cup butter or margarine
1½ teaspoons vanilla extract
Dash of salt

Combine all ingredients in large heavy saucepan; let stand for 1 hour, stirring occasionally. Cook over medium heat until mixture reaches soft-ball stage (240°). Remove from heat and beat until creamy.
Makes enough for one 2-layer cake.

Norma Clise
Romney, West Virginia

Jam Cake with Caramel Frosting

1 cup butter or margarine, softened
2 cups sugar
4 eggs
2½ cups all-purpose flour
1 teaspoon soda
1 teaspoon salt
1 teaspoon ground nutmeg
1 teaspoon ground cinnamon
1 teaspoon ground cloves
1 cup buttermilk
1 teaspoon vanilla extract
1 cup chopped pecans
1 cup raisins
1 cup strawberry or blackberry jam
Quick Caramel Frosting
   (recipe follows)

Cream butter in large mixing bowl; gradually add sugar, beating well. Add eggs, 1 at a time, beating well after each addition. Combine 2 cups flour, soda, salt, nutmeg, cinnamon and cloves. Add to creamed mixture alternately with buttermilk, beginning and ending with flour mixture. Beat well after each addition. Stir in vanilla. Dredge pecans and raisins in remaining flour; fold into batter. Stir in jam. Pour batter into 3 greased and floured 8-inch round cake pans. Bake at 350°F. for 25 minutes or until wooden pick inserted in center comes out clean. Cool in pans for 10 minutes. Remove from pans and let cool completely. Spread Caramel Frosting between layers and on top and sides of cake.
Makes one 3-layer cake.

Quick Caramel Frosting

⅔ cup butter or margarine
1 cup firmly packed brown sugar
Pinch of salt
⅓ cup milk
3 cups confectioners' sugar
1 teaspoon vanilla extract

Melt butter in large saucepan; add brown sugar and salt. Cook over low heat, stirring constantly, for 2 minutes. Add milk and bring to a boil, stirring constantly. Remove from heat and gradually add confectioners' sugar, beating well. Stir in vanilla.
Makes enough for one 3-layer cake.

Paul Justice
Theodore, Alabama

Pistachio Cake

1 (18-ounce) package golden butter
   cake mix
1 (3½-ounce) package instant
   pistachio pudding mix
3 eggs
1 cup sour cream
½ cup vegetable oil
½ cup chopped nuts
2 tablespoons sugar
2 tablespoons ground cinnamon

Combine cake mix, pudding mix, eggs, sour cream and oil; beat well. Combine nuts, sugar and cinnamon; mix well. Pour half the batter into greased and floured bundt pan; sprinkle with half the nut mixture. Spoon remaining batter over nuts; sprinkle with remaining nut mixture. Bake at 350°F. for 50 minutes or until wooden pick inserted in center comes out clean. Cool in pan for 1½ hours.
Makes one bundt cake.

Harry Muessner
Federal Way, Washington

Mexican Fruitcake

2 cups all-purpose flour
2 cups sugar
2 teaspoons soda
2 eggs
1 (16-ounce) can crushed pineapple,
   undrained
1 cup choped walnuts
Frosting (recipe follows)
½ cup chopped walnuts

Combine flour, sugar and soda in large mixing bowl; stir well. Add eggs, pineapple and 1 cup walnuts; beat well. Pour batter into a greased and floured 13x9x2-inch baking pan. Bake at 350°F. for 35 to 40 minutes or until wooden pick inserted in center comes out clean. Cool. Spread frosting over cake; sprinkle with ½ cup walnuts.
Makes one 13x9-inch cake.

Frosting

1 (8-ounce) package cream cheese,
   softened
½ cup butter or margarine, softened
2 cups confectioners' sugar
1 teaspoon vanilla extract

Beat cream cheese and butter until light and fluffy; gradually add confectioners' sugar, beating well. Stir in vanilla.
Makes enough for one 13x9-inch cake.

Gwen Bennett
Ann Arbor, Michigan

Italian Cream Cake

½ cup butter or margarine, softened
½ cup shortening
2 cups sugar
5 eggs, separated
2 cups all-purpose flour
1 teaspoon soda
1 cup buttermilk
1 teaspoon vanilla extract
1 (3½-ounce) can flaked coconut
1 cup chopped pecans
Frosting (recipe follows)

Cream butter and shortening in large mixing bowl; add sugar, beating well. Add egg yolks; beat well. Combine flour and soda. Add to creamed mixture alternately with buttermilk, beginning and ending with flour mixture; mix well. Stir in vanilla, coconut and pecans. Beat egg whites until stiff peaks form; fold gently into batter. Spoon batter into 3 greased and floured 8-inch round cake pans. Bake at 350°F. for 30 minutes or until wooden pick inserted in center comes out clean. Cool in pans for 10 minutes. Remove from pans and cool completely. Spread frosting between layers and on top and sides of cake.
Makes one 3-layer cake.

Frosting

1 (8-ounce) package cream cheese,
   softened
¼ cup butter or margarine, softened
3½ cups confectioners' sugar
1 teaspoon vanilla extract

Combine cream cheese and butter; beat until creamy. Gradually add confectioners' sugar, beating well; stir in vanilla.
Makes enough for one 3-layer cake.

Beth Hensley
Milford, Connecticut

Pumpkin Log

3 eggs
1 cup sugar
⅔ cup canned pumpkin
¾ cup all-purpose flour
1 teaspoon soda
½ teaspoon ground cinnamon
¼ teaspoon salt
½ cup finely chopped pecans
Confectioners' sugar
Filling (recipe follows)

Grease 15x10x1-inch jelly roll pan with vegetable oil and line with waxed paper. Grease waxed paper with vegetable oil; set aside. Beat eggs at high speed of electric mixer for 5 minutes or until pale yellow. Gradually beat in sugar. Stir in pumpkin. Combine flour, soda, cinnamon and salt; fold into pumpkin mixture. Pour batter into prepared pan, spreading evenly; sprinkle with pecans. Bake at 350°F. for 15 minutes or until top of cake springs back when lightly touched. Sprinkle confectioners' sugar on towel. Loosen edges of cake and immediately invert onto towel. Roll up cake in towel, beginning with narrow edge. Cool cake completely. Unroll cake; spread with filling to ½ inch of edges. Re-roll cake; chill. Store in refrigerator.
Makes 10 to 12 servings.

Filling

1 cup confectioners' sugar
1 (8-ounce) package cream cheese, softened
2 tablespoons butter or margarine, softened
¾ teaspoon vanilla extract

Combine all ingredients; beat at medium speed of electric mixer until smooth and creamy.
Makes about 1¼ cups.

Joseph McCord
Atlanta, Georgia

Kentucky Rum Cake

1 cup butter or margarine, softened
2 cups sugar
4 eggs
3 cups all-purpose flour
1 teaspoon baking powder
1 teaspoon salt
½ teaspoon soda
1 cup buttermilk
2 teaspoons vanilla extract
Sauce (recipe follows)
Confectioners' sugar (optional)

Cream butter in large mixing bowl; gradually add sugar, beating well. Add eggs, 1 at a time, beating well after each addition. Sift together flour, baking powder, salt and soda. Add to creamed mixture alternately with buttermilk, beginning and ending with flour mixture. Beat well after each addition. Stir in vanilla. Pour batter into greased and floured 10-inch tube pan. Bake at 325°F. for 1 hour or until wooden pick inserted in center comes out clean. Loosen cake from edges of pan; prick cake with tines of fork. Pour hot sauce over cake. Cool completely before removing cake from pan. Sprinkle with confectioners' sugar.
Makes one 10-inch cake.

Sauce

½ cup butter or margarine
1 cup sugar
¼ cup water
1 tablespoon rum extract

Melt butter in small saucepan. Add remaining ingredients, stirring until sugar dissolves.
Makes about 1 cup.

Patrick J. Kelly and Diane Keller
Boulder, Colorado

Sour Cream Pound Cake

1 cup butter
3 cups sugar
6 eggs
1 (8-ounce) carton sour cream
3 cups all-purpose flour
¼ teaspoon soda
⅛ teaspoon salt
1 teaspoon vanilla extract

Cream butter; gradually add sugar, beating until light and fluffy. Add eggs, 1 at a time, beating well after each addition. Stir in sour cream. Combine flour, soda and salt; add to creamed mixture, stirring well. Stir in vanilla. Pour batter into greased and floured 10-inch tube or bundt pan. Bake at 325°F. for 1 hour and 10 minutes or until wooden pick inserted in center comes out clean. Cool in pan for 10 minutes.
Makes one 10-inch cake.

Charles B. Whitehead
Nashville, Tennessee

Cookies and Candy

Austrian Fruit Bars

2 cups sifted all-purpose flour
½ cup sugar
Pinch of soda
½ cup butter, softened
4 eggs, separated
1 tablespoon lemon juice
1 (10-ounce) jar blueberry jam
½ cup sugar
2 (3-ounce) packages walnuts,
  coarsely chopped

Combine flour, ½ cup sugar, soda, butter, egg yolks and lemon juice in medium mixing bowl; mix well. Press mixture evenly into greased 13x9x2-inch baking pan. Bake at 350°F. for 10 minutes or until lightly browned. Spread jam over crust. Beat egg whites until foamy; gradually add ½ cup sugar, beating until stiff peaks form. Fold in walnuts. Spread mixture over jam, sealing to edges of pan. Bake at 325°F. for 30 minutes or until browned. Cool completely. Cut into bars.
Makes 20 servings.

Elizabeth Smith
Roslyn, New York

Butterscotch Delights

2½ cups shortening
2½ cups sugar
2½ cups firmly packed brown sugar
5 eggs
¼ cup milk
2½ teaspoons vanilla extract
5 cups all-purpose flour
2½ teaspoons soda
2½ teaspoons baking powder
2½ teaspoons salt
5 cups regular oats, uncooked
1 (12-ounce) package butterscotch
  chips (optional)

Cream shortening in large mixing bowl; gradually add sugars, beating well. Add eggs, milk and vanilla; beat well. Sift together flour, soda, baking powder and salt; add to creamed mixture, stirring well. Stir in oats and butterscotch chips. Drop by teaspoonfuls onto lightly greased cookie sheets. Bake at 375°F. for 8 to 10 minutes or until lightly browned. Remove to wire racks to cool completely.
Makes 10 to 12 dozen.

Robin Pimentel
Fort Worth, Texas

Choclava

1¼ cups butter or margarine, melted
1   (16-ounce) package frozen phyllo
     pastry, thawed
1   (16-ounce) package walnut halves,
     finely chopped
1   (6-ounce) package semisweet
     chocolate chips, finely chopped
¾ cup sugar
1½ teaspoon ground cinnamon
¾ cup orange juice
½ cup water
¾ cup sugar
½ cup honey
2 tablespoons lemon juice
2   (1-ounce) squares semisweet
     chocolate
2 tablespoons water

Brush 15x11x2-inch baking pan with melted butter. Layer 8 sheets phyllo pastry in pan, brushing each with melted butter. Combine walnuts, chocolate chips, ¾ cup sugar and cinnamon; stir well. Sprinkle about 2 cups nut mixture over phyllo in pan. Layer 4 sheets phyllo over nut mixture, brushing each with melted butter; sprinkle with 2 cups nut mixture. Repeat layers, using remaining phyllo and nut mixture, ending with phyllo. Cut into diamond shapes, cutting to but not through bottom layer. Bake at 325°F. for 1 hour. Remove from oven and finish cutting pieces. Combine orange juice, ½ cup water, ¾ cup sugar, honey and lemon juice in small saucepan. Bring to a boil. Reduce heat and simmer for 20 minutes stirring occasionally. Pour over choclava; cool completely. Combine semisweet chocolate and 2 tablespoons water in small saucepan. Cook over low heat, stirring constantly, until chocolate melts. Drizzle over choclava. Cover and refrigerate.
Makes 60 pieces.

Susan L. Horn
Ann Arbor, Michigan

Tom's "Award-Winning" Chocolate Chip Cookies

¾ cup margarine, softened
¼ cup shortening
¾ cup sugar
¾ cup firmly packed brown sugar
2 teaspoons vanilla extract
2 eggs
2¼ cups all-purpose flour
1 teaspoon soda
1 teaspoon salt
1   (12-ounce) package semisweet
     chocolate morsels
1 cup chopped nuts (optional)

Combine margarine, shortening, sugar, brown sugar and vanilla. Add eggs. Beat well by hand until creamy. Combine flour, soda and salt. Gradually add to creamed mixture and stir by hand until well blended. Stir in semisweet morsels and nuts. Drop by teaspoonfuls onto lightly greased cookie sheets. Bake at 375°F. for 8 to 10 minutes. Remove to wire rack to cool completely.
Makes about 8 dozen.

Tom Mathews
Huron, Ohio

Chocolate Drop Cookies

¾ cup shortening
1 cup firmly packed brown sugar
1 egg
½ cup milk
1 teaspoon vanilla extract
1½ cups all-purpose flour
½ teaspoon soda
2   (1-ounce) squares semisweet
     chocolate, melted
1 cup chopped pecans (optional)

Cream shortening in large mixing bowl; gradually add sugar, beating well. Add egg, milk and vanilla; beat well. Sift together flour and soda; add to creamed mixture, stirring well. Stir in chocolate and pecans. Drop by teaspoonfuls onto lightly greased cookie sheets. Bake at 325°F. for 10 to 12 minutes. Remove to wire racks to cool completely.
Makes 2½ dozen.

Ann Borchert
Ann Arbor, Michigan

Chocolate-Marshmallow Cookies

½ cup shortening
½ cup butter or margarine, softened
2 cups sugar
2 eggs
1½ cups milk
2 teaspoons vanilla extract
3½ cups all-purpose flour
¾ cup cocoa
1 teaspoon soda
1 teaspoon salt
1 cup chopped walnuts
1 (10-ounce) package marshmallows
Commercial chocolate fudge frosting

Cream shortening and butter in large mixing bowl; gradually add sugar, beating well. Add eggs, milk and vanilla; beat well. Sift together flour, cocoa, soda and salt. Add to creamed mixture, stirring well. Stir in walnuts. Refrigerate for 1 hour. Drop dough by heaping teaspoonfuls onto lightly greased cookie sheet. Bake at 375°F. for 7 minutes. Remove from oven and place 1 marshmallow on each cookie. Bake for 4 to 5 minutes longer or until marshmallows are puffed and golden brown. Remove to wire racks to cool completely. Frost each with chocolate fudge frosting.
Makes about 4½ dozen.

Deborah R. Rossolo
White Bear Lake, Minnesota

Chocolate Meringue Cookies

2 egg whites
¼ teaspoon cream of tartar
⅛ teaspoon salt
⅔ cup sugar
2 tablespoons cocoa
½ teaspoon almond extract
½ teaspoon chocolate extract
1 (6-ounce) package semisweet
  chocolate chips

Beat egg whites in large mixing bowl until foamy; add cream of tartar and salt. Gradually add sugar, 1 tablespoon at a time, beating until stiff peaks form. Fold in cocoa, extracts and chocolate chips. Drop by heaping teaspoonfuls onto greased cookie sheets. Bake at 200°F. for 1½ hours or until cookies are crisp. Remove to wire racks to cool completely.
Makes about 2½ dozen.

Nancy deJolsvay
Hopkins, Minnesota

Chocolate-Tipped Butter Cookies

1 cup butter or margarine, softened
½ cup sifted confectioners' sugar
1 teaspoon vanilla extract
2 cups all-purpose flour
1 (6-ounce) package semisweet
  chocolate morsels
1 tablesppoon shortening
½ cup finely chopped pecans

Cream butter; gradually add confectioners' sugar, beating until fluffy. Stir in vanilla. Gradually add flour to butter mixture; mix well. Shape dough into 2½x½-inch sticks. Place on ungreased cookie sheets and flatten ¾ of each cookie lengthwise with fork to ¼-inch thickness. Bake at 350°F. for 12 to 14 minutes. Remove to wire racks to cool. Combine chocolate morsels and shortening in top of double boiler; bring water to a boil. Reduce heat to low; cook until chocolate melts, stirring occasionally. Remove double boiler from heat, leaving chocolate mixture over hot water. Dip flattened tips of cookies in warm chocolate to coat both sides; roll tips in finely chopped pecans. Place cookies on wire racks until chocolate is firm. Arrange cookies between layers of waxed paper in an airtight container; store in cool place.
Makes 15 dozen.

Beckie Hibdon
Nashville, Tennessee

Coconut Chews

2/3 cup sweetened condensed milk
2 teaspoons vanilla extract
1/8 teaspoon salt
1/4 cup powdered milk
1/4 cup wheat germ
1 1/2 cups shredded coconut

Mix all ingredients except coconut until blended. Add coconut and mix well. Drop by teaspoonfuls onto greased baking sheets. Bake at 325°F. for 12 to 15 minutes. Remove to wire racks to cool completely. Makes 3 dozen.

Karen Moon
Auburn, Washington

St. Patrick's Clover Cookies

1 cup butter or margarine, softened
1 1/2 cups confectioners' sugar
1 egg
1 teaspoon vanilla extract
2 1/2 cups all-purpose flour
1 teaspoon soda
1 teaspoon cream of tartar
Sugar

Mix thoroughly butter, confectioners' sugar, egg and vanilla. Blend in flour, soda and cream of tartar. Cover; chill for 2 to 3 hours. Divide dough in half. Roll each half 3/16 inch thick on lightly floured cloth-covered board. Cut into desired shapes; sprinkle with sugar. Bake at 375°F. for 7 to 8 minutes or until lightly browned. Remove from cookie sheets and cool completely on wire racks. Makes about 5 dozen.

Karen Bassett
Ann Arbor, Michigan

Cut-Out Cookies

2 cups butter or margarine, softened
2 1/4 cups sugar
4 eggs
2 teaspoons vanilla extract
6 cups all-purpose flour

Cream butter in large mixing bowl; gradually add sugar, beating until light and fluffy. Add eggs and vanilla; beat well. Stir in flour. Cover and refrigerate overnight. Turn dough onto lightly floured surface; roll to 1/4-inch thickness and cut with floured cookie cutters. Place cookies on lightly greased cookie sheets. Bake at 350°F. for 12 to 15 minutes or until lightly browned. Remove to wire racks to cool completely. Makes about 6 dozen.

Christopher McCormick
Hendersonville, Tennessee

Italian Sesame Seed Cookies

4 cups all-purpose flour
1 cup sugar
2 tablespoons baking powder
3 eggs, beaten
1 cup butter or margarine, melted
1/2 cup milk
1/2 teaspoon vanilla extract
1/2 pound sesame seed

Combine flour, sugar and baking powder in large mixing bowl; stir well. Add eggs, butter, milk and vanilla; mix well. Shape dough into 1-inch balls; roll in sesame seed. Place cookies on ungreased cookie sheets. Bake at 350°F. for 15 to 20 minutes or until lightly browned. Remove to wire rack to cool completely. Makes about 5 dozen.

Ken Parry
Columbia, Georgia

Susie's Famous Cookies

2¾ cups all-purpose flour
1 tablespoon soda
1 tablespoon salt
2 cups butter, softened
1 cup firmly packed brown sugar
½ cup sugar
1 tablespoon vanilla extract
2 eggs
1 (12-ounce) package semisweet
  chocolate chips
1 package Heath Bits of Brickle
1 cup pecans or walnuts (optional)
1 (6-ounce) package peanut butter
  chips

Mix flour, soda and salt in large bowl; set aside. Beat butter, brown sugar, sugar, vanilla and eggs together well; fold in flour mixture. Stir in remaining ingredients. Drop dough onto ungreased cookie sheets, using ⅓ cup dough for each cookie. Bake at 275°F. for 20 to 25 minutes or until lightly browned. Remove to wire racks to cool completely.
Makes 1 dozen.

Susie Monaghan
Ann Arbor, Michigan

Lemon Snowflakes

1 cup butter or margarine, softened
1½ cups all-purpose flour
¾ cup cornstarch
½ cup confectioners' sugar
2 teaspoons grated lemon rind
1 cup finely chopped pecans
1 cup confectioners' sugar
2 tablespoons butter or margarine,
  melted
1 tablespoon lemon juice

Cream 1 cup butter in large mixing bowl. Combine flour, cornstarch, ½ cup confectioners' sugar and lemon rind; add to butter, beating well. Cover and refrigerate for 1 hour. Shape dough into 1-inch balls; drop dough into chopped pecans. Flatten each using bottom of glass. Place cookies, nut-side up, on greased cookie sheets. Bake at 350°F. for 15 minutes. Remove to wire racks to cool completely. Combine 1 cup confectioners' sugar, 2 tablespoons butter and lemon juice; mix well. Spread over cooled cookies.
Makes about 2 dozen.

Diane Black
Ann Arbor, Michigan

Mint Surprise Cookies

3 cups all-purpose flour
1 teaspoon soda
½ teaspoon salt
1 cup sugar
1 cup butter, softened
½ cup firmly packed brown sugar
2 eggs
1 teaspoon vanilla extract
35 to 45 Andes Chocolate Mints
70 to 90 walnut halves

Combine all ingredients except mints and walnuts in large mixer bowl. Mix at lowest speed until well blended. Drop by teaspoonfuls 2 inches apart onto ungreased cookie sheets. Press ½ Andes Mint on top of each cookie. Cover with teaspoonful of dough. Top each with walnut half; smooth edges. Bake at 375°F. for 9 to 12 minutes.
Makes about 7 dozen.

Diane Spicer
Forest Park, Illinois

No-Bake Cookies

½ cup milk
2 cups sugar
3 tablespoons cocoa
½ stick margarine
3 cups oats
½ cup peanut butter
1 teaspoon vanilla extract

Combine milk, sugar, cocoa and margarine in small saucepan. Bring to a boil and boil for 1 minute. Remove from heat and stir in oats, peanut butter and vanilla. Drop by spoonfuls onto waxed paper and allow to stand until firm.
Makes 10 servings.

Maryanne Josefczyk
Dexter, Michigan

Nutjammer Cookies

1 cup butter or margarine, softened
1 (8-ounce) package cream cheese, softened
2 cups all-purpose flour
½ teaspoon baking powder
2 cups finely chopped pecans
1 (12-ounce) jar strawberry jam (or any flavor)
2 teaspoons sugar
⅓ cup confectioners' sugar

Cream butter and cream cheese in large mixing bowl. Sift together flour and baking powder; add to creamed mixture, stirring well. Cover and refrigerate for 2 hours. Combine pecans, jam and sugar; stir well. Turn dough onto lightly floured surface. Roll dough to ⅛-inch thickness and cut into 2-inch squares. Place 1 teaspoon filling in center of each square; fold opposite corners of dough over filling, pressing to seal securely. Place cookies on lightly greased cookie sheets. Bake at 375°F. for 10 minutes or until lightly browned. Sprinkle with confectioners' sugar. Remove to wire racks to cool completely.
Makes about 4 dozen.

Gerry Boudrie
Saline, Michigan

Cape Cod Oatmeal Cookies

1½ cups all-purpose flour
1 teaspoon ground cinnamon
½ teaspoon soda
½ teaspoon salt
1 egg, lightly beaten
1 cup sugar
½ cup melted shortening
½ cup melted butter
1 tablespoon molasses
¼ cup milk
1¾ cups uncooked regular oats
½ cup raisins
½ cup chopped nuts

Mix flour, cinnamon, soda and salt together in large bowl. Stir in remaining ingredients. Drop by teaspoonfuls onto ungreased cookie sheet. Bake at 350°F. for 12 minutes or until edges are brown. Cool on wire rack.
Makes 5 dozen.

Julie Bennett
Statesboro, Georgia

Oatmeal Cookies

²⁄₃ cup flour
½ teaspoon soda
½ teaspoon salt
1 teaspoon cinnamon
¾ cup butter, softened
1 cup firmly packed brown sugar
½ cup sugar
2 eggs
2 tablespoons water
1 teaspoon vanilla extract
3 cups oats
1½ cups raisins

Sift together flour, soda, salt and cinnamon; set aside. Cream together butter and sugars. Add eggs, water, vanilla and flour mixture; mix well. Stir in oats and raisins until well blended. Drop dough by teaspoonfuls onto greased cookie sheets. Bake in preheated 350°F. oven for 10 to 12 minutes. Cool on wire racks.
Makes 4 to 5 dozen.

Eugene Powers
Ann Arbor, Michigan

Peanut Butter Crinkles

½ cup butter or margarine, softened
½ cup peanut butter
½ cup sugar
½ cup firmly packed brown sugar
1 egg
½ teaspoon vanilla extract
1¼ cups all-purpose flour
¾ teaspoon soda
¼ teaspoon salt

Cream together butter, peanut butter, sugars, egg and vanilla. Sift dry ingredients and add to creamed mixture, stirring well. Shape dough into 1-inch balls; roll in additional sugar. Place on greased cookie sheets. Bake at 350°F. for 10 minutes or until lightly browned. Remove to wire rack to cool completely.
Makes 2 dozen.

Peggy Hardley
Ypsilanti, Michigan

Mom's Pumpkin Cookies

½ cup shortening
1 cup sugar
1 cup canned pumpkin
1 teaspoon vanilla extract
2 cups all-purpose flour
1 teaspoon ground cinnamon
1 teaspoon baking powder
1 teaspoon soda
½ teaspoon salt
1 cup raisins (optional)
1 cup chopped pecans (optional)

Cream shortening in large mixing bowl; gradually add sugar, beating well. Stir in pumpkin and vanilla. Combine flour, cinnamon, baking powder, soda and salt; stir well. Gradually add to creamed mixture, stirring well. Stir in raisins and pecans. Drop batter by teaspoonfuls 2 inches apart onto greased cookie sheets. Bake at 350°F. for 10 minutes or until lightly browned. Remove to wire racks to cool.
Makes about 2 dozen.

Teresa Granado
Cucamonga, California

Raisin Jumbos

2 cups seedless raisins
1 cup water
4 cups sifted all-purpose flour
1 teaspoon baking powder
1 teaspoon soda
1 teaspoon salt
½ teaspoon ground cinnamon
½ teaspoon ground nutmeg
1 cup shortening or butter
1¾ cups sugar
2 eggs, beaten
1 teaspoon vanilla extract
½ cup nuts (optional)

Combine raisins and water in small saucepan; bring to a boil. Reduce heat and simmer for 3 minutes. Drain. Combine flour, baking powder, soda, salt, cinnamon and nutmeg; stir well. Set aside. Cream shortening in large mixing bowl; gradually add sugar, beating well. Add eggs and vanilla; beat well. Add reserved raisins, flour mixture and nuts; stir well. Drop batter by tablespoonfuls onto greased cookie sheets. Bake at 375°F. for 12 minutes. Remove to wire racks to cool completely.
Makes about 4 dozen.

Don and Pat Dufek
Ann Arbor, Michigan

Sugar-Nut Sticks

2 cups all-purpose flour
1 tablespoon sugar
¾ cup butter or margarine, softened
¼ cup milk
1 egg, beaten
½ cup sugar
¼ cup butter or margarine, melted
¼ cup raisins
¼ cup chopped pecans
1 teaspoon almond extract
½ cup confectioners' sugar
1 tablespoon warm water

Combine flour and 1 tablespoon sugar in medium mixing bowl; cut in butter, using a pastry blender, until mixture resembles coarse meal. Combine milk and egg; add to flour mixture, stirring with fork until dry ingredients are moistened. Divide dough into 2 equal portions. Roll 1 portion to 12x4-inch rectangle on lightly floured surface. Transfer dough to a baking sheet. Repeat procedure with remaining dough. Combine ½ cup sugar, melted butter, raisins, pecans and almond extract; stir well. Sprinkle mixture lengthwise down center of each portion of dough. Fold long sides of dough over filling, pressing to seal. Bake at 350°F. for 30 minutes or until lightly browned. Cool slightly. Combine confectioners' sugar and warm water, stirring well. Drizzle over pastry. Cut crosswise into 1-inch slices.
Makes 2 dozen.

Maria Lisa Blanka
Casa Grande, Arizona

Apple Brownies

¾ cup butter or margarine, softened
2 cups sugar
2 eggs
2 cups all-purpose flour
1 teaspoon baking powder
1 teaspoon soda
1 teaspoon ground cinnamon
½ teaspoon salt
2 cups chopped apples
1 cup chopped walnuts

Cream butter; gradually add sugar, beating until light and fluffy. Add eggs, beating well. Combine flour, baking powder, soda, cinnamon and salt. Add to creamed mixture, stirring well. Stir in apples and walnuts. Spoon mixture into greased 13x9x2-inch baking dish. Bake at 350°F. for 35 minutes. Cool completely. Cut into squares to serve.
Makes 20 squares.

Nanette B. Coté
Lynn, Massachusetts

Chocolate-Caramel-Nut Bars

1   (14-ounce) package caramels
⅓ cup evaporated milk
1   (2-layer) German's chocolate
   cake mix with pudding
⅓ cup evaporated milk
½ cup butter or margarine, melted
1 cup Planter's walnuts, chopped
1   (6-ounce) package semisweet
   chocolate pieces
½ cup walnuts, chopped

Preheat oven to 350°F. Melt caramels with ⅓ cup milk over low heat, stirring until smooth. Combine cake mix, ⅓ cup evaporated milk and butter; mix well. Press half the cake mixture into bottom of greased 13x9x2-inch baking pan. Bake at 350°F. for 6 minutes. Sprinkle 1 cup walnuts and chocolate pieces over crust; top with caramel mixture, spreading to edges of pan. Top with teaspoonfuls of remaining cake mixture; press gently into caramel mixture. Sprinkle with walnuts; press lightly into top. Bake at 350°F. for 20 minutes. Cool slightly; refrigerate. Cut into bars to serve.
Makes 2 dozen bars.

Substitute chocolate cake mix for German's chocolate cake mix or pecans for walnuts.

Judy Smith
Huntington Station, New York

$20,000 Chocolate Cherry Bars

1 chocolate fudge cake mix
1½ teaspoons almond extract
1   (20-ounce) can cherry pie filling
2 eggs, beaten

In medium mixing bowl, add cake mix, almond extract, cherry pie filling and eggs. Combine by hand until thoroughly mixed. (Do not add anything else to cake mix; the can of cherry pie filling will give it enough moisture.) Pour mixture into greased and floured 13x9-inch cake pan. Bake at 350°F. for 25 to 30 minutes, or until toothpick inserted in center comes out clean. Prick cake with a toothpick or fork and pour glaze over warm cake. Cut into 2-inch squares and ENJOY!
Makes 25 to 30 bars.

Glaze for $20,000 Chocolate Cherry Bars

1 cup sugar
5 teaspoons butter or margarine
⅓ cup milk
1   (6-ounce) package chocolate chips

Combine first 3 ingredients in saucepan. Bring to a boil and boil until sugar dissolves, being careful not to let burn. Stir in chocolate chips until thoroughly mixed.

Sharon Spires
Ypsilanti, Michigan

Fudge-Oatmeal Cookies

2 cups sugar
½ cup cocoa
½ cup milk
½ cup butter
½ cup crunchy peanut butter
2 cups quick-cooking oats, uncooked

Combine sugar, cocoa, milk and butter in large saucepan. Bring to a boil. Cook for 1 minute, stirring constantly. Stir in peanut butter and oats. Remove from heat. Press mixture into buttered 13x9x2-inch baking pan. Cool completely; cut into squares.
Makes 4 dozen.

Karen Boone
Kent, Ohio

Crème de Menthe Brownies

This recipe is made in three easy steps and must be allowed to cool between each step.

First Layer

1 cup sugar
½ cup butter, softened
4 eggs
1 (16-ounce) can Hershey's chocolate syrup
1 cup flour
½ teaspoon vanilla extract
½ cup nuts (optional)

Cream together sugar and butter. Add eggs, 1 at a time, beating well after each addition. Add Hershey's syrup, flour, vanilla and nuts. Pour into greased 13x9-inch baking pan. Bake at 350°F. for 30 minutes. Cool.

Second Layer

½ cup butter, softened
2 cups confectioners' sugar
2 tablespoons Crème de Menthe liqueur

Combine all ingredients; beat until smooth. Frost cold brownies.

Third Layer

1 (6-ounce) package chocolate chips
6 tablespoons butter

Melt together chocolate chips and butter. Cool and spread over second layer. Cut into squares.
Makes 2 dozen.

Denise Ralph
Ann Arbor, Michigan

Gold Rush Brownies

2 cups (about 18 crackers) packed graham cracker crumbs
1 (6-ounce) package semisweet chocolate pieces
½ cup coarsely chopped pecans
½ teaspoon ground cinnamon
1 teaspoon vanilla extract or rum flavoring
1⅓ cups sweetened condensed milk

Grease bottom of 8-inch square pan; line with waxed paper and grease again. Mix together graham cracker crumbs, chocolate pieces, pecans, cinnamon and vanilla. Blend in sweetened condensed milk. Pour mixture into prepared pan. Bake at 350°F. for 40 minutes or until golden brown. Remove from oven. Let stand in pan for 10 minutes. Turn out onto wire rack; remove waxed paper. Cut into 2-inch squares. Cool.
Makes 16 squares.

Fay Bundy
Winston-Salem, North Carolina

Michael's Anytime Bars

½ cup butter or margarine, melted
1 cup graham cracker crumbs
1 cup flaked coconut
1 cup chocolate chips
1 cup chopped pecans
1 (14-ounce) can sweetened condensed milk

Combine butter and graham cracker crumbs; mix well. Press mixture evenly into 9-inch square baking pan. Layer coconut, chocolate chips and pecans over graham cracker crust. Pour condensed milk over top layer. Bake at 350°F. for 30 minutes. Cool completely and cut into squares.
Makes 16 servings.

Michael Kelcourse
Ann Arbor, Michigan

Holidates

1¼ cups all-purpose flour
¾ teaspoon soda
½ teaspoon salt
½ cup water
1 cup pitted dates, chopped
¾ cup sugar
½ cup butter or margarine
1 tablespoon grated lemon rind
1 (6-ounce) package semisweet
   chocolate chips
2 eggs, beaten
1 cup water
1 cup chopped pecans

Sift together flour, soda and salt; set aside. Combine ½ cup water, dates, sugar, butter and lemon rind in large saucepan. Cook over medium heat, stirring occasionally, for 10 minutes or until dates soften. Remove from heat and stir in chocolate chips and eggs. Add reserved flour mixture alternately with 1 cup water, stirring well after each addition. Stir in pecans. Pour batter into 2 greased 13x9x2-inch baking pans. Bake at 350°F. for 25 minutes. Cool completely; drizzle with glaze if desired. Cut into squares to serve.
Makes about 4 dozen.

Annie McCauley
Manchester, Michigan

Michigan Brownies

1 stick margarine, softened
1 cup sugar
1 (16-ounce) can Hershey's
   chocolate syrup
4 eggs
1 cup unsifted flour
1 cup chopped pecans or walnuts

Cream margarine and sugar. Add syrup and beat well. Beat in eggs, 1 at a time. Add flour; mix well. Stir in pecans. Spread in greased and floured 13x9-inch baking pan. Bake in 350°F. oven for 25 minutes. Cool. Spread frosting on cooled cake at once. Cut into squares.
Makes 1 dozen.

Frosting

1 stick margarine
1½ cups sugar
½ cup evaporated milk
½ cup chocolate chips
1 cup flaked coconut

In saucepan, combine margarine, sugar and evaporated milk. Bring to a boil and boil for 1 minute. Remove from heat and stir in chocolate chips until melted. Add coconut.

Mille Schembechlen
Ann Arbor, Michigan

Orange Macaroon Bars

¼ cup butter or margarine, softened
1 cup sugar
1 egg
1 teaspoon grated orange rind
2 tablespoons frozen orange juice
   concentrate, thawed
1 cup all-purpose flour
1 teaspoon baking powder
½ teaspoon salt
1 cup flaked coconut

Cream butter in large mixing bowl; gradually add sugar, beating well. Add egg, orange rind and orange juice concentrate; beat well. Combine flour, baking powder and salt; add to creamed mixture, stirring well. Stir in coconut. Spoon mixture into greased 8-inch square baking pan. Bake at 350°F. for 30 to 35 minutes or until lightly browned. Cool completely and cut into squares.
Makes 3 dozen.

Eleanor Hansen
Seattle, Washington

Aunt Alice's Peanut Butter-Chocolate Bars

½ cup butter, softened
½ cup brown sugar
½ cup sugar
1 egg
⅓ cup peanut butter
½ teaspoon vanilla extract
1 cup flour
½ teaspoon soda
¼ teaspoon salt
1 cup rolled oats
1½ cups (12 ounces) chocolate bits

Cream together butter and sugars. Add egg, peanut butter and vanilla; beat well. Blend in flour, soda and salt. Add rolled oats. Spread in 13x9-inch greased pan. Bake in 350°F. oven for 20 minutes. Sprinkle on chocolate bits. Let stand for several minutes and spread with knife evenly. Let cool and cut into desired number of squares.
Makes 23 to 24 squares.

Sarah E. Cochran
Zelienople, Pennsylvania

World's Best Brownies

½ cup butter or margarine
1 (1-ounce) square unsweetened chocolate
1 cup plus 1 tablespoon all-purpose flour
1 cup sugar
2 eggs
1 teaspoon vanilla extract
Dash of salt

Combine butter and chocolate in small saucepan; cook, stirring constantly, over low heat until mixture melts. Remove from heat and stir in flour and sugar. Add eggs, 1 at a time, beating well after each addition. Stir in vanilla and salt. Pour batter into greased and floured 9-inch square baking pan. Bake at 325°F. for 35 to 40 minutes or until wooden pick inserted in center comes out clean. Cool and cut into squares to serve.
Makes 16 servings.

Catherine Bulla Rachide
Brandenton, Florida

Bourbon Balls

1 (6-ounce) package semisweet chocolate chips
1½ cups Jack Daniels
3 tablespoons light corn syrup
2½ cups vanilla wafer crumbs
½ cup confectioners' sugar
1 cup finely chopped pecans
½ cup confectioners' sugar

Place chocolate chips in top of double boiler. Place over hot water until chocolate melts. Add Jack Daniels and corn syrup, stirring well. Add vanilla wafer crumbs, ½ cup confectioners' sugar and pecans; stir well. Let stand for 30 minutes. Shape dough into 1-inch balls; roll in ½ cup confectioners' sugar. Store in airtight container for several days before serving.
Makes 15 to 20 balls.

Tewanna Douglas
Nashville, Tennessee

Buckeyes

1 pound butter, softened
2 pounds creamy peanut butter
3 pounds sifted confectioners' sugar
1 (24-ounce) package chocolate chips
⅔ bar parawax

Cream together butter and peanut butter. Add confectioners' sugar and blend well. Shape mixture by hand into size of small buckeyes. Place on cookie sheet and refrigerate for 1 hour. Melt chocolate chips and parawax in top of double boiler. Dip balls into chocolate, using toothpick. Place on waxed paper and allow to cool.
Makes 160 to 180 pieces.

Wayne J. Kleman
Columbus, Ohio

Campfire Foolproof Fudge

32 marshmallows
¼ cup water
2½ cups sugar
1   (5⅓-ounce) can evaporated milk
½ cup butter or margarine
¼ teaspoon salt
1½   (6-ounce) packages semisweet
    chocolate chips

Combine marshmallows and water in top of double boiler over boiling water. Cook, stirring occasionally, until marshmallows melt. Combine sugar, milk, butter and salt in large heavy saucepan; bring to a boil over medium heat. Boil for 8 minutes, stirring constantly. Remove form heat and stir in melted marshmallows and chocolate chips, stirring until chocolate melts. Pour mixture into buttered 12x8x2-inch baking pan. Cool completely and cut into squares. Makes 40 pieces.

Marge Monaghan
Ann Arbor, Michigan

Cocoa-Nut Candy

3 cups sugar
⅔ cup cocoa
Pinch of salt
1½ cups milk
½ cup butter or margarine
1 teaspoon vanilla extract
1½ cups chopped walnuts

Combine sugar, cocoa and salt in small Dutch oven; stir well. Add milk, stirring until smooth. Cook over medium heat, stirring constantly, until sugar dissolves. Continue cooking, without stirring, until mixture reaches soft-ball stage (236°F.). Remove from heat and stir in butter and vanilla. Cool for 10 minutes. Beat with an electric mixer or with wooden spoon until mixture is thick and creamy. Stir in walnuts. Pour into buttered 13x9x2-inch baking pan. Cool completely and cut into squares.
Makes 4 dozen pieces.

Elizabeth Gilley
Knoxville, Tennessee

English Toffee

1½ cups coarsely chopped pecans
    or almonds
2 cups butter
3 cups firmly packed brown sugar
1 teaspoon cream of tartar
1   (4-ounce) bar sweet baking
    chocolate
1½ cups coarsely chopped pecans
    or almonds

Sprinkle 1½ cups pecans in buttered 15x10x2-inch jelly roll pan; set aside. Melt butter in large cast-iron skillet over medium heat. Add brown sugar and cream of tartar. Cook over medium heat, stirring constantly, until mixture reaches soft-crack stage (285° to 290°F.). Quickly pour over pecans in prepared pan; let cool slightly. Place chocolate on toffee; spread melted chocolate over entire surface of toffee. Sprinkle with 1½ cups pecans. Cool completely. Break into pieces.
Makes about 3 pounds.

Rhea Y. Fetzer
Kalamazoo, Michigan

Five-Minute Peanut Butter Candy

⅔ cup evaporated milk
1⅔ cups sugar
Dash of salt
1½ cups diced marshmallows
1 cup creamy peanut butter (smooth)
1 teaspoon vanilla extract

Combine milk, sugar and salt in saucepan. Bring to a boil over low heat, stirring often. Boil for 5 minutes. Remove from heat and add marshmallows, peanut butter and vanilla, stirring until dissolved. Pour candy into buttered 8-inch square baking pan; cool. Cut into squares. Makes 2 dozen.

Susan Thomason
Elgin, Illinois

Creamy Mints

1 (16-ounce) package confectioners'
  sugar
¼ cup butter or margarine, softened
3 tablespoons boiling water
¼ teaspoon oil of peppermint
Few drops of food coloring
Sugar

Combine confectioners' sugar and butter, stirring well. Add water; stir until creamy. Stir in oil of peppermint and food coloring. Shape mixture into ½-inch balls; roll each in sugar. Press into candy molds; turn out onto waxed paper.
Makes about 80 mints.

Sally A. Blakely
Ann Arbor, Michigan

Mound Balls

½ cup butter or margarine, softened
1 (14-ounce) can sweetened
  condensed milk
4 cups confectioners' sugar
3 cups coconut
2 cups finely chopped nuts (optional)
1 bar paraffin
1 (12-ounce) package semisweet
  or milk chocolate chips

In large bowl, combine butter, condensed milk and confectioners' sugar. Add coconut and nuts. Drop by spoonfuls onto buttered cookie sheet. Freeze for 15 minutes or until easy to handle. In double boiler, melt paraffin. Add chocolate chips. Stir until melted. Dip candy, 1 at a time, into the chocolate. Place on waxed paper to dry. Refrigerate or freeze until serving time.
Makes about 5 dozen.

Randy Grooms
Louisville, Kentucky

Chocolate-Dipped Strawberries

2 pints strawberries with stems
½ cup semisweet chocolate chips
1 tablespoon corn syrup
1 tablespoon rum (optional)
5 tablespoons margarine or butter

Wash strawberries; gently pat dry. Combine chocolate chips, corn syrup, rum and margarine in small saucepan. Cook over low heat until chocolate melts, stirring constantly. Remove from heat. Set saucepan in pan of hot water to maintain dipping consistency. Dip each strawberry into chocolate mixture, coating ⅔ strawberry; allow excess chocolate to drip off. Place strawberries, stem-side down on waxed paper-covered wire rack. Refrigerate until chocolate is set, about 15 minutes.
Makes 36 to 48 strawberries.

Veronica McEachern-Kelly
Denver, Colorado

Sugar-Glazed Walnuts

½ cup butter or margarine
1 cup firmly packed brown sugar
1 teaspoon ground cinnamon
1 pound walnut halves

Place butter in microwave-safe 1½-quart baking dish; microwave at HIGH (100% power) for 1 minute or until butter melts. Stir in brown sugar and cinnamon; microwave at HIGH (100% power) for 2 minutes. Add walnuts, stirring to coat well. Microwave at HIGH (100% power) for 3 to 5 minutes. Spread on cookie sheet to cool completely. Store in airtight containers.
Makes about 1 pound.

Nancy Williams
Canton, Michigan

Pies

Candy Bar Pie

1 (8-ounce) milk chocolate bar
with almonds
1/3 cup milk
1½ cups miniature or 15 regular
marshmallows
1 cup whipping cream, whipped
1 (9-inch) baked chocolate pie shell
(recipe follows)
Additional whipped cream

Combine chocolate bar and milk in top of double boiler; cook over boiling water until chocolate melts. Add marshmallows, stirring until melted. Cool completely. Fold in whipped cream. Spoon mixture into pie shell. Chill for several hours or until firm. Garnish with additional whipped cream.
Makes one (9-inch) pie.

Chocolate Crust

½ cup butter or margarine, softened
1 cup sugar
1 egg
1 teaspoon vanilla extract
1¼ cups all-purpose flour
½ cup cocoa
¾ teaspoon soda
¼ teaspoon salt

Cream butter in medium mixing bowl; gradually add sugar, beating until light and fluffy. Add egg and vanilla, beating well. Combine flour, cocoa, soda and salt; stir into creamed mixture. Divide dough into 2 equal portions; shape each portion into roll 1½ inches in diameter. Wrap each in waxed paper; chill thoroughly. Slice 1 roll into ⅛-inch thick slices. Reserve remaining roll for other uses. Arrange slices in bottom and sides of 9-inch pie plate. Press edges together to seal. Bake at 375°F. for 8 to 10 minutes. Cool completely.
Makes two (9-inch) pie shells.

Louise Kaline
Bloomfield Hills, Michigan

Angel Pie

½ cup sugar
¼ cup flour
1 envelope Knox gelatin
½ teaspoon salt
1¾ cup milk
3 egg whites
¼ teaspoon cream of tartar
½ cup sugar
¾ teaspoon vanilla extract
1 pint whipping cream
⅓ cup sugar
¾ cup coconut
1   (9-inch) graham cracker crust

In saucepan, combine ½ cup sugar, flour, gelatin, salt and milk. Bring to a boil over low heat and boil for 1 minute. Cool completely. Beat egg whites, cream of tartar, ½ cup sugar and vanilla until stiff. Fold gently into cooled custard mixture. Beat whipping cream and ⅓ cup sugar until smooth and fold into mixture. Add coconut. Pour into graham cracker crust and chill. Garnish with raspberries or strawberries or serve plain.
Makes 6 to 8 servings.

Shirley Tranquill
Pittsburgh, Pennsylvania

Apple Pie

1 cup sifted all-purpose flour
1 cup whole wheat pastry flour
1 teaspoon salt
¾ cup shortening
5 to 7 tablespoons water
6 to 8 tart apples, pared, cored and
   sliced
1 cup sugar
2 tablespoons all-purpose flour
1 teaspoon ground cinnamon
¼ teaspoon ground nutmeg
1 tablespoon butter or margarine

Sift flours and salt together. Cut in shortening with pastry blender. Add water, 1 tablespoon at a time, gently tossing with fork. Form into ball. Divide dough in half. Flatten half the dough on lightly floured surface or pastry cloth. Roll from center to edge until ⅛ inch thick. Line 9-inch pie plate and trim extra dough around edge. Place apples, sugar, 2 tablespoons flour and spices in bottom crust. Dot with butter. Roll remaining dough to ⅛-inch thickness; cut slits in center of top crust. Lift pastry and place on top of pie. Trim ½-inch beyond edge. Tuck top crust under and flute edge. Bake at 400°F. for 50 minutes or until apple slices are tender.
Makes 6 to 8 servings.

Linda Mueller
Long Beach, Mississippi

No-Crust Apple Pie

8 or 9 apples, peeled, cored and
   sliced
1 tablespoon sugar
1 teaspoon ground cinnamon
½ cup butter or margarine, melted
1 cup all-purpose flour
¾ cup sugar
½ cup chopped pecans
1 egg, beaten
Pinch of salt

Fill 9-inch pie plate ¾ full with apples. Combine 1 tablespoon sugar and cinnamon; sprinkle over apples. Combine butter, flour, ¾ cup sugar, pecans, egg and salt; mix well. Spoon batter over apples. Bake at 350°F. for 45 minutes.
Makes 6 to 8 servings.

Gayle Ruby
Ponca City, Oklahoma

Butterscotch Pie

¼ cup sugar
1 (13-ounce) can evaporated milk
¼ cup water
½ cup sugar
3 tablespoons cornstarch
Dash of salt
¼ cup milk
2 eggs, separated
⅓ cup butter or margarine
1 teaspoon vanilla extract
1 (9-inch) baked pie shell
Pinch of cream of tartar
Dash of salt
⅓ cup sugar

Place ¼ cup sugar in heavy 2-quart saucepan. Cook over medium heat, stirring constantly with wooden spoon, until sugar caramelizes. Add evaporated milk and water, stirring well. Combine ½ cup sugar, cornstarch and salt in small mixing bowl; stir well. Stir in milk. Add to caramel mixture. Cook, stirring constantly, until thickened. Beat egg yolks; stir about ¼ of the hot mixture into egg yolks. Add to remaining hot mixture, stirring constantly. Cook, stirring constantly for 2 minutes or until mixture thickens. Remove from heat and stir in butter and vanilla. Pour mixture into pie shell. Combine egg whites, cream of tartar and salt; beat until foamy. Gradually add ⅓ cup sugar, beating until stiff peaks form. Spread meringue over filling, sealing to edge of pastry. Bake at 325°F. for 12 to 15 minutes or until meringue is lightly browned. Cool completely.
Makes one (9-inch) pie.

Alice Sloane
Detroit, Michigan

Pizza Grano

5 eggs
1¼ cups sugar
3 cups ricotta cheese
¼ cup fruit and peel mix (optional)
1 teaspoon grated orange or lemon rind
1 teaspoon vanilla extract
½ teaspoon ground cinnamon
¼ cup cold cooked rice
¼ cup milk
2 (8-inch) graham cracker pie shells

Combine eggs and sugar in large mixing bowl; beat until stiff. Add cheese, fruit and peel mix, grated rind, vanilla and cinnamon. Beat for 2 minutes. Cover and refrigerate for 4 hours. Stir in rice and milk. Pour mixture into pie shells. Bake at 350°F. for 1 hour or until set and golden brown. Let cool completely.
Makes two (8-inch) pies.

Joseph A. Umberto
Fresh Meadows, New York

Super-Size Toll House Walnut Pie

3 eggs
¾ cup all-purpose flour
¾ cup sugar
¾ cup firmly packed brown sugar
1½ cups butter, melted and cooled to room temperature
1½ cups semisweet chocolate morsels
1½ cups chopped walnuts
1 (10-inch) unbaked pie shell
Whipped cream or ice cream (optional)

Beat eggs until foamy in large bowl; beat in flour, sugar and brown sugar until well blended. Blend in melted butter. Stir in semisweet chocolate morsels and walnuts. Pour into pie shell. Bake at 325°F. for 1 hour 10 minutes to 1 hour 15 minutes. Serve warm with whipped cream or ice cream.
Makes 10 servings.

Kathy Bott
Westerville, Ohio

Minty Chocolate Pie

½ cup sugar
1 envelope unflavored gelatin
Dash of salt
1 cup milk
2 squares (2 ounces) unsweetened
  chocolate (cut up)
3 egg yolks, slightly beaten
¼ teaspoon peppermint extract
3 egg whites
¼ cup sugar
1   (4½-ounce) carton frozen
  whipped topping, thawed
1 (9-inch) baked pie shell
Crushed peppermint stick candy
  (optional)

Combine ½ cup sugar, unflavored gelatin and salt in medium saucepan. Add milk and chocolate. Cook and stir over low heat until gelatin is dissolved and chocolate is melted. Remove from heat; stir about half the hot mixture into egg yolks. Add to remaining hot mixture, stirring well. Return to saucepan; cook and stir until mixture thickens and bubbles. Remove from heat; stir in peppermint extract. Cool until partially set. Beat egg whites until soft peaks form; gradually add ¼ cup sugar, beating until stiff peaks form. Fold into chocolate mixture. Fold in whipped topping. Turn into baked pie shell. Chill until filling is set. Garnish with additional whipped topping and crushed peppermint candy.
Makes one (9-inch) pie.

Terri Rummer
Nashville, Tennessee

Mississippi Mud Pie

1 stick butter, softened
1 cup flour
1 cup chopped pecans
1   (8-ounce) package cream cheese
1 cup confectioners' sugar
1   (9-ounce) carton Cool Whip
2   (3-ounce) packages instant
  chocolate pudding
3 cups cold milk

Mix butter and flour with hands and add pecans. Press in 12½x8-inch pyrex dish. Bake at 350°F. for 20 minutes. Cool. Mix 8-ounce package cream cheese with 1 cup confectioners' sugar with mixer. Fold in 1 cup Cool Whip. Spread over cooled crust. Mix 2 packages chocolate instant pudding with cold milk with mixer until thick. Spread over Cool Whip. Top with remaining Cool Whip. Refrigerate and cut into squares to serve.
Makes 8 large servings.

Michael Smith
Bettendorf, Iowa

Old-Fashioned Chocolate Pie

1 cup sugar
¾ cup cocoa
½ cup all-purpose flour
½ teaspoon salt
2 cups milk
2 eggs, separated
3 tablespoons butter or margarine
1 teaspoon vanilla extract
1   (9-inch) baked pie shell
1 teaspoon sugar

Combine 1 cup sugar, cocoa, flour and salt in medium saucepan; stir well. Combine milk and egg yolks, beating well; add to sugar mixture. Cook over medium heat, stirring constantly, until mixture thickens. Remove from heat and stir in butter and vanilla. Pour mixture into pie shell. Beat egg whites until foamy; gradually add 1 teaspoon sugar, beating until stiff peaks form. Spread over filling, sealing to edge of pastry. Bake at 425°F. for 6 minutes or until meringue is lightly browned. Cool to room temperature.
Makes one (9-inch) pie.

Marjorie Bates
Godfrey, Illinois

Coconut Macaroon Pie

2 cups all-purpose flour
½ teaspoon salt
½ cup chilled butter or margarine
3 tablespoons lard or shortening
5 to 6 tablespoons cold water
Sugar
Ground cinnamon
3 eggs
1½ cups sugar
1⅓ cups flaked coconut
½ cup butter or margarine, melted
⅓ cup buttermilk
1 teaspoon vanilla extract

Combine flour and salt in medium mixing bowl; cut in chilled butter and lard with pastry blender until mixture resembles coarse meal. Sprinkle water evenly over surface; stir lightly with fork until dry ingredients are moistened. Shape dough into ball. Cover and refrigerate for 2 to 36 hours. Roll pastry to ⅛-inch thickness on surface sprinkled with sugar and ground cinnamon. Fit pastry into 9-inch pie plate; flute edges. Beat eggs until light and fluffy; stir in remaining ingredients. Pour mixture into pie shell. Bake at 350°F. for 1 hour or until set. Serve warm or at room temperature.
Makes one (9-inch) pie.

Judith A. Nelson
Ann Arbor, Michigan

Cream Pie

5 tablespoons flour, (heaping)
2 cups sugar
1 cup whipping cream
1 cup half and half
⅛ teaspoon nutmeg
⅛ teaspoon cinnamon
1 (9-inch) pie crust

In bowl, combine flour and sugar; mix well. Add cream, half and half and sprinkle with nutmeg and cinnamon. Stir until mixture is dissolved. Set aside and stir again in 5 minutes. Pour into pie crust. Bake in 400°F. oven for 15 minutes; reduce temperature to 350°F. and bake for 45 minutes longer.
Makes one (9-inch) pie.

George Griffith
Ann Arbor, Michigan

Grasshopper Pie

16 to 18 Oreo cookies
3 tablespoons margarine, melted
20 large marshmallows
⅔ cup coffee cream
2 teaspoons Creme de Menthe
  liqueur
2 teaspoons Creme de Cacao
  liqueur
1 cup heavy whipping cream, whipped

Crush cookies with rolling pin and mix with melted margarine. Press into 8-inch pyrex pie plate. Melt marshmallows with coffee cream and allow to cool. Add liqueurs; fold in whipped cream. Pour over crust and sprinkle with additional Oreo crumbs. Keep refrigerated and serve chilled.
Makes 8 servings.

Cheryl L. McCormick
Hendersonville, Tennessee

Key Lime Pie

1 (14-ounce) can sweetened
  condensed milk
Grated rind from 1 key lime
½ cup key lime juice
2 eggs, separated
1 egg
1 (9-inch) graham cracker crust
¼ cup sugar

Combine condensed milk, lime rind and juice; add egg yolks and egg, beating well. Spoon mixture into crust. Beat egg whites until foamy; gradually add sugar, beating until stiff but not dry. Spread meringue over filling, sealing to edge of pastry. Bake at 350°F. for 10 minutes or until meringue is golden brown. Cool to room temperature. Chill.
Makes one (9-inch) pie.

Mike Keuper, Sr.
Fort Worth, Texas

Key Lime Pie

1 envelope unflavored gelatin
½ cup sugar
¼ teaspoon salt
4 eggs, separated
½ cup lime juice
¼ cup water
1 teaspoon grated lime rind
Few drops of green food coloring
½ cup sugar
1 cup whipping cream, whipped
1   (9-inch) baked pastry shell
1 cup whipping cream, whipped
Lime slices

Combine gelatin, ½ cup sugar and salt in large saucepan; stir well. Add egg yolks, lime juice and water, beating well. Cook over medium heat, stirring constantly, until mixture comes to a boil. Remove from heat and stir in rind and food coloring. Chill until mixture mounds when dropped from spoon. Beat egg whites until foamy; gradually add ½ cup sugar, beating until stiff peaks form. Fold beaten egg whites and whipped cream into gelatin mixture. Spoon mixture into pastry shell. Chill until set. Spoon 1 cup whipped cream in center of pie, leaving 2 inches of filling uncovered around edge of pie. Garnish with lime slices.
Makes one (9-inch) pie.

Mary Gay Jerue
Boca Raton, Florida

Kiwi Pie

2 cups all-purpose flour
½ teaspoon salt
¾ cup butter or margarine, softened
¼ cup cold water
¼ cup plus 2 tablespoons cornstarch
½ cup water
1 cup sugar
1¾ cups water
¼ cup lemon juice
Dash of salt
1 tablespoon butter or margarine
1 cup (about 3 kiwi) mashed kiwi
1 cup whipping cream
½ cup confectioners' sugar
1 or 2 kiwi, peeled and sliced

Combine flour and salt in medium mixing bowl. Cut in ¾ cup butter with pastry blender until mixture resembles coarse meal. Sprinkle ¼ cup cold water evenly over surface; stir with fork until dry ingredients are moistened. Shape dough into ball; chill. Roll dough to ⅛-inch thickness on lightly floured surface; fit into 9-inch pie plate. Flute edges. Bake at 425°F. for 18 to 20 minutes or until golden brown. Dissolve cornstarch in ½ cup cold water. Combine sugar, 1¾ cups water, lemon juice and salt in small saucepan; bring to a boil. Add cornstarch mixture. Cook, stirring constantly, until mixture returns to a boil. Remove from heat and stir in 1 tablespoon butter. Cool. Stir in mashed kiwi. Spoon mixture into pie shell; chill thoroughly. Beat whipping cream until soft peaks form; gradually add confectioners' sugar, beating until stiff peaks form. Pipe whipped cream onto pie, using pastry bag or cookie press. Garnish with sliced kiwi.
Makes one (9-inch) pie.

To make 12 tart shells, press dough into muffin pans. Bake at 425°F. for 12 to 14 minutes or until golden brown.

Barbara Little
Redondo, Washington

Macaroon Pie

12 saltine crackers
3 egg whites
1 cup sugar
¼ teaspoon baking powder
1 teaspoon almond flavoring
12 dates, chopped
½ cup nuts, chopped
Whipped cream

Crush crackers very fine with rolling pin; place in bowl. Beat egg whites until stiff, gradually adding sugar, baking powder and almond flavoring. Add dates and nuts to crackers. Fold egg whites into cracker mixture and pour into buttered 9-inch pie pan. Bake at 350°F. for 25 minutes to 30 minutes. Top with whipped cream and serve.
Makes one (9-inch) pie.

Jackie Webb
Smyrna, Georgia

Lemon Meringue Pie

1½ cups sugar
⅓ cup cornstarch
1½ cups water
3 egg yolks, beaten
3 tablespoons butter or margarine
1 tablespoon grated lemon rind
¼ cup lemon juice
1 (9-inch) baked pie shell
3 egg whites
¼ teaspoon cream of tartar
¼ cup sugar

Combine 1½ cups sugar and cornstarch in medium saucepan; stir well. Gradually add water, stirring well. Cook over medium heat, stirring constantly, until mixture thickens and boils. Boil for 1 minute. Stir about ¼ of the hot mixture into egg yolks; add to remaining hot mixture, stirring constantly. Bring to a boil, stirring constantly, and boil for 1 minute. Remove from heat. Stir in butter, lemon rind and juice. Pour mixture into pie shell. Combine egg whites and cream of tartar in large mixing bowl; beat until foamy. Gradually add ¼ cup sugar, beating until stiff peaks form. Spread meringue over filling, sealing to edge of pastry. Bake at 400°F. for 8 to 10 minutes or until meringue is lightly browned. Cool.
Makes one (9-inch) pie.

Craig Schubert
Carmichael, California

Maple Chiffon Pie

1½ cups hot milk
2 eggs, separated
1 envelope Knox's gelatin
¼ cup water
1 cup maple syrup
¼ teaspoon salt
½ teaspoon vanilla extract
¼ cup chopped nuts (optional)
1 (9-inch) baked pie shell
½ cup whipping cream, whipped
  (optional)

In top of double boiler, add hot milk slowly to slightly beaten egg yolks. Cook until of custard consistency. Sprinkle gelatin on cold water. Add softened gelatin to custard mixture and stir until dissolved. Add maple syrup and salt. Cool. When mixture begins to congeal, fold in stiffly beaten egg whites, vanilla and nuts. Pour into baked pie shell and top with whipped cream.
Makes 6 servings.

Whipped cream may be folded into mixture before chilling, if desired. Nuts add flavor and texture. Mixture may also be served as a pudding in glass dishes.

Aaron Kaufer
Ann Arbor, Michigan

From The South–Old-Fashioned Pear Cobbler

4 pears, halved and cored
¼ cup plus 2 tablespoons frozen
  orange juice concentrate,
  thawed and undiluted
½ cup all-purpose flour
½ cup uncooked regular oats
½ cup firmly packed brown sugar
¼ teaspoon ground cinnamon
⅛ teaspoon ground nutmeg
⅛ teaspoon salt
¼ cup plus 2 tablespoons butter or
  margarine, softened

Arrange pears, skin-side down, in greased 3-quart baking dish. Pour orange juice concentrate over pears. Combine flour, oats, brown sugar, cinnamon, nutmeg and salt; stir well. Cut in butter with pastry blender. Sprinkle mixture over pears. Bake at 375°F. for 30 minutes or until pears are tender. Serve warm.
Makes 8 servings.

Larry C. Stark
Long Beach, Mississippi

Mystery Pecan Pie

1   (8-ounce) package cream cheese,
      softened
⅓ cup sugar
4 eggs
1 teaspoon vanilla extract
¼ teaspoon salt
½ cup sugar
1 cup light or dark corn syrup
1 teaspoon vanilla extract
1   (9-inch) pie crust
1¼ cups chopped pecans

Beat cream cheese with ⅓ cup sugar, 1 egg, 1 teaspoon vanilla and salt until thick and creamy. Set aside. Beat remaining eggs only until blended; add ½ cup sugar, corn syrup and vanilla. Blend well. Spread cream cheese mixture on bottom of pastry-lined pan. Sprinkle with pecans. Gently pour syrup mixture over pecans. Bake at 375°F. for 35 to 40 minutes or until center is firm to touch.
Makes one (9-inch) pie.

Mary Rowley
Columbia, South Carolina

Mile-High Strawberry Pie

1½ cups all-purpose flour
1½ teaspoons sugar
½ cup vegetable oil
2 tablespoons milk
2 egg whites
1   (16-ounce) package frozen
      strawberries, thawed
1 cup sugar
1 tablespoon lemon juice
1 cup whipping cream, whipped
Fresh strawberries
Mint leaves

Sift together flour and 1½ teaspoons sugar into 10-inch pie plate. Combine oil and milk; add to flour mixture. Stir until dry ingredients are moistened. Press mixture evenly into pie plate. Bake at 400°F. for 10 to 15 minutes or until golden brown. Cool completely. Beat egg whites until light and fluffy in large mixing bowl. Add strawberries, 1 cup sugar and lemon juice; beat at high speed on electric mixer for 15 minutes. Fold in whipped cream. Spoon mixture into pie shell. Freeze for 6 hours. Garnish with fresh strawberries and mint leaves.
Makes one (10-inch) pie.

A great light summer dessert.

Susan S. Piekenbrock
Arlington Heights, Illinois

Quick And Easy Strawberry Pie

1 cup water
1 cup sugar
2 tablespoons light corn syrup
3 tablespoons cornstarch
1   (3-ounce) package strawberry
      gelatin
1   (8-inch) baked pie crust
3 cups fresh strawberries
Whipped cream

Combine water, sugar, corn syrup and cornstarch in saucepan. Boil until thick, stirring constantly. Remove from heat. Stir in strawberry gelatin. Fill baked pie crust with strawberries. Spoon gelatin mixture over strawberries; cool. Top with whipped cream.
Makes one (8-inch) pie.

Martha Zeeb
Ann Arbor, Michigan

Miscellaneous

Miscellaneous

Beet Jelly

3 cups beet juice
1 (1¾-ounce) package Sure Gel
¼ cup lemon juice
1 (1½-ounce) package unsweetened
 raspberry drink mix
1 (3¾-ounce) package raspberry-
 flavored gelatin
4 cups sugar

In medium saucepan, combine beet juice, Sure Gel and lemon juice. Bring mixture to a boil. Add drink mix, gelatin and sugar; continue to boil mixture for 6 minutes. Remove pink foam. Pour into hot sterilized jars, leaving ½-inch headspace; seal.
Makes 4 to 6 jars jelly.

Tess Bommarito
Ann Arbor, Michigan

Blueberry Marmalade

1 medium orange
1 lemon
¾ cup water
3 cups crushed blueberries
5 cups sugar
½ (6-ounce) bottle liquid fruit
 pectin

Peel orange and lemon, scraping excess white membrane from rind; cut rind into fine shreds. Place in large saucepan with water; bring to a boil. Simmer, covered, for 10 minutes, stirring occasionally. Remove white membrane from fruit; finely chop fruit and discard seeds. Add fruit to rind mixture with blueberries. Cover; simmer for 12 minutes. Add sugar. Bring to a full rolling boil; boil for 1 minute, stirring constantly. Remove from heat and immediately stir in fruit pectin. Skim foam; stir and simmer for 7 minutes. Ladle mixture into hot sterilized jars, leaving ½-inch headspace. Seal jars at once.
Makes 6 ½-pint jars.

June Bales
Ann Arbor, Michigan

Strawberry Soup

1 quart fresh strawberries
1 quart heavy cream
1 cup sugar
1 cup rum
Dash of ginger
7 sliced strawberries
7-Up

Combine strawberries, cream, sugar, rum and ginger in blender. Process until smooth. Pour into serving bowls. Top with sliced strawberries and serve with splash of 7-Up.
Makes 8 to 10 servings.

Lorin Frye
Rochester, New York

◀*Dinnerware in this photograph by Franklin Lloyd Wright.*

Kaernaemaelk Koldskaal
(Cold Buttermilk Soup)

4 cups buttermilk
3 eggs
4 tablespoons sugar
Juice of 1 lemon
1 teaspoon vanilla extract
Whipping cream, whipped

In large bowl, beat buttermilk. In separate bowl, beat eggs, sugar, lemon juice and vanilla together. Add egg mixture to buttermilk, a little at a time, beating well after each addition. Chill and serve in bowls topped with whipped cream.
Makes 4 servings.

Esther Swanson
Kent, Washington

Cucumber Soup (Hot or Cold)

5 cucumbers
2 shallots, chopped
7 cups chicken broth
¼ cup butter
2 tablespoons all-purpose flour
Salt and pepper to taste
3 egg yolks
1 cup heavy cream
8 tablespoons fresh chives, chopped

Peel, seed and coarsely chop 4 cucumbers, reserving 1 for garnish. Combine cucumbers with shallots and chicken broth in large saucepan or Dutch oven. Simmer mixture for 15 to 20 minutes. Cool slightly and purée in blender. Melt butter in large saucepan over low heat. Add flour; stir and cook gently until straw-colored. Add cucumber purée. Increase heat and stir until boiling. Reduce heat and simmer for 2 to 3 minutes. Season with salt and pepper to taste. Whisk egg yolks and cream together in bowl. Add a little of the hot soup to egg mixture, mixing well. Add egg mixture to soup. Heat gently while stirring but do not boil. Chill for several hours or overnight. Just before serving, peel, seed and chop reserved cucumber for garnish. Add approximately 2 tablespoons chopped cucumbers to each chilled serving bowl. Pour soup on top and garnish with 1 tablespoon chopped chives.
Makes 4 to 6 servings.

Excellent hot too! Remember flavor loses intensity when chilled, so salt well. Use your good judgement.

Sharon Horn Madsen
Aberdeen, South Dakota

Canadian Vichyssoise

4 potatoes, peeled and cut into pieces
1 cup parsley, chopped
½ head lettuce, shredded
1 onion, sliced
5 to 6 cups well-seasoned chicken broth
1½ cups milk or cream
Dash of nutmeg, cayenne pepper, thyme, salt and pepper to taste
Snipped chives
Grated raw carrot

In large saucepan, combine potatoes, parsley, lettuce, onion and chicken broth. Bring to a boil; reduce heat. Simmer until vegetables are tender; cool slightly. Place mixture in blender or food processor; blend until smooth or press through a food mill. Return to saucepan; add milk and season to taste. Reheat to serve warm or place in refrigerator for at least 2 hours until thoroughly chilled to serve cold. Sprinkle each serving with chives and carrots.
Makes 8 servings.

For a lighter soup, use milk; for a thicker consistency, use cream.

Susan L. Parker
Bedford, Ohio

Princess Di's Watercress Soup

2 tablespoons butter
2 tablespoons flour
2 cups warmed chicken stock
2 bunches fresh watercress, washed,
  thick stems removed
1 cup heavy cream
Salt and pepper to taste

Melt butter in saucepan; add flour and cook over low heat for about 2 minutes, stirring gently. Slowly add chicken stock, whisking constantly until thickened. Add watercress to mixture; cook slowly for about 20 minutes. Remove from heat; allow to cool. Blend mixture in blender or food processor, then press through a fine sieve into bowl. Add cream. Season with salt and pepper. Cover and chill until ready to serve.
Makes 4 servings.

Diane Allan
England, United Kingdom

Cauliflower Soup

½ cup butter or margarine
4 tablespoons flour
4 to 6 chicken bouillon cubes
2 cups milk
2 small potatoes, chopped
1 small onion, chopped
2 stalks celery, chopped
1 small carrot, thinly sliced
3 cups boiling salted water
1 medium head cauliflower, washed
  and cut into small pieces
Salt to taste

In large saucepan or Dutch oven, melt butter and stir in flour. Add chicken bouillon cubes and milk. Stir mixture over medium to medium-high heat for approximately 15 minutes until thick. (Do not let mixture brown). Set aside. Cook potatoes, onion, celery and carrot in boiling water until tender. Drain vegetables, reserving liquid; add to cream sauce. Steam cauliflower until tender. Add cauliflower to cream sauce. If mixture looks thick, add vegetable water to thin.
Makes 4 to 6 servings.

Ann Litzler
Ann Arbor, Michigan

Cheese Soup

1 chicken bouillon cube
1 cup water
¼ cup diced onion
½ cup diced celery
½ cup diced carrots
3 cups cubed potatoes
3 cups milk
2 tablespoons flour
½ pound Velveeta cheese, cubed

In medium saucepan, dissolve bouillon in water. Add remaining ingredients except cheese. Simmer until vegetables are soft, about 15 minutes. Add cheese and heat over low heat until melted.
Makes 4 to 6 servings.

Amy Hamill
Brighton, Michigan

Kangaroo Tail Soup

1 kangaroo tail
2 pounds ground beef
Salt and pepper
8 cups water
2 carrots, finely chopped
2 turnips, finely chopped
6 whole cloves
1 clove garlic
1½ teaspoons fresh lemon juice
1 cup port wine

Chop tail and beef into small pieces. Place in deep saucepan. Add salt and pepper to taste. Cover with water. Bring to a boil. Simmer for 2 hours. Strain. Add carrots, turnips, cloves, garlic, lemon juice and wine to stock. Cook until vegetables are tender. Serve with toast.
Makes 6 servings.

David and Sallyanne Robin
Parramatta Sydney, Australia

Caramel Corn

1⅓ cups sugar
1 cup butter or margarine
½ cup light corn syrup
1 teaspoon vanilla extract
8 cups popped popcorn
  (keep warm in oven)
1 cup peanuts (optional)

Combine sugar, butter and corn syrup in 3-quart saucepan. Cook over medium heat, stirring constantly, until mixture comes to a boil; reduce heat. Continue boiling, stirring occasionally, until mixture reaches hard-ball stage (270° on a candy thermometer). Remove from heat and stir in vanilla. Place popcorn and peanuts in large bowl. Pour sauce over popcorn and stir until evenly coated. Store in airtight container. Makes 8 cups.

Linda Mueller
Long Beach, Mississippi

Crazy Corn

8 cups popped popcorn
1⅓ cups chopped pecans
⅔ cup chopped almonds
1⅓ cups sugar
1 cup (2 sticks) corn oil margarine
½ cup light corn syrup
1 teaspoon vanilla extract

Combine popcorn and nuts in large bowl. In medium saucepan, combine sugar, margarine and corn syrup; cook until mixture turns light caramel color. Remove from heat and add vanilla. Pour over corn and nuts. Spread mixture on buttered cookie sheet. Let cool; break into chunks.
Makes about 10 cups.

Makes a nice Christmas gift.

Susan Webb
Long Beach, Mississippi

Deviled Eggs

6 hard-cooked eggs
¼ cup mayonnaise
2 tablespoons butter or margarine,
  melted
¼ teaspoon salt
Dash of pepper
¼ teaspoon prepared mustard
1 teaspoon minced onion
Olives with pimentos (optional)
Parsley (optional)
Watercress (optional)

Cut eggs in half lengthwise. Place yolks in small bowl. Mash yolks; add mayonnaise, melted butter, salt, pepper, mustard and minced onion; mix well. Fill egg white halves with mixture. Garnish each egg half with olives, parsley or watercress.
Makes 12 egg halves.

Jennifer Menges
Dunkirk, New York

Granola

4 cups rolled oats
1½ cups flaked coconut
1 cup sunflower seed
1 cup wheat germ
½ cup bran
1 cup toasted salted soybeans
½ cup chopped cashews
½ cup chopped almonds
½ cup sesame seed
1 teaspoon cinnamon (optional)
½ cup peanut oil
½ cup honey
½ teaspoon vanilla extract
½ cup brown sugar
1 cup raisins

Combine oats, coconut, sunflower seed, wheat germ, bran, soybeans, cashews, almonds, sesame seed and cinnamon. Heat oil and honey until hot; add vanilla. Pour over oat mixture. Spread out on two 11x6-inch baking sheets with sides. Bake in preheated 250°F. oven for 1½ hours, stirring occasionally. Remove from oven and add brown sugar and raisins; stir to combine. Cool and package to store.
Makes 20 servings.

Beverly Switzer
Ann Arbor, Michigan

Coleslaw Dressing

1 cup mayonnaise
½ teaspoon onion salt
½ teaspoon celery salt
½ teaspoon pepper
⅛ cup vinegar
⅛ cup oil
¼ cup milk
⅛ cup sugar

Combine all ingredients in blender container; process until well blended.
Makes 1½ cups dressing.

Therese Laurin
Burlington, Vermont

Great Garlic Dressing

1 cup mayonnaise (or low-calorie
   mayonnaise)
¼ cup fresh chopped parsley
1½ teaspoons Dijon-style mustard
1 to 2 cloves garlic, minced
¼ teaspoon leaf oregano, crumbled
⅛ teaspoon pepper

Combine mayonnaise, parsley, mustard, garlic, oregano and pepper in bowl; beat until blended. Store in airtight container in refrigerator.
Makes 1 cup.

Suzanne Gibson
Hamden, Connecticut

Lazy Housewife's Pickles

4 medium onions, sliced
10 to 12 cucumbers
2½ teaspoons dillseed
2½ teaspoons celery seed
¼ plus ¹⁄₁₆ teaspoons alum
4 cups sugar
1 quart vinegar
1 quart water
½ cup salt

In bottom of 5 sterilized jars place 4 slices onion. Cut cucumbers into quarters lengthwise; place in jars (enough to fill each jar). Add ½ teaspoon dillseed, ½ teaspoon celery seed and ¹⁄₁₆ teaspoon alum to each jar. In large saucepan combine sugar, vinegar, water and salt. Bring to a boil. Pour boiling liquid over cucumbers in each jar, leaving ½-inch headspace; seal. Let stand for 2 weeks before using.
Makes 5 quarts.

Louise Martin
Columbia, Missouri

Mexican Madness (Kiss)

1 medium onion
2 cloves garlic
1 teaspoon salt
1 tablespoon sugar
2 teaspoons crushed dried red pepper
  (no substitutions)
1 (14½-ounce) can whole red
  tomatoes

Chop onion and garlic in food processor, using sharp blade, for 8 seconds or until mixture is coarse. Add salt, sugar, red pepper and tomatoes with liquid. Process in food processor for 10 to 15 seconds until blended. Place mixture in medium saucepan; cook over medium heat for approximately 8 minutes.
Makes about 2 cups.

May be cooked in microwave on High for 6 to 7 minutes.

Jean Wilcox
Jasper, Indiana

Ravioli Pasta

4 eggs
2 teaspoons salt
3 tablespoons vegetable oil
1 cup boiling water
5 cups flour

Beat eggs. Add salt, oil and boiling water, beating well. Add flour slowly. Knead on floured surface for about 10 minutes or until elastic and smooth. Roll dough to ¹⁄₁₆ or ⅛-inch thick. Cut into desired size.
Makes about 1½ pounds pasta.

Great for Ravioli pasta.

JoAnn Godwin
Adrian, Michigan

Red Wine Marinade

1 cup onions, thinly sliced
¼ cup olive oil
2 large cloves garlic, minced
½ cup red wine vinegar
1 crumbled bay leaf
½ teaspoon thyme
¾ cup dry red wine
½ cup beef broth
Salt and pepper to taste

Sauté onions in olive oil until golden. Add garlic and sauté for 2 minutes longer. Add red wine vinegar and cook over medium-high heat until liquid is reduced by half. Add bay leaf, thyme, red wine and beef broth. Simmer for 5 minutes. Add salt and pepper to taste. Cool. Pour over beef or lamb. Marinate, covered, overnight.
Makes about 3 cups marinade.

Lorraine Galloway
St. Louis, Missouri

Teriyaki Marinade

2 cloves garlic, minced
¼ cup soy sauce
¼ cup tomato juice
2 tablespoons oil
1 teaspoon lemon juice
3 tablespoons brown sugar
1 tablespoon catsup
Meat or chicken

Combine garlic, soy sauce, tomato juice, oil, lemon juice, brown sugar and catsup; mix well. Pour over meat or chicken and marinate for 1 hour, at room temperature, turning once; or in refrigerator for 1 to 3 days, covered. Remove meat from marinade; broil or barbecue. Brush meat with marinade during cooking.
Makes ¾ cup sauce.

Nancy Dotson
Canoga, California

Barbecue Marinade

2 teaspoons salt
4 tablespoons Worcestershire sauce
1 teaspoon paprika
2 or 3 cloves garlic, minced
1 teaspoon black pepper
1 tablespoon molasses
2 tablespoons vinegar
2 teaspoons prepared mustard
1 cup cold water

In bowl, combine all ingredients; mix well. Pour marinade over pork, beef or chicken. Marinate for 30 minutes to 1 hour.
Makes about 2 cups sauce.

Nanette B. Coté
Lynn, Massachusetts

Plantation Hot Sauce (for Seafood)

½ cup honey
½ cup prepared mustard
½ cup cider vinegar
¼ cup Worcestershire sauce
1 tablespoon parsley, chopped
2 teaspoons Tabasco sauce
1 teaspoon salt

In small saucepan, blend honey and mustard; stir in vinegar, Worcestershire sauce, parsley, Tabasco sauce and salt; bring to a boil. Remove from heat and cool. Serve with smoked fish, shrimp or seafood.
Makes about 1½ cups.

Christi Orcutt
Norcross, Georgia

Susie's Orbital Mustard (Sweet-Hot)

1   (4-ounce) can dry mustard
1 cup white wine vinegar
3 eggs, beaten
1 tablespoon molasses
1 tablespoon honey
¾ cup sugar
1 tablespoon whole mustard seed
2 cups mayonnaise

Mix dry mustard and vinegar; cover. Let stand for 8 hours or overnight. In medium saucepan, mix eggs, molasses, honey, sugar and mustard mixture. Stir over low heat until thickened, about 20 minutes; allow to cool. Add whole mustard seed and mayonnaise; cover and refrigerate.
Makes about 4 cups.

Susan Peterson
Diamond Bar, California

Barbecue Sauce For Baby Back Ribs

1 cup barbecue sauce
1 tablespoon spicy mustard
1 teaspoon Worcestershire sauce
1 teaspoon lemon juice
½ teaspoon liquid smoke
1 teaspoon wine vinegar
1 teaspoon seasoned salt
¼ teaspoon ground black pepper

Combine all ingredients in bowl; stir well. When ready to grill, brush parboiled baby back ribs with sauce. Brush occasionally throughout cooking.
Makes about 1 cup sauce.

Donna Haley
Columbus, Ohio

Chicken Barbecue Sauce

½ cup cooking oil
1 cup white vinegar
2 tablespoons salt
1½ teaspoons poultry seasoning
¼ teaspoon pepper
1 egg

Place all ingredients in deep bowl, mixing well. Make sure egg is well mixed into mixture. Dip chicken pieces into sauce; place under broiler or on barbecue grill. Turn chicken every 10 minutes, basting each time.
Makes 1¾ cups sauce.

This is an excellent sauce for those who don't like the "tomato" based sauces.

Gayle Ruby
Ponca City, Oklahoma

Honey Glaze

¼ pound butter
½ cup brown sugar
1 tablespoon honey
Juice of 1 lemon

Melt butter; add brown sugar, honey and lemon juice. Heat until hot, stirring occasionally.
Makes about ¾ cup glaze.

Use as glaze to grill salmon steaks on barbecue. Brush on both sides while grilling.

Anna Schmitt-Heatlie
Ann Arbor, Michigan

Potpourri For Use In Home

2 cups dried thyme
1 cup dried rosemary
½ cup dried lavender
1 cup dried mint
¼ cup dried tansy
¼ cup whole cloves
½ ounce orris root

Mix all ingredients together.
Makes 5 cups.

A very pleasant-smelling potpourri for use in drawers, bathrooms, kitchen and windows.

Donna Haley
Columbus, Ohio

Bachelor's Delight Breakfast "Just For Fun"

4 eggs
½ cup milk
½ cup all-purpose flour
½ cup salt
Pinch of brown sugar
Handful of peanuts
2 cups (8 ounces) shredded Cheddar cheese
4 ounces sausage, cooked and drained
Leftover Domino's Pizza

Beat eggs in medium mixing bowl; gradually add milk and flour, beating well. Stir in salt, brown sugar and peanuts. Pour mixture into greased microwave-safe 9-inch square baking dish. Top with cheese and sausage. Microwave at Medium (50% power) for 20 minutes; let stand for 5 minutes. Throw mixture away. Microwave Domino's Pizza at High (100% power) for 30 seconds. Devour. Serve with coffee, orange juice or coke.
Makes 1 serving.

Michael L. Orcutt
Norcross, Georgia

Nutrition Conversion Chart

Chocolate	Carob Powder (3 tablespoons plus 2 tablespoons milk = 1 square of chocolate)	
Cocoa	Carob Powder (equal amounts)	
Cornstarch	Arrowroot Powder Brown Rice Flour; Whole Wheat Flour;	
Fats and Shortenings, Hydrogenated	Unrefined Oils: Safflower, Corngerm, Olive Oil, Sesame	Requires Less Liquid
All-Purpose Flour	Whole Wheat Flour	Requires Additional Liquid
Rice, White	Brown Rice or Whole Grain Rice	
Salt	Kelp Powder; Sea Salt (equal amounts); Sesame Salt; Tamari Soy Sauce	
Sugar	Raw Unfiltered Honey (½ cup instead of 1 cup sugar) Pure Maple Syrup	Requires Less Liquid

Jane M. Tilford
Nashville, Tennessee

Equivalent Chart

When the recipe calls for . . .   **You need . . .**

When the recipe calls for . . .	You need . . .
½ cup butter	1 stick
2 cups butter	1 pound
4 cups all-purpose flour	1 pound
4½ to 5 cups sifted cake flour	1 pound
1 square chocolate	1 ounce
1 cup semisweet chocolate pieces	1 6-ounce package
4 cups marshmallows	1 pound
2¼ cups packed brown sugar	1 pound
4 cups confectioners' sugar	1 pound
2 cups granulated sugar	1 pound
3 cups tapioca	1 pound

1 cup fine dry bread crumbs	4 to 5 slices
1 cup soft bread crumbs	2 slices
1 cup small bread cubes	2 slices
1 cup fine cracker crumbs	28 saltines
1 cup fine graham cracker crumbs	15 crackers
1 cup vanilla wafer crumbs	22 wafers
1 cup crushed cornflakes	3 cups uncrushed
4 cups cooked macaroni	1 8-ounce package
3½ cups cooked rice	1 cup uncooked

1 cup freshly grated cheese	¼ pound
1 cup cottage cheese	1 8-ounce carton
1 cup sour cream	1 8-ounce carton
1 cup whipped cream	½ cup heavy cream
⅔ cup evaporated milk	1 small can
1⅔ cups evaporated milk	1 13-ounce can

4 cups sliced or chopped apples	4 medium
1 cup mashed banana	3 medium
2 cups pitted cherries	4 cups unpitted
3 cups shredded coconut	½ pound
4 cups cranberries	1 pound
1 cup pitted dates	1 8-ounce package
1 cup candied fruit	1 8-ounce package
3 to 4 tablespoons lemon juice plus 1 teaspoon grated rind	1 lemon
⅓ cup orange juice plus 2 teaspoons grated rind	1 orange
4 cups sliced peaches	8 medium
2 cups pitted prunes	1 12-ounce package
3 cups raisins	1 15-ounce package

4 cups diced cooked chicken	1 5-pound chicken
3 cups diced cooked meat	1 pound, cooked
2 cups ground cooked meat	1 pound, cooked

1 cup chopped nuts	4 ounces, shelled
	1 pound, unshelled

2 cups cooked green beans	½ pound fresh or 1 16-ounce can
2½ cups lima beans or red beans	1 cup dried, cooked
4 cups shredded cabbage	1 pound
1 cup grated carrot	1 large
1 4-ounce can mushrooms	½ pound, fresh
1 cup chopped onion	1 large
4 cups sliced or diced	4 medium raw potatoes
2 cups canned tomatoes	1 16-ounce can

VEGETABLES

Substitution Chart

Instead of . . . | *Use . . .*

BAKING

Instead of	Use
1 teaspoon baking powder	¼ teaspoon soda plus ½ teaspoon cream of tartar
1 tablespoon cornstarch (for thickening)	2 tablespoons flour or 1 tablespoon tapioca
1 cup sifted all-purpose flour	1 cup plus 2 tablespoons sifted cake flour
1 cup sifted cake flour	1 cup minus 2 tablespoons sifted all-purpose flour
1 cup fine dry bread crumbs	¾ cup fine cracker crumbs

DAIRY

Instead of	Use
1 cup buttermilk	1 cup sour milk or 1 cup yogurt
1 cup heavy cream	¾ cup skim milk plus ⅓ cup butter
1 cup light cream	⅞ cup skim milk plus 3 tablespoons butter
1 cup sour cream	⅞ cup sour milk plus 3 tablespoons butter
1 cup sour milk	1 cup sweet milk plus 1 tablespoon vinegar or lemon juice or 1 cup buttermilk

SEASONING

Instead of	Use
1 teaspoon allspice	½ teaspoon cinnamon plus ⅛ teaspoon cloves
1 cup catsup	1 cup tomato sauce plus ½ cup sugar plus 2 tablespoons vinegar
1 clove of garlic	⅛ teaspoon garlic powder or ⅛ teaspoon instant minced garlic or ¾ teaspoon garlic salt or 5 drops of liquid garlic
1 teaspoon Italian spice	¼ teaspoon each oregano, basil, thyme, rosemary plus dash of cayenne
1 tablespoon lemon juice	½ teaspoon vinegar
1 tablespoon prepared mustard	1 teaspoon dry mustard
1 medium onion	1 tablespoon dried minced onion or 1 teaspoon onion powder

SWEET

Instead of	Use
1 1-ounce square chocolate	3 to 4 tablespoons cocoa plus 1 teaspoon shortening
1⅔ ounces semisweet chocolate	1 ounce unsweetened chocolate plus 4 teaspoons sugar
1 cup honey	1 to 1¼ cups sugar plus ¼ cup liquid or 1 cup molasses or corn syrup
1 cup granulated sugar	1 cup packed brown sugar or 1 cup corn syrup, molasses or honey minus ¼ cup liquid

Index

APPETIZERS
Antipasto, 24
Artichoke Dip, 14
 Spread, Hot, 24
Benedictine Sandwich
 Spread, 11
Celery Sticks, "There's-Never-
 Any-Left," 24
Cheese
 Ball, 12
  Hot, 12
  Microwave, 12
  Taco, 12
 Beer, in Rye Boat, 11
 Chili Dip, 14
 Fondue
  Beer Cheese in
   Rye Boat, 11
  Mary's, 19
 Fried, 14
 Pastry Hors d' Oeuvres, 13
 Sables, 13
 Slices, Puffy, 14
 Spread, 13
 Stuffed Mushrooms, 25
Chicken
 Sweet and Sour
  Wing Dings, 23
Clam
 Bites, 19
 Dip, 15, 17
Crab
 Dip, 15
 Meatballs, Elegant, 20
 Mold, Company, 20
Dips
 Artichoke, 14
 Chili con Queso, 14
 Clam
  Company, 15
  Slow-Ball, 17
 Crab, 15
 Dill Mustard, 15
 Egg, Festive, 16
 Horseradish and
  Cream Cheese, 16
 Jalapeño, 16
 Mock Oysters
  Rockefeller, 21
 Mushroom, 16
 Pumpernickel, 17
 Shrimp, 17
 Spinach, 17
 Taco Party, 18
 Tuna, Tantalizing, 18
 Vegetable, 18
Easy and Good, 18
Eggs, Deviled, 216
Finger Steaks, 20
Ground Beef
 Meatballs
  Mom's Spicy Recipe, 21
  Party, Quick, 21
 One-Pounder, the, 20

Meatballs
 Crab, Elegant, 20
 Mom's Spicy Recipe, 21
 Quick Party, 21
Mock Oysters Rockefeller, 21
Mushrooms, Stuffed
 Cheese, 25
 Sausage, 25
 Spinach-Crab, 25
Nuts, Spiced, 19
Seasoned Oyster Crackers, 23
Shrimp
 Filipino Raw-Style,
  Exotic, 23
 Mini Quichettes, 22
 Mold, 22
 Spread, 22
Spiced Nuts, 19
Spinach
 Balls, 26
 Crab Stuffed Mushrooms, 25
 Squares, 26
Spreads
 Artichoke, Hot, 24
 Benedictine Sandwich, 11
 Cheese, 13
  Ball, 12
 One Pounder, the, 20
 Shrimp, 22
Steaks, Finger, 20
Supervisors, 11
Sweet and Sour Wing Dings, 23
Water Chestnut, 26
Won Ton, 23
Bachelor's Delight Breakfast, 220
BEEF
Barbecue, Brisket, 80
Boliche, 81
Bourguignon, 79
Bul-Go-Gi, 81
Burgundy, 80
Roast, Grilled Marinated
  Chuck, 81
Roladen, 82
Scallopine, 80
Steak
 Finger, 20
 Flank
  Marinated, 83
  Stuffed, 84
 Mexican, 82
 Stuffed, and Parsley
  Potatoes, 83
BEVERAGES
Cold
 Aunt Julie's Bloody
  Mary Mix, 29
 Chocolate
  Irish Cream, 29
  Milk Shake, 30
  Peanut Butter Cup, 31
 Eggnog
  Boiled Custard, 29
  Ultimate, 31

 Uncle Bob's Moose
  Milk, 31
 with Ice Cream
  Merry Berry Mint, 30
  Orange Cow, 31
  Peanut Butter Cup, 31
 Irish Cream, 29
 Merry Berry Mint, 30
 Multi-Flavored Juice, 35
 Orange
  Cow, 31
  Julius, 35
 Peanut Butter Cup, 31
 Punch, 36
  Candy Apple, 34
  Fruit, 34
  Peppermint Twist, 35
  Strawberry Citrus, 36
 Root Beer, 30
 Shakes
  Banana Milk, 30
  Chocolate Milk, 30
  Health, 34
 Slushes
  Brandy, 33
  Strawberry, 36
 Sunshine, 36
Hot
 Buttered Rum, 32
 Chocolate Mix, 32
 Cider, 32
  Candy Apple Punch, 34
 Mama's Good Tea, 33
 Spiced Mocha, 33
 Tom and Jerry Mix, 30
Kahlua, 29
Mixes
 Aunt Julie's Bloody Mary, 29
 Hot Chocolate, 32
 Mama's Good Tea, 33
BREADS
Biscuits, 96
 Angel, 151
 Molasses, Mum's, 157
Coffee Cake
 Cherry, 160
 Cinnamon Bubble Ring, 160
 Crumble, 161
 Deutsch Kuchen, 160
 Monkey Bread, 161
 Shoo Fly, 162
Corn Bread
 Hush Puppies, 151
 Johnny Cake, 152
 Mexican, 152
 Spoon, 154
Doughnuts
 Potato, 162
 Southern, 162
French Toast, 153
Fritters
 Apple, 153
 Old Tavern, 153
Hush Puppies, Baked, 151

Loaves
  Quick
    Apple, 157
    Banana-Nut, 158
    Breakfast, 158
    Lemon, 158
    Pumpkin Spice, 159
    Sausage, 156
    Zucchini, 159
      Pineapple, 159
  Yeast
    Cheese
      Golden Wheel, 154
      Swiss, Onion, 156
    Wheat Germ Herb,
      Homemade, 155
    Whole Wheat-
      Granola, 155
Muffins
  Banana-Oatmeal, 163
  Blueberry-Orange, 163
  Bran, 163
    Six-Week, Jackie's, 164
  Oatmeal
    Banana, 163
    Crescent, 164
    Sunshine, 164
Pancakes
  Apple, Baked, 165
  English, 165
  Potato, Jewish, 165
  Pumpkin, 165
  Strawberry, 166
Popovers, Blender, 153
Pretzels, German, 166
Rolls
  Mexican Sweet, 161
  Parker House Potato, 156
  Pull-Apart Breakfast, 157
  Refrigerator Yeast, 157
Scones, 154
Spoon Bread, 154
Sticks, 152
Breakfast Casserole, 67

CAKES
  Butterscotch, 181
  Carrot, 182
  Chocolate
    Devil's Food
      Peanut Layer, 182
    Mahogany, 183
    Mississippi Mud, 183
    Sandwich Cookie, 184
    Tennessee, 184
    Turtle, 185
    Viennese Torte, 185
    White, 186
  Fruitcake
    Golden, 184
    Mexican, 187
  Italian Cream, 187
  Jam, 186
  Kentucky Rum, 188
  Pistachio, 187
  Pound, Sour Cream, 188
  Pumpkin Log, 188
Calf Liver with Red Wine
    Sauce, 88

CANDIES
  Bourbon Balls, 200
  Buckeyes, 200

Cocoa-Nut, 201
Fudge, Campfire Foolproof, 201
Mints, Creamy, 202
Mound Balls, 202
Peanut Butter, Five-Minute, 201
Strawberries, Chocolate-
    Dipped, 202
Toffee, English, 201
Walnuts, Sugar-Glazed, 202

CHEESECAKES
  Blender, 175
  Chocolate, 176
  Mocha, Frozen, 176
  Old-Fashioned, 176

CHICKEN
  Arroz con Pollo, 92
  Breast
    Casserole, 104
    Crab-Stuffed, 101
    with Tarragon, 98
  Broccoli
    Casserole, 98
      Cheese, 92
    Divan, 93
  Casserole
    Breast, 104
    Broccoli, 98
      Cheese, 92
    Leftover, 96
    One-Cup, 96
  Continental, 92
  Cordon Bleu, 98, 99
  Crescents, 93
  Divan, 93
  Drumstick Ragoût, 94
  Dumplings, and, 93
  Enchilada Pie, 94
  Hawaiian, Smothered, 103
  Jalapeño, 95
  Juliet, 99
  La Scala, 100
  Lemon, 91
    Grilled, 95
  Mexican, 96
  Oven-Fried, Golden, 95
  Pam's, 102
  Peking Imperial, 102
  Poppy Seed, 91
  Puerto Rican, 97
  Quiche, Great, and Spinach, 104
  Quick-n-Easy, Gourmet, 103
  Ragoût, 94
  with Rosemary Cream
    Sauce, 100
  Sherry
    Baked, with, 97
    French, in, Sauce, 102
  Sour Cream Sauce, in, 99
  Spaghetti, 103
    Shrimp, 71
  Supreme, 101
  Swiss, 97, 104
  with Tarragon, 98
  Wings, Sweet and Sour,
    Dings, 23

COOKIES
  Apple Brownies, 196
  Austrian Fruit Bars, 189
  Bars
    Anytime, Michael's, 198
    Apple Brownies, 196

Austrian Fruit, 189
Brownies
  Apple, 196
  Creme de Menthe, 198
  Gold Rush, 198
  Michigan, 199
  World's Best, 200
Chocolate
  Brownies, see Brownies
  Caramel-Nut, 197
  Cherry, 197
  Creme de Menthe, 198
  Fudge-Oatmeal, 197
  Peanut Butter, Aunt
    Alice's, 200
  Holidates, 199
  Orange Macaroon, 199
  Peanut Butter-Chocolate
    Bars, 200
Butterscotch Delights, 189
Chocolate
  Butter-Tipped, 191
  Chip, Award-Winning, 190
  Choclava, 190
  Drop, 190
  Marshmallow, 191
  Meringue, 191
Clover, St. Patrick's, 192
Coconut Chews, 192
Cut-Out, 192
Famous, Susie's, 193
Lemon Snowflakes, 193
Mint Surprise, 193
No-Bake, 194
Nutjammer, 194
Oatmeal, 195
  Cape Cod, 194
Peanut Butter Crinkles, 195
Pumpkin, Mom's, 195
Raisin Jumbos, 196
Sesame Seed, Italian, 192
Sugar-Nut Sticks, 196
Cornish Game Hens in Flaming
    Cherry Sauce, 105

DESSERTS
Apple
  Bavarian Torte, 169
  Cinnamon, 169
  Sauce, Campfire, 169
Bananas, Caramel with
    Rum, 170
Blueberry Torte, 170
Broken Glass, 171
Cakes, see Cakes
Cheesecakes
  Blender, 175
  Chocolate, 176
  Mocha, Frozen, 176
  Old-Fashioned, 176
Chocolate
  Blender Mousse, 170
  Cheesecakes, 175, 176
  Chocolatissimo, 172
  Heavenly Surprise, 172
  Hot Fudge, 179
  Oreo Cake, 172
  Paté, 171
  Peanut Butter Pizza, 171
Cobbler, Pear, Old-
    Fashioned, 209
Cranberry Ice, 179
Custard, Baked, 177

Ice Cream
    Chocolate-Peanut Butter
            Cookie, 180
    Coffee, 180
    Cranberry, 179
    Mocha, 180
    Peach, Fresh, 180
    Sandwiches, Cookie, 173
    Snow, 179
Lorna Doone, 173
Orange Refrigerator, 173
Pear, Cobbler, Old-
        Fashioned, 209
Pizza, Fruit Spectacular
        Platter, 174
Puddings
    Bread
        New Orleans, 178
        Raisin-Honey, 178
    Noodle, 178
Raspberry Delight, 174
Soufflés
    Blintz, 177
    Lemon, 177
Strawberries Susan, 175
Sunshine Pine, 175
Fancy Dogs, 68
FROSTINGS
Butter Cream, 181, 185
Caramel, 186
Chocolate, 183, 184, 185
Cream Cheese, 182, 183, 187
GROUND BEEF
Casseroles, 85
    and Bean, 86
    Cabbage, 85
    Enchilada, 73
    Italian, 73
    Plummerville, 75
    Sweet and Sour, 88
    Taco, 90
Chalupas, 70
Chili
    Soup, Trail, 90
    Tigress II, Black Bean, 90
    Topping For Chili Dogs, 68
Chop Suey, American, 83
Chow Mein, Chop Chop, 85
Dip, Jalapeño, 16
Lasagne, 74
Meatballs
    Cheese, with Spaghetti
            Sauce, 72
    Homemade Spaghetti Sauce
            with, 82
    in Onion Gravy, 86
    Polish, 86
    Sculer, 87
    Spicy, Mom's Recipe, 21
Meat Loaf with Rice Wafers, 87
Pie
    Cincinnati, 84
    Tortilla, 72
Sauce
    Baked, Randy's Italian, 71
    Spaghetti
        Cheese Meatballs, 72
        Homemade, with
                Meatballs, 82
Seven-Layer Beef and Rice, 87
Sloppy Joes, 88
Stuffed Green Peppers, 78

HAM
Broccoli Bake, 70
Kentucky Country, 115
Loaf, 113
Pie, 113
    Easter, My Mom's, 70
Quiche, Impossible, 114
Roll-Ups, 114
Sandwiches, Croissant, 113
Spaghetti, Lanterna Blu, 69
Tetrazzini, 114
ICE CREAM
Chocolate-Peanut Butter
        Cookie, 180
Coffee, 180
Cranberry Ice, 179
Mocha, 180
Peach, Fresh, 180
Sandwiches, Cookie, 173
Snow, 179
LAMB
Moussaka, 75
Roast Leg of, 76
with Spaghetti, 75
MARINADES
Barbecue, 219
for Leg of Lamb, 76
Red Wine, 218
Teriyaki, 218
MEATLESS
Broccoli-Cheese Burritos, 77
Chili-Cheese Pie, 67
Eggplant
    Aubergines Baigan
            Tamatar, 77
    Parmigiana, 78
Glop, 69
John Wayne Cheese
        Casserole, 68
Zucchini
    Casserole, 78
Nutritional Conversion
        Chart, **221**
Pheasant, Jubilee, 105
PIES
Angel, 204
Apple, 204
    No-Crust, 204
Butterscotch, 205
Candy Bar, 203
Chocolate
    Minty, 206
    Mississippi Mud, 206
    Old-Fashioned, 206
    Toll-House Walnut, Super-
            Size, 205
Coconut Macaroon, 207
Cream, 207
Grasshopper, 207
Key Lime, 207, 208
Kiwi, 208
Lemon Meringue, 209
Macaroon, 207, 208
Maple Chiffon, 209
Pecan, Mystery, 210
Pizza Grano, 205
Strawberry
    Mile-High, 210
    Quick and Easy, 210
PORK
Chops
    Company, 108

with Paprika, 108
'n' Potato Bake, 109
Saucy Baked, 109
Sausage Jambalaya, 109
Chow Mein, Pineapple, 111
Haole Lau Lau, 108
Korean Pork Pagogie, 110
Mandarin, and Vegetables, 110
Maui Chow-Funn, 112
Moo Shu Pork, 111
Ribs
    with Bourbon Marinade, 117
    Country Joe's, 117
Roast, 110
Sausage
    Alice's Breakfast
            Casserole, 67
    Crêpes, Filled, 116
    Frittatas, 115
    Manicotti, Spinach-
            Stuffed, 118
    Meatballs, Quick Party, 21
    Mushrooms, Stuffed, 25
    Pork Chop-Jambalaya, 109
    Ring, Apple-, 116
    Stuffing Bake, 116
    Sweet 'n' Sour Smoked, 69
    The One Pounder, 26
    and Zucchini, 117
Spanish, with Olives, 107
Sweet and Sour, 112
Sweet,-Colli, 107
Potpourri for Use in Home, 220
PRESERVING
Jelly, Beet, 213
Marmalade, Blueberry, 213
Pickles, Lazy Housewife's, 217
PUDDINGS
Bread
    New Orleans, 178
    Raisin Honey, 178
Custard, Baked, 177
Mousse, Blender, 170
Noodle, 178
QUICHE
Chili-Cheese Pie, 67
Great Chicken and
        Spinach, 104
Ham Pie, 113
Impossible, 114
Mini, 22
My Mom's Easter Pie, 70
SALADS
Dressings
    Coleslaw, 217
    French, 55
    Garlic, Great, 217
    Honey Cream, 52
    Poppy Seed, 58
    Sweet and Sour, 58
    Vinaigrette, Fresh Basil, 60
Fruit
    Cranberry Holiday, 49
    Garden, 49
    Mandarin
        Congealed, 50
        Orange, 49
    Mom's Special, 51
    Papaya-Avocado, 50
    Pretzel, 50
    San Francisco Bowl, 51
    Sawdust, 51

Strawberry-Nut, 52
Summer, 52
Waldorf, 52
Main Dishes
    Chicken
        Artichoke-Rice, 53
        Hot, 62
        Mexican, 62
        Nutty, 62
        and Pineapple, 63
        Shrimp and Rice, 61
        Taco, 64
        Tomato Fans, 58
        Tortellini, 64
        Wild Rice, 61
    Pasta
        Curried, Beth's, 60
        Layered Garden, 61
        Linguine, 60
        Macaroni-Shrimp, 59
        Pizza, 59
        Primavera, 60
        Rotini, 61
    Vegetable
        Broccoli, 53
            Cauliflower, 54
        Carrots, Marinated, 54
        Cauliflower-Broccoli, 54
        Cucumber, 54
        Fumi-Fumi, 55
        Lentil, 55
        Lettuce, Red Leaf
            and Mushroom, 58
        Pebble, 56
        Potato, Hot, 56
        Spinach
            Korean, 57
            with Sweet and Sour
                Dressing, 57
        Tomato Fans, 58
        Vegetable
            Molded, 59
            Twenty-Four Hour, 58

SAUCES
Barbecue
    for Baby Back Ribs, 219
    Chicken, 220
Bourbon, 178
Hollandaise, 101
Honey Glaze, 220
Hot Sauce, Plantation, 219
Mexican Madness, 218
Mustard, Orbital, 219

SEAFOOD
Fish
    Cod, Fisherman's
        Curried, 121
    Flounder
        with Lemon Broccoli, 121
        Stuffed, 122
            with Cheese Sauce, 122
    Grilled, with Herbs, 120
    Icelandic, Dish, 120
    Pie, 120
    Redfish Court Bouillon, 123
    Salmon Loaf, 121
    Sauté, 120
    Sole en Papillote, 123
    Tuna
        Biscuit-Topped, 124
        Casserole, 124
        Dip, Tantalizing, 18

Shellfish
    Clam
        Bites, 19
        Dip
            Company, 15
            Slow-Ball, 17
            Linguine and, Sauce,
                Captain Paul's, 125
    Crab
        Cakes, Chesapeake
            Bay, 125
        Deviled, Easy, 126
        Dip, 15
        Meatballs, Elegant, 20
        Mold, Company, 20
        Soufflés, 126
    Lobster Seviche, 126
    Scallops
        California-Style, 119
        Scalloped, 127
    Shrimp
        Alfredo, 127
        Boiled "Spicy," 127
        Casserole, 128
        de Jonghe, 129
        Dip, 17
        Etouffée, 129
        Filipino Raw-Style, 23
        Marguerite, 129
        Mold, 22
        Quichettes, Mini, 22
        Sauté, 128
        Soufflé, 128
        Spread, 22
        Stuffed Eggplant, 130
        Sweet-Sour
            (Low-Cal), 130

SIDE DISHES
Dressing, Applesauce, 146
Dumplings, 147
Fruit, Curried Baked, 146
Grits Casserole, 147
Pasta
    with Cream Sauce, 148
    Macaroni and Cheese,
        California, 147
    Noodles, Madame's, 147
    Ravioli, 218
Rice
    Green, 148
    Scalloped, 148
    Wild Rice Casserole, 148

SNACKS
Corn
    Caramel, 216
    Crazy, 216
Granola, 217

SOUPS
Bean, Navy, 41
Broccoli, Cream of, 42
Buttermilk, Cold, 214
Cauliflower, 42, 215
Cheese, 42, 215
Chicken
    Jewish-Style with
        Matzo Balls, 39
    Mom's, 39
Chili
    Tigress II-Black Bean, 90
    Trail, 90
Crab, Gumbo, 40
Cucumber, 214

Gazpacho, 43
Gumbo
    Crab, 40
    Seafood, 41
    Italian, 40
    Lentil, 43
Kangaroo Tail, 215
Lentil
    Italian, 43
    Sweet and Sour, 44
Onion, French, 43
Potato
    Egg Drop, 44
    Polish, 44
    Vichyssoise, Canadian, 214
Strawberry, 213
Vegetable, Jim's, 45
Watercress, Princess Di's, 215
Wedding, 40
Zucchini, Curried Cream of, 45

STEWS
Beef
    Bourguignon, 80
    Burgundy, 80
    World's Easiest, 46
Ground Beef
    Tater, 46
Jambalaya, Pork Chop-
        Sausage, 109
Lamb
    Irish, 46
Shrimp
    Etouffée, 129
    Marguerite, 129

TURKEY
Spanish, 106
Waffles, Pecan, 105

VEAL
Crêpes with Mornay Sauce, 89
Parmigiana, 89

VEGETABLES
Artichokes, 133
Asparagus with Mustard
        Sauce, 133
Beans, Baked
    Calico, 133
    Casserole, 134
    Home-, Mother's, 134
Beans, Green
    and New Potatoes, 135
    Sweet and Sour, 135
Broccoli
    Casserole, 135
    Soufflé, 136
Cabbage, 136
Carrots
    Glazed, 136
    Olé, 136
    Sweet and Tangy, 137
Corn
    Creamed, Gulliver's, 137
    Pudding, Liz's, 137
Cucumber, Pickled with
        Long Rice, 137
Easy Garden Pie, 145
Eggplant a la Italiano, 138
Frijoles Refritos, 134
Garden Delight Casserole, 146
Lentils, Sweet and Sour, 44
Mushrooms
    with Basil Cream, 138
    Puff, 138

Onions
    au Gratin, Baldwin's, 139
    Vidalia Pie, 139
Potatoes
    Giselle's, 139
    Irish, 139
    Mashed
        Casserole, 140
        Make-Ahead, 140
    Scalloped, 141
    Soufflé, Vegetable, 140

Stuffed, 141
    Twice-Baked, 142
Swedish Baked, 142
Tennessee Spuds, 142
Spinach
    Casserole, 142
    Spanakopita, 143
Squash
    Casserole, 143
    Stuffed Acorn, 143
Sweet Potatoes

    Casserole, 143
        and Apple, 144
    Soufflé, 144
Yam and Cranberry
        Casserole, 144
Tomatoes Country-Style, 145
Zucchini, J. R.'s, 145
VENISON
    Pepper Steak, 77
    Stir-Fry, 76
Vlcek's Wild Fowl Recipe, 106

Index of Contributors

A

Adamson, Bill—Regional Director Adamson Region, 152
Adamson, Nancy—Wife of Regional Director
    Bill Adamson, 112, 174
Allan, Diane—Franchisee, Tuskpride Ltd., 107, 215
Allen, Elaine—McCormick Region, 165
Allen, Judie—Orcutt Area, 103
Anderson, Lou—Shipman Region, 70
Archenbronn, Joyce A.—World Headquarters, 15, 51, 151
Arky, David—Garland Texas, 39
Armbruster, Julie—World Headquarters, 77
Arnowitz, Tala—Franchisee, Western Ohio
    Pizza Inc., 12, 81, 119
Ashford, Denise Marie—World Headquarters, 60, 115
Ashley, Barbara—World Headquarters, 99

B

Baker, Doris Ann—Fort Worth, Texas, 73
Bales, June—World Headquarters, 213
Bassett, Karen—World Headquarters, 192
Bates, Marjorie—Seiber Region, 206
Baum, Barbara—Franchisee, 179
Belknap, Becky—Franchisee, Ann Arbor Pizza Inc., 23, 170

Bender-Hutmier, Sarah L.—McCormick Region, 142
Benjamin, Becky—World Headquarters, 63
Bennett, Gwen—World Headquarters, 187
Bennett, Julie—McCord Region, 194
Bertram, Rita—Rossolo Region, 169
Binderman, Bruce—Franchisee, Subec Region, 147
Bitner, Christina Marie—Carol Stream, Illinois, 68
Black, Beth—Ebert Area, 44
Black, Diane—Wife of Executive Vice President
    Dave Black, 92, 193
Blakely, Sally A.—World Headquarters, 202
Blanka, Maria Lisa—Dotson Region, 196
Bloodworth, Helen R.—McCord Region, 53
Board, Barb and Dave—Vice President, International, 81
Bommarito, Tess—World Headquarters, 52, 213
Boone, Karen—Nickep Region, 144, 197
Borchert, Ann—World Headquarters, 51, 92, 190
Bores, Debra—Franchisee, Blue Earth
    Enterprises, Inc., 15, 61, 136
Bott, Kathy—Nickep Region, 51, 205
Boudrie, Gerry—World Headquarters, 194
Bradley, Gwendolyn G.—Nickep Region, 56
Bradley, Janet M.—McCord Region, 80, 128

Briggs, Sara Ann—World Headquarters, 19, 35, 59, 162
Brock, Robert B.—Franchisee, Doughmatic Pizza, Inc., 81
Brown, Rhonda—Franchisee, Adamson Region, 54, 96, 156
Brueggeman, Mary C.—World Headquarters, 53
Brusinski, Deanna—World Headquarters, 20
Bundy, Fay—Winston-Salem, North Carolina, 198
Burgerhoudt, Susan—World Headquarters, 104
Bussey, Marianne—Kuehn Region, 18
Butterfield, Mary—St. Cloud, Minnesota, 176
Butterick, Coleen—Franchisee, Rock River Pizza, 31
Butterick, Merle—Franchisee, Rock River Pizza, 123

C

Caldwell, Carla—World Headquarters, 45
Callicotte, Kimberly—World Headquarters, 154
Calta, Donna—McCormick Region, 171
Cangialosi, Joseph S.—Nickep Region, 146
Caputo, Barbara—DNC, North Carolina, 88, 171
Carmichael, Pam—Jefferson City, Missouri, 41
Carpenter, Cindy—McCord Region, 91
Carpenter, Pat—McCord Region, 55, 147
Carr, Carol—Wife of Vice President, Tim Carr, World
    Headquarters, 17
Chaparro, Jennifer N.—World Headquarters, 128
Chapekis, Anna M.—World Headquarters, 75, 143
Clise, Margaret—Franchisee, M Pizza, Inc., 165
Clise, Norma Lee—Franchisee, M Pizza, Inc., 134, 186
Cochran, Sarah E.—Western Pennsylvania Pizza, Inc., 49, 200
Cole, Ellen R.—Franchisee, Tilley Region, 62
Collins, Connie—McCormick Region, 129
Cone, Joanne—Kuehn Region, 172
Corbin, Sue—World Headquarters, 143
Coté, Nanette B.—Franchisee, Tilley Region, 196, 219
Cromer, Janet—World Headquarters, 49
Cromer, Joan M.—World Headquarters, 87, 159
Curby, Jill—World Headquarters, 14, 75
Curran, Joan—World Headquarters, 21, 67, 141
Curtis, Katherine Hilboldt—World Headquarters, 13, 60
Cymes, Onda—World Headquarters, 70, 107

D

Daniel, Robert—World Headquarters, 12
David, Michael D.—Gas City, Indiana, 90
Dawson, Sue—Wife of Vice President
    Doug Dawson, 85, 130, 136, 177
Dean, Vicki—McCormick Region, 18, 111, 142
De Gaeta, Captain Paul—Captain of Tigress II, 125
De Gaeta, Joyce—Wife of Captain of Tigress II, 90
de Jolsvay, Nancy—Franchisee, River City Pizza, Inc., 176, 191
DeMoss, Debby—World Headquarters, 63
Derouin, Paul K.—Dotson Region, 25
DeVantier, Connie—World Headquarters, 55, 155
DeWeese, Nancy—Kuehn Region, 20
Dixon, Sue—Nickep Region, 84
Domingues, Roileen—Meussner Region, 13, 101
Donze, Sue—Franchisee, 95
Dotson, Nancy—Wife of Regional Director John Dotson, 218
Douglas, Tewanna—McCormick Region, 200
Doyle, Linda—World Headquarters, 161
Dufek, Don and Pat—World Headquarters, 196

E

Ebert, Joan—Wife of Area Vice President Gale Ebert, 42
Eckel, Barbara—World Headquarters, 16, 98
Edgell, Joyce—Rossolo Region, 117
Elbert, Rachel—McCord Region, 30, 33
Ereddia, Laura—Franchisee, East Carolina Pizza, 120
Ernst, Lily—Adamson Region, 22, 78
Evans, Mary Jo—Franchisee, Fast and Free, Inc., 74

Faeth, Teresa—Nickep Region, 178

Fast, Tom—Seiber Region, 34
Fernandez, Franfisca—Kuehn Region, 61
Ferns, Karen Lynn—DNC,Southern California, 72, 144
Fetzer, Rhea Y.—Wife of John Fetzer, Board of Directors,
    Detroit Tigers, 19, 87, 201
Fiedler, Eileen B.—World Headquarters, 82
Findley, Earnestine—Nickep Region, 179
Fine, Peggy—Wife of Vice President Sam Fine, 83
Frisbee-Goden, Connie Lynn—Oney Region, 14
Frye, Lorin—Franchisee, B. G. and L. Enterprises, Inc.,
    Tilley Region, 180, 213
Fulcher, Sandra F.—World Headquarters, 54
Funkhouser, Naomi—Wife of Damon Funkhouser, Franchisee,
    Funkhouser, Inc., 11, 97

G

Gabriel, Daphne—World Headquarters, 44
Galdikas, Tammy Jo—Nickep Region, 26
Galloway, Lorraine—Franchisee, One-Way Pizza, Inc., 154, 218
Galusha, Doug—Nickep Region, 12
Gardner, Jack—World Headquarters, 46
Gast-Kolecki, Sandra—World Headquarters, 175
Gates, Susan J.—McCord Region, 23
Gee, Mary E.—World Headquarters, 120
Geisler, Aletha—Rossolo Region, 121
Gentner, Jan—World Headquarters, 57
George, Janet—Glen Falls, New York, 59
Gephart, Katherine—World Headquarters, 88, 160
Germond, Kathy—Seiber Region, 160
Gerstein, Dona—McCord Region, 164, 165
Gibson, Suzanne—Tilley Region, 36, 107, 117, 217
Gilley, Elizabeth—McCormick Region, 201
Goad, Mary—McCormick Region, 184
Godwin, JoAnn—World Headquarters, 85, 162, 218
Golzan, Sharon—International, 24
Goodson, Regina—DNC, Illinois, 116
Gottsche, Lucy Kay—Adamson Region, 170
Govaere, Lois—World Headquarters, 97, 116
Grabbe, Barbara K.—World Headquarters, 86
Graf, Jerry and Nancy—World Headquarters, 95
Graham, Catherine N.—World Headquarters, 154
Granado, Teresa—Dotson Region, 25, 195
Griffith, Beverly—Wife of George Griffith,
    Board of Directors, 64, 181
Griffith, George—Board of Directors, 207
Grooms, Randy—McCormick Region, 28, 202
Grove, Yvonne—Dotson Region, 35

H

Hanna, Annastasia—Franchisee, Hanna Creative
    Enterprises, Inc., 93, 110
Haley, Donna—Nickep Region, 158, 219, 220
Hamill, Amy—World Headquarters, 42, 215
Hansen, Eleanor—Muessner Region, 109, 199
Hardin, Tammy Jo—Franchisee, Dotson Region, 109
Hardley, Peggy—World Headquarters, 195
Harvey, Lisa G.—Seiber Region, 99, 129
Heitger, Hope—Franchisee, Dotson Region, 101
Hendricksen, Ruth—World Headquarters, 26, 140, 146
Henerdine, Peg—Seiber Region, 20, 172
Hensley, Beth—Cohen Area, 187
Herz, Jackie—Oney Region, 103
Hibdon, Beckie—Madison, Tennessee, 82, 191
Hickey, Sara—World Headquarters, 21
Hingst, Ron—World Headquarters, 135
Holder, Debra—World Headquarters, 78
Holliday, Ann M.—McCormick Region, 41, 135
Holmes, Howard S.—Board of Directors, 124
Holmes, Mary B.—Wife of Howard S. Holmes,
    Board of Directors, 18
Holtz, Nancy—Kuehn Region, 174
Horn, Susan L.—World Headquarters, 190

Houseman, Pat—Franchisee, Middle Tennessee Pizza, Inc., 138
Hughes, Marguerite M.—World Headquarters, 161

I

Ikle, Marsha—World Headquarters, 42
Isemann, Betty L.—Beavercreek, Ohio, 125

J

Janis, Cindy—World Headquarters, 173
Jenks, Linda—Franchisee, Boston Pie, Inc., 165
Jerue, Mary Gay—Oney Region, 208
Jewell-Greer, Tammy—Pasadena, California, 33, 72, 138
Johnson, Marcia L.—Rossolo Region, 157, 162
Johnson, Mary—Franchisee, Dotson Region, 94, 145
Jasefczyk, Maryanne—World Headquarters, 137, 194
Justice, Paul—McCord Region, 186

K

Kaline, Louise—Detroit Tigers, 129, 203
Kane, Lois—Franchisee, O.A.E. Pizza, Inc., 177
Kane, Mary Anne—World Headquarters, 86
Kanitz, Betsy—World Headquarters, 179
Kaufer, Aaron—World Headquarters, 209
Keith, John P.—Meussner Region, 173
Kelcourse, Michael—World Headquarters, 198
Keller, Diane—Roberson Region, Boulder, Colorado, 188
Kelly, Patrick J.—Area Vice President, 188
Kemppainen, Jolene—Domino's Lodge, 77, 100, 178
Kuehn, Kenneth R.—Regional Director, 184
Keuper, Mike, Sr.—DNC, North Texas, 207
King, Barbara A.—Nickep Region, 140
King, Randy—International, 86, 151
Kleman, Wayne J.—Nickep Region, 200
Knapp, Denise—Franchisee, Knapp Co., McCord Region, 69
Kogelschatz, Mary—World Headquarters, 43, 89, 96, 156
Krivatsy, Serge—Dotson Region, 108
Krpan, Kathleen—Seiber Region, 31, 32, 153
Krueger, Ann—World Headquarters, 12, 134, 142, 164
Kruer, Denise—Nickep Region, 146
Kubota, Mrs. Scott—Pearl City, Hawaii, 23
Kuz, Kim—World Headquarters, 31

L

LaButte, Gail—Rossolo Region, 50, 83
Lake, Kimberly Breeding—Franchisee, Nickep Region, 84, 157
LaRosa, Lynn—Dotson Region, 43
LaScola, Marlena—Nickep Region, 60
Laughlin, Diane Lyon—Franchisee, Subec Region, 102, 148
Laurin, Therese—Tilley Region, 217
LeClair, Jennifer—Tilley Region, 102
Ley, Stephen—Nickep Region, 29, 133
Lipinski, Steve—Nickep Region, 44
Lipschutz, Sheila—Dotson Region, 80, 91
Litman, Susan—Franchisee, Golden Brown Pizza, Inc., 53
Little, Barbara—Muessner Region, 208
Litzler, Ann Lovernick—World Headquarters, 109, 215
Lombardi, Michael—Tilley Region, 122
Lykins, Lorie—World Headquarters, 93
Lynn, Tammy R.—Wife of Danny Lynn,
    Franchisee, Ebert Area, 15

M

Madison, Teena—Dotson Region, 180
Madsen, Sharon Horn—Franchisee, Ebert Area, 214
Manders, Mark—World Headquarters, 114
Marcus, Ildiko—Franchisee, Western Ohio Pizza, Inc., 26, 147
Martel, Lynne L.—Ebert/Seiber Region, 153
Martin, Louise—Ashland, Missouri, 217
Matthews, Tom—Rossolo Region, 190
McAteer, Gene—Rossolo Region, 95
McCauley, Annie—World Headquarters, 199
McCord, Joseph—Regional Director, 188

McCord, Nancy—Wife of Regional Director Joseph McCord, 56
McCormick, Cheryl L.—Wife of Regional Director
    Christopher McCormick, 43, 67, 97, 207
McCormick, Christopher—Regional Director, 164, 192
McCracken, Kathy—Kuehn Region, 34, 35, 36
McEachern-Kelly, Veronica—Wife of Area Vice President
    Pat Kelly, 202
McHale, Brian—Orcutt Area, 116
McHale, Susana Hernandez—Orcutt Area, 92
McIntire, Dan—Dotson Area, 120
McMichael, Ronnie—Adamson Region, 169
McNulty, Helen—Assistant to President, 80
Menges, Jennifer—Franchisee, Tilley Region, 22, 89, 141, 216
Merkerson, Gracie—McCord Region, 183
Metro, Karen—Franchisee, Nickep Region, 64
Meussner, Harry—Regional Director, 187
Miller, Claudia—World Headquarters, 110, 144
Miller, Joan Hocker—McCord Region, 122
Miller, Sylvia—DNC, Colorado, 31, 166
Minick, Polly—World Headquarters and Wife of
    Vice President Tom Minick, 40, 176, 177
Minick, T. R.—Vice President, World Headquarters, 152
Mitchell, Anita J.—Dotson Region, 128
Monaghan, Barbie—World Headquarters, 173
Monaghan, Marge—Chairman of the Chairman
    of the Board, 68, 181, 201
Monaghan, Maggie—World Headquarters, 36
Monaghan, Susie—World Headquarters, 180, 193
Monaghan, Thomas—Chairman of the Board of
    Domino's Pizza, 46, 124, 139
Moon, Karen—Meussner Region, 192
Montoya, Darla—Dotson Region, 183
Mudd, James J.—Franchisee, Ebert Area, 184
Mueller, Linda—RPM Pizza, 96, 204, 216
Mueller, Valerie—Franchisee, RPM Pizza, 24, 82
Mull, Colleen—World Headquarters, 17
Murphy, Mary Ann—Ohio Commissary, 113

N

Nagle, Philip James—Kuehn Region, 104
Nakamura, Dane—Dotson Region, 112
Nelson, Judith A.—World Headquarters, 104, 207
Nelson, Randall and Linda—Dotson Region, 17, 67
Newby, Jay—Franchisee, Valley Pizza, Inc., 45
Newsome, Gail—Wife of Mike Newsome,
    Franchisee, McCord Region, 15, 113
Noeker, Jill—World Headquarters, 139

O

Olenski, Bobbi—McCormick Region, 120
Ondusky, Linda—World Headquarters, 79
Orcutt, Christi—Wife of Area Vice President
    Michael Orcutt, 62, 139, 151, 219
Orcutt, Michael L.—Area Vice President, 68, 220
Ostulund, Randy—World Headquarters, 71
Ott, Mary L.—McCormick Region, 21, 115
Oudehengle, Petra—International, 52, 160
Owen, Donna—Vice President, World Headquarters, 182

P

Pagniano, Sue—Franchisee, PM Pizza, Inc., 40
Paris, Linda, J—Rossolo Region, RPM, 58
Parker, Susan L.—Nickep Region, 30, 214
Parray, Christopher—Tilley Region, 70
Parry, Ken—McCord Region, 192
Perkowski, Linda—Wife of Robert Perkowski,
    Franchisee, Subec Region, 74
Peters, Chris—Adamson Region, 163
Peterson, Susan—Dotson Region, 20, 111, 219
Piekenbrock, Susan S.—Seiber Region, 210
Pimentel, Robin—Adamson Region, 189
Pope, Susan T.—Kuehn Region, 153
Porter, Paula K.—McCormick Region, 158

Powers, Eugene—Board of Directors, 195
Presnar, William H.—Kuehn Region, 76, 77
Press, Barbara—Dotson Region, 102
Przybyski, Janet—World Headquarters, 22, 29

R

Rachide, Catherine Bulla—Franchisee, Oney Region, 200
Ralph, Denise—World Headquarters, 198
Recker, Patty—Franchisee, Roberson Region, 54
Rector, Catherine—World Headquarters, 69, 117
Reed, Monica—Franchisee, Tilley Region , 127
Richwine, Sharon—Tilley Region, 13, 127
Ricketts, John—Franchisee, Big Yellow Pie, Inc., 105, 135
Riddle, Cheryl A.—Ebert Area, 118
Riley, Carol Ann—Adamson Region, 113
Roberson, Cyndie—Wife of Regional Director Alan Roberson, 135
Robin, David and Sallyanne—Franchisee, International, 175, 215
Robinson, H. D., Jr.—Adamson Region, 148
Rogers, Michelle, R.—Nickep Region, 157
Romano, Peggy—J.A.R. Pizza, 145
Romano, Timothy and Patrick—Children of Joe Romano, 11
Rommelfaenger, Roger L.—Subec Region, 87
Romyananda, Terri—Wife of Regional Director
    Nickep Romyananda, 172
Rouse, Dan—Carlsbad, California, 50
Rossolo, Deborah R.—Wife of Regional Director
    Ron Rossolo, 191
Rowland, Anne—Wife of William Rowland, Franchisee,
    Adamson Region, 114, 180
Rowley, Mary—DNC, South Carolina, 108, 210
Ruby, Gayle W.—Adamson Region, 32, 204, 220
Rummer, Terri—McCormick Region, 58, 59, 206
Russell, Valeria—World Headquarters, 29, 34
Ryan, Erica Noreen—World Headquarters, 136
Ryan, Timothy J.—World Headquarters, 29

S

Sanders, Susan—Roberson Region, 153
Santamaria, Salvador—McCord Region, 106
Sassano, Donna—Tokyo, Japan, 103
Scarlett, Ramona—D R Pizza, Inc., Adamson Region, 94
Schaub, Brenadette A.—Meussner Region, 171
Schlembechlen, Mille—Wife of Bo Schlembechlen,
    Board of Directors, 199
Schlemmer, Karo—Ebert Area, 105
Schmitt-Heatlie, Anna—World Headquarters, 14, 220
Schopen, Birgitta—International, 126, 140
Schubert, Barbara—Muessner Region, 148, 159, 209
Schubert, Craig—Muesnner Region, 209
Scott, LaVay M.—Seiber Region
Seals, Jennifer—Rossolo Region, 40
Segrist, Don—World Headquarters, 134
Seiber, Sherri—Wife of Regional Director Geoff Seiber,
    Subec Region, 19, 108, 126, 138
Serrano, Norma—DNC, Illinois, 170
Seufert, Chris—World Headquarters, 175
Silva, Richard—Dotson Region, 137
Shaw, Miriam—World Headquarters, 178
Shefte, Daniel R.—Franchisee, Danrik, Ltd., 39
Shipman, Alison A.—Wife of Regional Director
    Peter Shipman, 148, 156
Shipman, Karen—McCord Region, 25, 46
Shook, Kay—World Headquarters, 25, 121
Silvey, Yvonne—DNC, Georgia, 36
Sims, Billie Jo—Adamson Region, 100
Sloane, Alice—Detroit Tigers, 76, 205
Smith, Brenda K.—Nickep Region, 88, 124
Smith, Elizabeth—Tilley Region, 189
Smith, Judy—Wife of Regional Vice President Dave Smith, 197
Smith, Michael—Ebert Area, 206
Smith, Nancy—McCord Region, 183
Smoak, Elberta—Wife of Robert Smoak, Franchisee,
    Roberson Region, 106

Soignet, Mary Beth—Wife of Mike Soignet, Regional Manager,
    Distribution, 123, 133, 185
Sootin, Karen—McCormick Region, 130
Spicer, Diane—Wife of Glen Spicer, Franchisee,
    Subec Region, 193
Spires, Sharon—World Headquarters, 197
Stansik, Sally—Ebert Area, 57, 58
Stark, Larry C.—RPM Pizza, Inc., 209
Stevens, Craig—Meussner Region, 14
Stewart, Suzanne—International, 98, 141
Stover, Anne—McCord Region, 93
Sutton, Patricia—World Headquarters, 90
Swanson, Esther—Meussner Region, 136, 214
Swanson, Kim—World Headquarters, 145, 179
Swanson, Susan—Meussner Region, 121
Swanton, Wanda—McCord Region, 49, 83
Switzer, Beverly—World Headquarters, 155, 166, 217
Swisher, Gail—L.A. Pizza, Inc., 137

T

Tabor, Jeanne—McCormick Region, 75
Takessian, Adam—Dotson Region, 182
Talledo, Mario—Dotson Region, 23
Tanner, Sally—Franchisee, Inflated Dough, 16
Thomason, Susan—Seiber Region, 11, 201
Thorp, Diana—Adamson Region, 33
Tilford, Jane M.—McCormick Region, 221
Tilley, Janet—Wife of Regional Director Jim Tilley, 30
Tilley, Jim—Regional Director, 41
Topping, Patricia—World Headquarters, 185
Totte, Bob—World Headquarters, 169
Tovo, Patricia A.—Ebert Area, 98
Tranquill, Shirley—Pittsburgh, Pennsylvania, 24, 50, 204
Trapnell, Pat—Rossolo Region, 143

U

Umberto, Joseph A.—Tilley Region, 205

V

Vallance, Mary—World Headquarters, 69
Viers, Sara—McCormick Region, 153
Villarreal, Bonnie—Franchisee, Ebert Area, 161
Villarreal, Michael J.—Franchisee, Ebert Area, 127
Villarreal, Robyn—Franchisee, Ebert Area, 30
Vincent, Dave—Franchisee, Oney Region, 126
Virgilio, Angela—Tilley Region, 133
Vlcek, Don—Vice President Distribution, 106
Vlcek, Suzanne Mae—World Headquarters, 147

W

Waleri, Pam—Marcris Enterprises, Inc., 17, 52, 110
Warner, Lempe—Hog Town Pizza, Shipman Region, 163
Wasczenski, Virginia—Garden City, Michigan, 159
Watson, Sally A.—Franchisee, Rossolo Region, 16, 152, 163
Waltz, Rebecca—Roberson Region, 32
Webb, Jackie—McCord Region, 70, 208
Webb, Susan—Long Beach, Mississippi, 137, 216
Whitehead, Charles B.—McCormick Region, 188
Whitelock, Rebecca W.—Franchisee, Dotson Region, 73
Wilcox, Jean—Franchisee, McCormick Region, 218
Williams, Nancy—World Headquarters, 56, 139, 202
Witte, Keith—Ebert Area, 157
Witzky, Touby—McCormick Region, 85
Wright, Anne M.—Wife of Gordon Wright,
    North Aurora, Illinois, 61
Wright, Cindi L.—Oney Region, 16

Y

Yaney, Sharon—Celeni, Ohio, 78
Yost, Tracey E.—McCormick Region, 99

Z

Zeeb, Martha—World Headquarters, 210

For information on how to obtain the
Domino's Pizza 25th Anniversary Cookbook

Write to:
Domino's Pizza Cookbook
PO Box 997
Ann Arbor, MI 48106